BERTIE AHERN
THE AUTOBIOGRAPHY

Bertie Ahern has been at the cutting edge of Irish politics for over three decades. Ireland's youngest ever Taoiseach, he presided over a time of unprecedented progress in Irish society. In 1998, working closely with Bill Clinton and Tony Blair, he won widespread acclaim for his perseverance and skill in negotiating the Good Friday Agreement, which has provided the political framework for a lasting peace in Northern Ireland. On the international stage, he is a respected figure who enjoyed an acclaimed Presidency of the European Council in 2004. There, he oversaw the completion of the largest ever expansion of the EU and concluded negotiations on a European constitution.

Bertie Ahern resigned on 6 May 2008, having served for ten years, ten months and ten days as Taoiseach.

In preparing his autobiography Bertie Ahern worked in partnership with UCD historian, Professor Richard Aldous.

BERTIE AHERN
THE AUTOBIOGRAPHY

Bertie Ahern
with Richard Aldous

arrow books

Published by Arrow Books 2010

2 4 6 8 10 9 7 5 3 1

First published in Great Britain in 2009 by
Hutchinson
Random House, 20 Vauxhall Bridge Road,
London SW1V 2SA

www.rbooks.co.uk

Addresses for companies within The Random House Group Limited can be found at:
www.randomhouse.co.uk/offices.htm

The Random House Group Limited Reg. No. 954009

A CIP catalogue record for this book
is available from the British Library

ISBN 9780099539254

The Random House Group Limited supports The Forest Stewardship Council (FSC),
the leading international forest certification organisation. All our titles that are
printed on Greenpeace approved FSC certified paper carry the FSC logo. Our paper
procurement policy can be found at www.rbooks.co.uk/environment

Mixed Sources
Product group from well-managed
forests and other controlled sources
www.fsc.org Cert no. TT-COC-2139
© 1996 Forest Stewardship Council

FSC

Typeset in Bembo by Palimpsest Book Production Limited,
Falkirk, Stirlingshire

Printed and bound in Great Britain by
CPI Bookmarque, Croydon CR0 4TD

For my daughters, Georgina and Cecelia.
And to the memory of my parents, Julia and Con.

CONTENTS

ILLUSTRATIONS

With Pope Benedict XVI
With Hillary Clinton
With Sir Alex Ferguson
Put me in coach!
GAA All-Stars
With Celia Larkin (Photo: Priory Studios)
Inspecting Irish UN Forces
St Columba's Christian Brothers School, New Delhi
President of the European Council
Day of Welcomes
G8 Conference
With George W. Bush
With Tony Blair
With Ian Paisley
With John Hume and Gerry Adams
Georgina's wedding (Photo: John Ryan Photography)
New additions to the family: Jay and Rocco
Addressing the US Congress
Addressing the Houses of Parliament at Westminster
United Nations AIDS Conference
With President McAleese
Last Cabinet
St Catherine's Infant School

The author thanks Tony and Mark Maxwell for their considerable help with the photographs in this book.

ACKNOWLEDGEMENTS

For help in a variety of ways, thanks to: Cecelia Ahern; Maurice Ahern; Miriam Ahern; Elizabeth Aldous; Kathryn Aldous; Patricia Aldous; Audiotrans, Cyprian Brady; Rory Brady; Kate Breslin; Maurice Bric; Robert Brigham; David Byrne; Georgina Byrne; John Byrne; Georgina Capel; Tess Callaway; Sandra Cullagh; Loughlin Deegan; Eoghan Harris; Karyn Harty; Mandy Johnston; Celia Larkin; Liam Mac Mathúna; Martin Mansergh; Maxwell Photography; Olive Melvin; Brian Murphy; Eileen O'Donovan; Niamh Puirseil; Susan Sandon; and Tony Whittome.

1

A BOY FROM DRUMCONDRA

Drumcondra. It's where I'm from. And it's who I am.

I was born Bartholomew Patrick Ahern in Dublin's Rotunda Hospital on 12 September 1951. Home was 25 Church Avenue, Drumcondra, on the north side of the city, which remained the hub of family life until my mother died in 1998. It was a small red-brick terraced house – two-up two-down – dating from around 1900 and it was a bit of squash for a family of seven. I used to sleep in the front bedroom with my parents and two brothers, Maurice and Noel. The two girls, Kathleen and Eileen, took over the smaller room at the back. In those days before central heating, I would sleep with a big coat pulled over me to keep warm in winter. I had a happy childhood. As the youngest of the five children in the house, I was a bit spoilt by my brothers and sisters. Eileen, especially, would mammy me in the way that only little girls can.

Living in Drumcondra, I always felt I lived somewhere special. It's only a twenty-five-minute walk from the city centre, but it had its own presence and a real sense of identity. A private Act of Parliament had brought the 'township' into existence in 1878 and it felt more like a village than part of the city. There were historic colleges at the front and side of us in Church Avenue. The front of the house overlooked the mature orchard of All Hallows College. The gardens of Clonturk House were on the other side of our back wall. The Archbishop of Dublin's residence was around the corner on Drumcondra Road. The Botanic Gardens were nearby. It was a short cycle ride to Dublin Zoo. Croke Park was just a stone's throw away. Nothing much happened at Croker that we in Church Avenue didn't know about. Even when we couldn't get to matches, we could still hear the cheers of the crowd as the fortunes of the teams rose or fell. The roar of that crowd – I like to think it must have been for the great Dublin player Kevin Heffernan – is one of my earliest memories. Another is of the distinctive smell of my mother's baking. Even now when I'm out campaigning, a constituent might open the door and I'll catch the familiar waft of home-made brown bread or apple tart to take me right back to the kitchen in Church Avenue.

My mother was a quiet, patient person but immensely strong-willed. Like most women of her generation, she was always working to look after her family. She baked, cooked, cleaned, washed, ironed – struggling from morning till night to keep us all going. She cycled to 7 a.m. Mass each day. The house was always immaculate, with the step bleached, the letter box polished with Brasso and the windows gleaming. It was about self-respect. Even though there was not much money about, we knew who we were and what we were about. And there was always time for the neighbours, especially Mam's great friend Sheila Booth. There was one great sadness though. My parents' third child, John Joseph, who was born on Christmas Day 1942, had died as a baby. It was only as I got older that I began to notice the pain in my mother when she spoke of him or said a rosary for the peaceful repose of his soul.

Mam's own upbringing in Cork had been tough. She was born Julia Hourihane in 1911, hailing from Garranes North, beside

Castledonovan near Dromdaleague in the west of the county. Her family were rural. Growing up there in the early twentieth century was hard. The farmland was not particularly good and they struggled to make ends meet. There was a long history of emigration in the area and a lot of her family, including three of her four brothers, went to England to look for work. She was aged forty when she gave birth to me. Her mother was the only one of my grandparents I knew when I was growing up. Her father, after whom I was named, died when I was a toddler. I remember going down to Cork as a child and, in the way you do when you're young, thinking my grandmother was the oldest, toughest person I had ever seen. She had the shawl and a very strong rural accent, talked a hundred words a minute, and had the kind of deeply creased face that spoke of a life which had seen little in the way of comfort. It was like the pictures of nineteenth-century women in the history books I had at home. No doubt the setting helped, but when I looked at that small old lady it got me thinking about what the famine must have been like. So in her own way, my grandmother ignited her own little spark of nationalism in me.

Not that I needed much of a spark. Later on in my political life, a lot would be made about my father's IRA activities during the civil war, but in reality he was the moderate one in comparison to my mother. When she told stories about the Black and Tans, the look in her eyes turned to hatred. Her small farm was suspected of being a hideout used by IRA men on the run during the war of independence. When the Tans raided the house, they found nothing, so the soldiers slaughtered all the animals, including the geese and turkeys that the family had reared to sell off at Christmas. My grandfather was taken into the yard and a gun put to his head before eventually he was let go. I was very small when Mam told me these stories. The images were so vivid that they burned their way in. Staunch Republicanism, staunch Old IRA. Even in the weeks before her death in 1998, as I was negotiating the Good Friday Agreement, she quizzed me about whether changing Articles 2 and 3 of the Constitution undermined our commitment to a united Ireland. 'Are you sure that it's what Mr de Valera would have wanted, Bertie?' she demanded to know.

Although my father was also from Cork, he had met my mother right here in Drumcondra. Mam left Cork for Dublin in 1929, seeking new opportunities. She was employed as a children's nurse and for a few years worked the summer season on the Isle of Man. The move to Dublin was not easy and Mam often talked of how homesick she felt each time she boarded the Cork train for Dublin. Although she ended up living in Drumcondra for almost seventy years, Mam never lost her Cork accent or pride in her roots. Nobody was surprised when she fell in love with a good Cork man, who she met in 1932 in the parish of St Columba's Church, Iona. My parents would talk of this year as one of great weather and even greater excitement, because the Eucharistic Congress took place in Dublin that summer. It was a good omen for them. In 1937, Julia and Cornelius Ahern married in the Pro-Cathedral and moved into Church Avenue, where they lived happily together all their married life until my father's death in 1990.

My father's people were definitely that bit better off than my mother's. They were a hurling family, Mam's football. The Aherns were farmers from Ballingarry in the parish of Ballyfeard, near Kinsale. 'Con' was born in 1904 and could trace back his roots in the parish for at least two hundred years. I've got cousins who are still farming in the area to this day, including my first cousin on the home farm. It's good agricultural land compared to other parts of the west of the county, so while they were not wealthy people, the family was self-sufficient. Whereas most on my mother's side were forced to emigrate, on my father's the majority were able to stay. I used to visit Cork as a child and got to know the place like a second home. It's so beautiful, just a stone's throw from the Atlantic Ocean, where the family would swim. I spent many happy summers of my childhood there, staying with my aunt and uncle, May and Ted Lyons. The sun always seemed to be shining and my accent got more 'Cork' as each day went by. Like my father before me, I played underage hurling and football for Tracton GAA club and even managed to win a medal. They were idyllic times and reinforced the sense of my roots that I had already developed growing up in the 'little Cork' on Church Avenue.

I say idyllic, but there was one thing that marred those happy summer days. My father never returned to Cork with me. Memories of the civil war cast a shadow over the lives of so many families in Ireland. Mine was no different.

Growing up, my dad naturally spoke about the principles of Republicanism and sometimes even told me a bit about what it had been like in Cork. He told me how fields were never crossed, headlands never walked, about hiding in dykes and trees, and how he had sheltered in bushes for days. Out walking one day, he pulled me back by my collar and told me, 'Never walk straight into the middle of a field. It makes you an easy target.' For a boy, these were good stories, but for him it had been deadly serious. He had lived through the war of independence and the civil war. He had seen friend and foe killed. Getting my father to talk about those days was all about timing. Even as a young lad I learnt to come at it in a roundabout fashion, usually by getting him to talk about Cork. He was too young to have fought actively in the early years of the war of independence, but he would tell me about how the local IRA would get him to run dispatches, taking messages between men in the field. A farm boy, he was a good horseman, so he would gallop around the place. By the time the civil war broke out in 1922, he had become a Volunteer on the Anti-Treaty side, fighting with the Cork 1st and 3rd Brigades.

A lot went on in Cork during the civil war that's controversial to this day. Close to his death, my father warned me not to let the revisionists rewrite the history of the 1920s. But as hard as I tried, I could never get him to talk about his own role in the conflict. Obviously he was closely associated with the flying columns. Perhaps he was even a member. As I got older, I soon learnt that the best way to get Dad to talk about those times was to bring up Tom Barry, commanding officer of the 3rd (West) Cork Brigade flying column. Barry was deeply respected in our house. Dad always said what an honour it had been to know him. No criticism was allowed. Barry had this incredible aura about him. He was hard but his charisma inspired a kind of respect in my father that I rarely saw him show with anyone else. Barry by the late 1940s and 1950s had lost a lot of support among veterans of the civil war. He had run in the 1946 Cork City by-election and been absolutely hammered. But in our house he was still given the respect accorded a former IRA leader. When I was a young TD, I visited Barry a few times at his home in Cork City in 1979. He hadn't much time for Fianna Fáil, but he chatted to me out of loyalty to my father. When I asked Barry about what Dad had done during the civil war, he just replied, 'His patriotic duty, boy.'

Whatever that may have been, it had made Dad a target in West Cork. He was picked up and imprisoned by Free State forces in the summer of 1922. He always used to joke that it wasn't so bad as he was the first man to be locked up in the Cork women's jail. Then he was moved to the infamous 'Tintown' internment camp at the Curragh. In Church Avenue, Dad ran a tight ship. You never stepped out of line without getting a clout. He expected you to do what he said and when he said it. One look from him was enough to quieten us down. I'm sure that tough attitude came from the experience of Tintown. Discipline was how those men survived. You stuck to the cause. You obeyed your commanders. Your duty was to keep the Republican movement going at all costs.

And you honoured 'the dead generations', including your own. After news came through in August 1922 that Michael Collins had been killed at Béal na Bláth, Dad told me he saw some of the hardest men he knew cry. There was certainly no sense of triumph or celebration. Many of those in the Curragh had fought alongside Collins during the war of independence. The fact that Collins was a West Cork man meant that many had known him as a friend. That night the Cork IRA men all knelt down and prayed, and said a rosary for the repose of his soul.

Dad made his own sacrifices in the Curragh too, notably by going on hunger strike. Twice he did it, until the IRA commanders ordered them all off. That was tough and had an impact on his health for the rest of his life. He was a well-built man – and athletic – and he never moaned in his life, but he did tell me that it was the hardest thing he had done. Interrogation techniques were harsh too, and he got roughed up a fair few times. They must have targeted him as a leading man in his own area on the Anti-Treaty side. At the end of the civil war he was one of the last prisoners from Cork let out of the Curragh.

Thinking about the hunger strikes and the interrogations, you can understand why Dad felt so bitter. A lot of that was directed towards the Free Staters and Cumann na nGaedheal. Until the day he died, you'd do well to get through the door in Church Avenue if you were a Fine Gaeler. But there was even frustration about the Republican leadership itself. I once asked Dad if he had any regrets about fighting in the civil war. 'None!' he fired back. Then he added more quietly but with anger, 'Just the one: they gave up.' He always believed the struggle should have gone on until Ireland was united. He admired de Valera for everything he had done from the Easter Rising to the civil war. If anyone deserved to be Taoiseach it was Dev. But when Fianna Fáil came to power in 1932, Frank Aiken became the new Minister for Defence. A message was got to Dad that they would be recruiting for the military and that he should apply, but Dad wasn't interested. He never said it, but I think he had seen enough.

There were a lot of memories for Dad down in Cork as well. After each happy boyhood summer, back in Dublin my father would quiz me for hours. He could recall everything as he had left it – the bends in the road, the old schoolhouse, the lie of the land – and needed to know every detail of how it had changed – what had been built, how people were getting on. It was the same when anyone from Cork came into the house. He wanted every last story out of them. And you could tell that he could still see it all, right there in his mind. I didn't think much about it at the time, but it makes me sad when I remember it now. One of the rituals in our household every Sunday night was to listen to Seán Óg Ó Ceallacháin's sports round-up programme on Radio Éireann. We'd sit there listening in dead silence until Dad had got all the local club scores from home. Somehow it always marked the formal end of the weekend.

Dad loved Cork, kept his accent and proudly declared himself a Cork man all his life. But he never went back, not even for important family occasions. He would never say why. Even my mother said she did not know the reason, although that must have been out of loyalty and discretion. Certainly it pained her that he would not return. I remember being down in Cork one summer around 1964. Dad was on the phone in Drumcondra talking to me in the house in Ballingarry. Dad's brother was right there beside me, so I thought here's my opportunity, and blurted out, 'Da, do you want to talk to David?' He didn't, and hung up straight away. I never got another chance. My uncle died at the end of the sixties and there was no reconciliation. Dad did not go to the funeral.

It was only recently that I began to piece bits of the picture together. In the end it seems to have come down to land. Dad, who was the eldest son, lost his inheritance to his brother David on entering religious life in Dublin. When he came out three years later, his brother, now married with a family, was firmly in possession of the home farm. To make matters worse between them, Dad wrote to David in 1944 during the Emergency asking for shelter for Mam and my siblings if they were to be evacuated from Dublin. That didn't work out and it was the end of the relationship between the two brothers. Fortunately, the bad feeling did not cross the generations and I remain close to my cousins to this day.

I don't know exactly when Dad left the IRA, but from the moment

Fianna Fáil started he was supportive of the party. It must have been the late 1920s when he finally got out. He was not active in the border campaign of the 1950s, but he did work closely with people associated with the National Graves Association, and there was no hiding our Republican sympathies. There were always lilies in the house for the anniversary of the Rising – something I still do to this day – and we'd sing the old Rebel songs, including those of the flying columns like 'On the 28th day of November, the Tans left the town of Macroom'. Well into the 1960s, Dad was still selling raffle tickets to raise funds for the Cork Old IRA. One time around 1970 we did get a visit from the Special Branch when they were updating their lists. By that stage he had been out for decades. Dad always told me that you had to be careful with the IRA that you weren't kept in longer than you wanted. 'When you get away, God, you get away completely,' he said.

I was lucky growing up that I got to spend so much time with him. He worked just yards away from the house, at All Hallows College, one of Ireland's first Catholic missionary seminaries and a prominent fixture in Drumcondra since 1842. After my father gave up training for the religious life – he never told me why he left – he was given a job at All Hallows on the college farm. He stayed there for the next fifty years, eventually becoming farm manager.

A good few years later, some politicians tried to score points off me by saying I thought I could get the farmers' vote just because my father was 'some kind of gardener'. But All Hallows was a real farm, feeding more than four hundred people in the college. It had cows, pigs and chickens, row after row of vegetables, a fantastic orchard. There would have been few places around as self-sufficient in feeding hundreds of mouths. At thirty acres, with another two-hundred-acre site out near Dublin airport, it was probably one of the biggest farms in the city.

I worked alongside Dad every weekend and during the holidays. I would get up early to work on the farm. We'd be milking the cows, filling buckets for the feed and cleaning out the sheds. There was calving in spring. Even the slaughtering held a grisly fascination. I used to love feeding the cats, robbing bits of meat from the swill for them. I had a favourite cat, a granny cat, who lived into her twenties, and years later when I was Taoiseach I would get my own cat, Ben, who probably knew more about what I was thinking than anyone in Leinster House.

Every summer, before I went down to Cork, we'd drive the cattle through the streets of Drumcondra up to the Fairview convent and hospital where they'd keep them until the new term began. My mates – some of them very refined people now – would all line the streets for a laugh, shouting, 'Bertie, you feckin culchie!'

And in a way I suppose I was. My life was a mixture of town and country. All around me in Dublin, things were very, very tough for ordinary people. Unemployment was high; nearby in the inner city there was terrible poverty. On a fairly regular basis, kids would just disappear from our school because their families had emigrated to get work. The fifties were a bad time economically for Ireland and you saw it in people's everyday lives.

Although we didn't have much money, life in Church Avenue was good. With a plentiful supply of fruit and vegetables from the farm at All Hallows, there was always nutritious food to put on the table. That made me stronger and fitter than many of the lads in Drumcondra, which was handy enough when it came to sport or even getting into a fight. Mam always insisted that the whole family ate our main meal together at one o'clock, and because her cooking was so good, we looked forward to it. We weren't short of treats either. Lemon's sweet factory was just over the road and we would stand outside the windows calling to the girls to throw out broken toffee. They would make the Easter eggs about a month early, so we would all be bundling after the chocolate and scoffing ourselves.

All Hallows was the best playground a boy could ask for. Sometimes the president of the college, Father Purcell, would stop to talk and always seemed happy to let us have the run of the place. We'd tie ropes to the chimney pots and hike ourselves up onto the roof of the farm sheds. We'd jump off the walls of the hay sheds, never breaking a bone. I shudder now when I think about myself and my brother Noel taking the large bales of hay and straw to make long dark tunnels, which we'd plunge into without so much as a second thought. There were plenty of pheasants and rabbits. And I developed a great interest in birdwatching, and became good at identifying eggs. I would look into the blackthorn bushes and climb the trees to find as many nests as I could, and then kept going back to them to see the young.

All Hallows gave me a real feel for the practices of rural life, reinforced by the summers spent down in Cork. But the college also gave me a look at the world outside Ireland. Students came from across the globe to train in Drumcondra. There were many English students, and a lot from Newfoundland. They were very bright and devoted guys, who were brilliant about spending time talking to me. They must have thought I was a bit cocky, because I was always the one for a cheeky answer, especially about football. They would use me and a small group of my friends to get fizzy drinks and chocolates from the local shops for them, and afterwards they let us keep the 'money back' on the bottles.

Sports Day was always a great occasion. Those students were very competitive for guys learning to 'love thy neighbour'. There would be a big marquee with tables groaning with cakes and home-made lemonade. We always came home sick. Sports Day was at the end of the year, and this was always a sad time for me. There would be a *Te Deum* sung in the chapel on the last day of the academic year, and I would stand outside listening and then shake hands with the students when they came out. Many of them would be getting ordained, so I knew I might never see them again. All of a sudden this place, filled with people who you knew, playing matches and everything, would go very quiet. Even the cows would be gone. It wasn't just about missing out on earning a few extra bob in weekly pocket money or playing sports, it was also the long chats I would have with the students about religion or politics and history. It would take me a week to understand that I had the place to myself. Then the priests' diocesan summer retreat would happen in the college and it would be all go again.

Being brought up in Church Avenue, there was a particular way of seeing the world and All Hallows added to that. Every student was adopted by an overseas diocese, so there was always a strong sense of being part of a large international community. The college also gave me a different way of looking at life – a recognition that not everything was as cut and dried as I thought. If I got my convictions from my parents, it was the seminarians of All Hallows, such as my life-long friend Father Martin O'Connor, who taught me to think for myself.

As the baby of the Ahern house, that came in handy. There were almost thirteen years between me as the youngest child and Maurice as the eldest. Although outward signs of affection were unusual in those times, we always felt cared for and loved. And the parents had definitely got a bit less strict as they'd gone along. I know the others all thought I got away with murder because I was the young fella. Mind you, if I annoyed Dad, he still gave me a wallop quick enough. Around the dinner table, the debate would fly. Politics, sport and religion: it was always the same. Usually when I tried to butt in, I was told to shut up by my brothers, so I learnt when to come in. It's something that's carried on all my life. I went to St Patrick's National School at just three and a half, so I was the smallest in the class then. Even when I turned up at Leinster House in 1977 I was one of the youngest TDs. So I learnt always to watch first, get my bearings and try not to attract too much in the way of attention. Then when I'd got the lie of the land, I would have my say. It's right back to walking the edge of those fields, really, and avoiding going across the middle of them.

Debate in the house would get even more rowdy when our cousins came. Mam's sister, Molly Horgan, lived in Cabra. She was a very kind woman, who usually slipped me a few bob when she came to visit. 'Good God tonight!' she would say whenever anything out of the ordinary occurred. The Horgans were a large family and they visited regularly. Then there would be the family up from Cork or over from England. So it was a busy and welcoming house, always full of conversation and banter. Gossip would fly; there would be arguments about the usual topics. One thing though – no one was ever drunk. Although Dad was a very gregarious and sociable man, he was fiercely opposed to alcohol. I don't think I ever had a drink in Church Avenue. It just wasn't worth it. He kept a bottle of Paddy to offer someone if they came in. No sooner had they taken a mouthful than he'd be saying, 'Jesus, you'll be drunk there if you're not careful.' He'd have loved the rules today where you can't even have 'one for the road' because you'll be stopped by the Guards. Almost sixty years he lived on Church Avenue and he was never in the Cat and Cage. That was one of the reasons I started drinking Bass. 'Weak as water,' I would tell him.

Maybe he was frightened about what the drink might do to him. He was a big man, physical and well able to look after himself. I know he could be handy at matches when provoked. If any of us gave Mam lip then he would stop us in our tracks. They were so close. He started work at six but would be backwards and forwards to the house all day; for breakfast at nine in the morning, in for his dinner at one and home for his tea at 6 p.m. I don't remember him ever spending a night away. I never thought about what it must have been like for them to be separated when we went down to Cork for our holidays. The only consolation must have been that it gave him a few extra nights at the greyhounds.

At weekends, when my father had milked the cows, we would all go out for walks together, over to Fairview Park, down to the 'Bots' or – my favourite – to the zoo. A lot of these places would get badly run down over the years, so it was really satisfying as

Taoiseach to help restore them to their full glory. That felt like paying off a childhood debt, letting today's kids get the pleasure out of them that I did. It was one of the great things about living in Drumcondra – fantastic facilities as soon as you stepped out of your front door. And we had religion, big time. Obviously there were the Vincentian Fathers at All Hallows. Just outside the door was the Drumcondra Church, which is Church of Ireland. Beside that was the famous graveyard where the remains are buried of the architect James Gandon and the musician Patrick Heeney, who helped compose the national anthem, 'Amhrán na bhFiann'. The Hampton Carmelite monastery and the Sisters of Our Lady of Charity of Refuge at High Park were both close by. The Christian Brothers were in nearby Marino. The famous teacher training college, St Pat's, was across the road from Church Avenue, with Belvedere House and St Patrick's National School on the same site. The Rosminian Fathers were at St Joseph's School for the Blind opposite All Hallows. Around the corner was Clonliffe College, the Catholic diocesan seminary for Dublin founded by Cardinal Cullen, and the palace of the Catholic Archbishop of Dublin. No wonder locals called it the Holy Land.

Every Sunday morning we would go to Mass. It didn't matter if you were dying with the flu, you still went. You would never think of not going, and God help you if you ever complained about it. We went to Corpus Christi on Griffith Avenue, an art deco church built around the 1940s, with a dome that you can see across the city. At other times we might go to one of the college chapels or to the 'Blind'. You would change the church or the priest maybe, for certain festivals, like St Blaise's Day and the blessing of the throats, but you always went. During Lent we would go every day. My first Holy Communion was a big occasion in the house. I had a smart little suit with short trousers, and a big white rosette. It was in the chapel at St Pat's, which was usually private, so it was a big deal to go in. Afterwards I got an apple and an orange.

My favourite day in the liturgical calendar was always Holy

Thursday. That day we would visit the Altar of Repose at seven different churches, following the tradition of visiting the seven pilgrim churches in Rome to gain indulgences. It was a real Drumcondra event. We would go to different churches every year, so it would be one of the rare times to see some of the private chapels like that in the Redemptorist monastery. It was a great Dublin tradition and I was sad when it died out in the 1970s. The changes to the timetable for Holy Thursday introduced after Vatican II had been the beginning of the end for this custom. Mind you, for us as children, it wasn't about having a good laugh or a day out. Our parents were very pleased that we took it so seriously.

It was the same for the Novena of Grace, which begins on 4 March and ends on the 12th, the day of the canonisation of St Francis Xavier. It was first held in Dublin in 1712 in the church at Mary's Lane, now in Halston Street parish, and has taken place in the city every year since. I've done the novena each year since before I was even ten. There's nothing comes close for getting you back to what matters. In 2008, just weeks before I resigned, when I was coming under real political pressure, I would go to one of the three daily devotions at the Gardiner Street church. Whatever difficulties you might be facing in your own life, the novena puts them into perspective. I always felt a special connection with St Francis Xavier's Church in Gardiner Street and in my last speech in the Dáil as Taoiseach, I would quote from Father John Sullivan, a Jesuit whose remains lie in the church. 'Take life in instalments,' he said. 'This day now, at least let this be a good day. Be always beginning, let the past go. Now let me do whatever I have the power to do.'

I might have been brought up as a bit of a culchie, and definitely as a Catholic, but living in Drumcondra also meant that the world would sometimes arrive on your doorstep. I remember going up to the airport perimeter in July 1960 to see the huge UN jets that would take the Irish soldiers out to the Congo. A few months later, in November, I stood on the corner of Blessington Street and Dorset

Street to watch the funeral cortège of some of the nine soldiers who had been killed in the Niemba Ambush. After school, it was always my job to go up to the shop to get the *Evening Press*. I remember seeing the headline 'TRIBESMEN KILL IRISH SOLDIERS' and running up to All Hallows to tell Dad the news. One of the survivors, J. P. Fitzpatrick, was later a constituent of mine and is still affectionately known as 'Congo Joe'.

President Kennedy came in 1963. Dad had already seen him once, when Kennedy visited All Hallows as a senator in the 1950s. Now the sense of excitement was like nothing I had ever seen before. No one could talk of anything else. Just a year before everyone had thought we were going to die in the the Cuban Missile Crisis. We had been told that we were to shelter in the Vincentians' cold stone cellar. So JFK came to Ireland as a hero to us in more ways than one. I stood below the Cat and Cage to watch the cavalcade ride past. Crowds were lining the streets as far as I could see in both directions. When the car arrived, he was standing, looking happy and apparently with no worries for his personal security. I had never seen anyone so glamorous in all my life. I was only beginning to realise the importance of the United States, just getting to grips with how it was so vital in the world. Now here was the US President in Dublin telling us that 'Ireland's hour has come'. Later on, I would use that phrase myself in a speech to the joint Houses of Parliament in Westminster in 2007. I tried to learn Kennedy's speech to the Oireachtas off by heart, reciting bits of it in the bedroom in Church Avenue. As he did for a lot of schoolboys around the country, Kennedy became an obsession for me.

Along with everyone else, I can remember where I was when I heard the desperate news from Dallas on 22 November 1963. My brother Noel was into radios in a big way. He had a state-of-the-art transistor and had rigged up a huge aerial on the shed in the garden. After tea, we were listening to a sports programme on RTÉ previewing the weekend matches, when they cut in to say that Kennedy had been shot. Then, unbelievably, they went back to the sport. We ran out to the shed to get Noel's radio to try and get Voice of America. The reception was awful. Then we heard that President Kennedy was dead. So we took off round the houses telling everyone. The father of a friend of mine, Dermot Lawlor, didn't believe me, but I said, 'No, it's true, we just heard it on Voice of America. Go over to the house.' He welled up, which was not something you would see men do then. By the time we got back, there was a crowd. I think it was about half an hour later that RTÉ finally announced it. That seemed to make it official. Instead of staying around to talk as we normally would when somebody died, everybody just drifted away. I watched the funeral on our rented television in Church Avenue. It just didn't seem real. Kennedy had only been in Drumcondra five months earlier. Later, when I was Taoiseach, I would go to early-morning Mass in St Matthew's Cathedral, Washington, around St Patrick's Day every year. A Monsignor would bring me to my place and I would always read the inscription on the ground which marked where Kennedy's coffin had stood for his Requiem Mass in 1963. Kennedy's reputation has gone up and down at different times in the years since his death, but I have never lost my childhood admiration for this great president.

Political events in Ireland made an impact on me as well. The first election I can remember is when de Valera ran for president in 1959. A few years later, in May 1963, I got my first chance to do a bit of campaigning. A teacher of mine at St Patrick's National School, 'Stan the Man' O'Brien, ran in a by-election in Dublin North East after the death of the sitting TD, Jack Belton. Stan was a member of the local O'Donovan Rossa Cumann, so all the Fianna Fáil kids in the school were up and down lamp posts for him, putting up posters. This was my first time out, but it was not a good start to my political career: Stan lost to Paddy Belton, Jack's brother, so the seat stayed with Fine Gael.

This was all a bit of fun, but what really began to develop my political thinking was the fiftieth anniversary of 1916. Everyone in our house was aware of just how important that was. We had the tricolour flying from the window. It was a big event for Fianna Fáil in our area as well. The two local cumainn were both named for men with 1916 connections: Dick McKee, who had fought with Thomas MacDonagh, and O'Donovan Rossa, whose funeral in 1915 had inspired Pearse's greatest speech – 'The fools! The fools! They have left us our Fenian dead.' That was another one I learnt by heart.

Dad had been taking me to commemorations for years – even as a young boy I remember going to the Martin Savage memorial on the Navan Road on the last Sunday before Christmas. Savage had fought with Pearse in the GPO and later died in 1919 trying to assassinate the viceroy, Lord French, in an ambush. When I was a bit older, we would go up to Boland's Mills and the Custom House, and to the annual commemoration at Arbour Hill. But 1966 was something really special. Every week in the run-up to Easter Sunday there was some kind of commemoration. RTÉ broadcast hours of programmes with veterans recalling the events. We all went to O'Connell Street for the ceremonial parade past the GPO. When the army fired the *feu de joie* from the roof of the GPO it sent a thrill right through me. I looked up at Dad, wondering what he was thinking, and his face showed how proud he was to be there.

That was a great day, but the real highlight of 1966 for me was the Croke Park pageant, Aiséiri. They had built a replica of the GPO. The great actor Ray McAnally played the role of Pearse. There were explosions and everything. James Connolly was carried in for his execution. It was a real drama. I had never seen anything like it in all my life. We were in the Hogan Stand, mostly schoolchildren, and when they read out the names of the executed there was absolute silence. It was like everyone was holding their breath. A stadium of thousands of people that is suddenly quiet is always moving, but this was something else. It left a lasting impression.

This was when my interest in the Rising really took off. A few months later, in November, I went to the Pro-Cathedral on my own for the lying-in-state for Seán T. O'Kelly, who had been involved in 1916 and had been president from 1945 to 1959. My real passion was for Pearse. I got my hands on everything I could. Books, pamphlets, even bits of memorabilia if I could afford them (I've quite a collection now). I would go on little pilgrimages to places associated with him. Years later, I even got to meet a woman who had the two revolvers that had been fired over O'Donovan Rossa's grave after Pearse's oration. She had lived in St Joseph's Cottages in Berkeley Road and smuggled the guns in under her drawers when she was pregnant. What attracted me to Pearse was not just his fine oratory, but also his energy. He promoted Gaelic games, because they taught you self-discipline, to play for the team, and the importance of using your head, your heart and your physical fitness. I understood from an early age that Pearse was a patriot and a visionary. He is truly an inspiring figure to me.

Pearse's self-discipline was something I recognised too in the Taoiseach, Seán Lemass, and around this time he became the political hero to match my historical champion Pearse. What really appealed was that he had been just a couple of years older in 1916 than I was then and that he had carried Connolly's wounded body from the GPO. That was enough to make him my idol, just as Dev was for my parents' generation. Only later would I discover that my schoolboy belief that he was Ireland's most capable Taoiseach was absolutely right. Years afterwards I was delighted to launch John Horgan's biography of Lemass, and also a collection of essays entitled *The Lemass Era*. Then and now, I never miss a chance to state my belief that Lemass was in the vanguard of almost every great event and decision that shaped the Ireland in which we live. As a child of the Lemass era, I could see Ireland prosper under his leadership, and his philosophy that 'a rising tide lifts all boats' would become mine.

It was around this time, newly inspired, that I started to get an interest in debates, always arguing the Lemass line. I was at St Aidan's

Christian Brothers School by this stage. Bridget Sweeney, a teacher at Mercy Beaumont School for Girls, put a team together with St Aidan's and we began going round Dublin debating other schools. There was nothing we liked better than crossing the river and trouncing teams from the south side. Even back then they liked to give us a right slagging for being Northsiders. But growing up in Church Avenue had given me a good training in how to deal with those tactics, so we'd just be nice and polite until kick-off, and then try to land a few blows.

St Aidan's was good for me, even if I didn't get off to a good start there. My brothers had both gone to O'Connells School, whose alumni included Seán Lemass and the former Fine Gael Taoiseach, John A. Costello. The year I was due to go, the Christian Brothers from O'Connells decided to set up a new school up the road in Whitehall. I say school, but really it was two prefabs – 'the huts' – in the grounds of Larkhill Boys' National School. With my name beginning with 'A', I was the first boy enrolled. Thirty years or so later, as Taoiseach, I would help them finally get permanent buildings for the school, and would bring Tony Blair along for a visit.

St Patrick's National School had been very easy-going, but this new school – it didn't even have a name when we arrived – was very tough. For the first time I was exposed to guys from all over the north city. I'd come from a very protected world – Drumcondra all the way – so it was a shock not to know everyone. And because I'd started school so young, a lot of these guys were a year or two older than me. Fortunately I was good at sport, so this meant even the hardest fellas often wanted me on their team. If not, I was on the school cross-country team and could run very fast if I needed to.

The principal, Brother Hayes, was a dynamic character. Brother Clarke was the funny one, always saying things like, 'God gave me terrible eyes, but a brilliant pair of glasses.' There was one teacher, though, who didn't seem to like any of us in that first class. For sure he didn't like me. He would set on me, ripping into me hard. That was enough to make me hate the school to begin with. When we got back for the start of the second year, it turned out that he'd gone off to get married. Perhaps I'd put him off his vocation. In any case I was delighted. Once he'd gone, I settled into the school, and even though they worked me hard, I enjoyed it.

One teacher was a real inspiration. Mr Coughlan came into the school to teach us commerce. He was an accountant who spotted that I was good with figures, and he would really encourage me to take an interest in business and finance. When the school stopped doing Saturday mornings in 1968–69, he would still come in to give extra classes to get us ready for our Leaving Cert that year. He was the first one to suggest that I might think about accountancy as a career, suggesting I enrol in the College of Commerce in Rathmines. We all need a push. He did it for me.

Not that I was just working at my books. That last year at Aidan's was also when I began to get interested in girls. Every school around that time used to organise regular discos, so there'd always be one to go to somewhere each weekend. I don't know if she will thank me for outing her, but my first real girlfriend was Helen Stenson. She was a lovely girl. A blonde from Beaumont.

So I'd got off to a cracking start.

2

I'M YOUR MAN

Bord Bainne Cheantar Bhaile Átha Cliath. You might think that the Dublin District Milk Board doesn't sound like a glamorous place for an ambitious young man straight out of school to start his working life. But you would be wrong.

No sooner had I done my Leaving Cert than I got a job as an accounts clerk there, making the trek out to the Naas Road every morning. I finished my last exam at five o'clock on the Saturday – it was English and we were repeating it because some of the papers had been stolen that year – and started work at eight-thirty the following Monday morning. My sister Eileen had worked at the Milk Board and got me a summer job. When a position came up for an accounts clerk, I went for it and got it. It was nice to think that the Milk Board was also where the Taoiseach of the day, Jack Lynch, had started his own career. Of course as well as being the party leader, Lynch was a Cork All-Ireland hurling and football star, and loving sport and politics like I did, I felt I was following in good footsteps. You can imagine the banter that the office new boys had to put up with. 'Ah, sure you'll be all right,' they would say. 'One fella in here ended up running the country.' Needless to say it never crossed my mind that I would eventually overtake Jack as the second longest leader of Fianna Fáil after de Valera.

It was at the Milk Board I first got a taste for organised politics, although that came through the union not the party. I was convinced by the younger staff and by one of the older hands, Yam Cashin, to put my name forward as a rep on Branch 15 of the Federated Workers' Union of Ireland – Jim Larkin's old union. Then I became the scrutineer. That was how I got to know Roddy Connolly, the son of one of my heroes from 1916, James Connolly. Roddy claimed he had taught Lenin to speak English with a Rathmines accent. He had certainly lost none of his passion for socialism. I think he was impressed that I knew so much about the Rising, and we talked a lot about it. Roddy was hostile to Fianna Fáil. My comeback to him was straight from Seán Lemass: 'The real Labour Party in Ireland is Fianna Fáil!' Roddy always struggled with that one. I enjoyed our discussions. We mostly talked about the union, and he taught me how proportional representation worked. Even now some people say to me, 'You should have been Labour.' But I never had any time for David Thornley, Conor Cruise O'Brien and all those intellectual types – I thought they were going to ruin the country. I respected the Workers' Union. Given my own background, I understood what they were doing and knew that without them ordinary working people would just get walked on. I made some friendships through the unions that have lasted throughout my political career.

Most nights after work, I would take the bus across the city to the College of Commerce in Rathmines to prepare for my accountancy exams. Even though I had a job, it did not cross my mind to stop studying. Education was important in the Ahern household. All five children had completed the Leaving Cert. Except for my last couple of years, when I benefited from the free secondary education scheme introduced by Donogh O'Malley as Minister for Education, my parents had made financial sacrifices to put us all through school. They were progressive too, with the girls as well as the boys encouraged to make the most of ourselves. And it did not stop with the Leaving Cert. We were all prodded onto third level at night. Maurice and Kathleen did accountancy. Noel went to University College Dublin and also to Rathmines to study transport. Eileen did her BA at UCD.

Studying at night was what most people like us did if we wanted to get on. I would finish at 10 p.m. and then get the bus back to Drumcondra. The next morning it was up to do some swotting before heading back into work for half eight. Work, study, work. That would be the pattern of my life for the next few years. This was when I started to appreciate what I had learnt from my parents: that you had to put in the hours and that success came from hard work.

In April 1974, just as I was finishing my training, a job as assistant accountant came up at the Mater Hospital. The Sisters of Mercy had been running the hospital for more than a century, and by the 1970s they were putting it through a process of modernisation. I was thrilled, because it was a job on my patch in a prestigious institution. As a trainee at the Milk Board I had been on IR£1,500 a year. Now I started on IR£2,200 and got another raise when they promoted me to cost accountant. The hours were longer. I would be in at eight in the morning and would stay working into the night. On Saturdays, I would drop in for a few extra hours. It was hard work but I enjoyed the challenge. It reinforced my belief in putting in the effort to get results. I would stay at the Mater until 1987, when I got my first cabinet appointment.

When I wasn't at my desk, I was out on the sports pitch. At school I had come up through the age groups with Home Farm FC and the Whitehall Gaels (later Whitehall Colmcille). The year after we left school, a crowd of us including Paddy Dalton, Pat Byrne, Brian Hawkins, Fintan Diggins and Michael Lenihan decided to set up our own team in the amateur league. We called it All Hampton, a name that combined All Hallows College and the Hampton Convent that was next to it. I was still well in at the college, so we negotiated a deal on the pitch and even paid a bit extra to use the changing rooms.

Every team loved coming to us because we were one of the few outfits with hot showers. We got off to an awful start, losing our first twelve games, some of them big drubbings. But then we got it going, reached the semi-final of the Leinster Shield. After that, we went from strength to strength. The next year we put out two teams. I wasn't a particularly skilful player, but I was hard. I played left back, although I was no Denis Irwin. There was a great social life around the matches, and we would go out drinking afterwards. I got a lot of ribbing because I was always moaning that people didn't take the matches seriously enough. We were a good team and did well, but we should have done better with what we had.

If I wasn't playing matches at weekends I was watching them. I had a season ticket to support Drumcondra FC in the League of Ireland since I was old enough to go, and would keep that up until their last season in 1971–72. Shelbourne were our tenants in Tolka Park at the time, so with each team playing home games on alternate Sundays, there was a game to go to every week. Then there was the GAA. I had played a bit, and of course I had grown up with it with Dad at home. For us it was Dublin for the football and Cork for the hurling. I had certainly roared myself hoarse when Cork won the hurling in 1966, just as I had done when Dublin won the Sam Maguire in 1963. Later, in the mid-seventies, there would be tremendous excitement when Dublin won the All-Ireland three championship seasons out four. We always went to the Canal End. Dad had his spot, eight steps down from the scoreboard. Very organised. Most of the time it was a pretty small crowd, but for big matches, we would be there when the gates opened at twelve o'clock. God help anyone who was in Dad's place. He wasn't against a bit of pushing to make sure he got his spot. Croker was not as plush in those days, but the atmosphere was great and that has not changed. Just before they knocked down the Canal End in 1998, I went back with my brother Maurice for one last time. Eight steps down, just like the old days.

And of course there was also Manchester United. Every Saturday after getting in from an All Hampton or Gaels match, I would throw down the kitbag in front of the television to get the result. It doesn't take much working out why so many in my generation supported United. I was six years old when the Munich air crash happened. I didn't know much about the Football League then, but I remember Dad telling me about the crash and that Liam Whelan, one of the players who died, was a local lad from Cabra who had started out at Home Farm. We went out to watch the hearse go past. It paused outside Home Farm, with all their players forming a guard of honour. That was the moment I decided I would always support United.

Inevitably, I started following the Irish players in the team. Noel Cantwell was a Cork man. Tony Dunne went to Old Trafford from Shels. Shay Brennan was in the Ireland team. There was even the older brother of a kid I used to play football with near his house at 'the dumps' in Drumcondra, who had gone to the same school as me. He started out at United in the 1960s before moving on to other clubs, including Millwall. I knew his dad and his brother, but Eamon Dunphy would crop up later in my political career. I also had a soft spot for Hull City when the goalkeeper Maurice Swan, who played for Drums, went there in the early 1960s. Hull were in the Fourth Division at the time, so I always had to wait ages for their result to be read out on Saturday, which made everyone laugh.

Then there was George Best. Not only was Bestie one of the greatest footballers this island has ever produced, he was also one of the finest of all time. Words can hardly describe his talent. He was a football genius. To say that his performance in the 1968 European Cup Final was one of the highlights of my teenage years would be an understatement. Best came from a working-class family, so I felt we shared a similar background, and the fact that he was from a Unionist tradition gave me a different perspective on the North.

It was through sport I met my wife Miriam. She was eighteen and some girl: good-looking with long blonde hair, a wonderful personality and a terrific sense of humour. The first time I really sat up and paid attention was at an All Hampton dinner dance at the North Star Hotel on the North Strand. It was near the end of the 1971–72 season. Everyone met for a few jars beforehand near the Five Lamps and that was when I saw her, all dressed up and looking like a million dollars. 'Jesus,' I said to myself, 'is that Miriam Kelly?' One of the other lads, Frank Little, was her partner for the night and so I had to bide my time. Although I was never much of a rugby man, I made sure I got myself invited to the end-of-season club dinner at the Suttonians, where Miriam's brother played. That was when I got my first dance with her and it took off from there. We got engaged in March 1974, and married at St Columba's Church in September the following year on my birthday. Dáithí Ó Broin was my best man. Miriam was twenty-one. We went to Malta for our honeymoon and got back just in time for the All-Ireland final on 28 September. There was a shocking tackle on the Kerry captain, Mickey Ned O'Sullivan, and Dublin lost the match, so it wasn't a good day. But nothing was going to spoil our good humour.

On our return, we moved into our new house, 133 Pinebrook Road, Artane. My sister Kathleen put up the deeds to part of her farm to bridge the small difference between the mortgage and the cash deposit that we had saved. It was a lovely place, but I think we both felt a shock being away from Drumcondra. Miriam came from a family of eleven, who had all had grown up in a house near Croke Park. Now we were on our own in the suburbs and we knew no one. It really wasn't that far from home, but it felt like a different world. After a year or so, we got to know our neighbours, Joe and Helen Burke, and finally we started to settle. We even got a dog, Blondie. Every weekend we would head back to Drumcondra, going for dinner on alternate Sundays to Miriam's and Church Avenue. The two families got on really well. The Kellys were great people and they really welcomed me into their home. Like the Aherns, they were ordinary working people who knew that hard work and education were the only way to get on, and they did that extremely success-fully. In Church Avenue, they all took to Miriam. She got close to my sisters. And Dad absolutely adored her. Miriam's own father was an older man, so she knew just how to handle mine, teasing him and listening to his stories. In fact, everyone loved Miriam. I was lucky to have her.

A few years later we would have the girls, Georgina first in 1979 and then Cecelia in 1981. Georgina was born six weeks premature, and that gave us a bit of a scare. We named her after Miriam's aunt, who was a nun, although I would be lying if I said there wasn't a bit of 'George' Best in there when I agreed, 'Yeah, that's nice.' Right from the start, she had such a winning personality, always smiling and looking at you all soft with her big eyes. Cecelia arrived just after a general election, so her poor mam had been out canvassing when she was six months pregnant, with the little one in tow in the buggy. If Georgina was calm, Cecelia was into everything. She wanted to climb up ladders, stand on her head, jump into the sea. It was the old story: we were careful with the first one, more relaxed the second time round. Whatever mistakes we made – and most of them were mine – we didn't do too badly. They've both turned out to be wonderful young women. No wonder their mam and dad are so proud of them.

As a family, we spent some of our happiest times in Kerry. I had first started going down to Ballybunion in the early 1970s. Then we discovered Dingle. There was a special little B & B run by Tom and Muiríde Crowley. They were lovely people and it became our hide-away. The year Georgina was born, Charles Haughey, being friendly to a first-term TD, brought us all out to Inishvickillane, one of the most remote of the Blasket Islands. Georgina, who was the youngest baby on the island in a hundred years, was the definite star of the show, putting even Charlie in the shade. Over the years he would have us back and the girls became very fond of him. Most of the time on holidays, though, we just kept to ourselves, enjoying being together. For at least a few weeks, Kerry was the real thing: a proper holiday. Even now the girls will come down with me every year. They've got such busy lives, but for me it's just like it was when they were kids. I think it's the same for Miriam, who I know still goes some summers. We've both got such lovely memories of that time when we were a young family all together.

By the time I had met Miriam in 1972, I had been a member of Fianna Fáil for over a year. I joined the O'Donovan Rossa Cumann, which had a long history in Drumcondra. It had previously been a Sinn Féin cumann and could trace its origins back to a Fenian group in the area from the nineteenth century. Lorraine Booth, with whom I had grown up in Church Avenue, was the recruitment officer. She took me to my first monthly meeting in Amiens Street. Years later, an old lady called Emma Murphy sent me a letter saying that she remembered me going to my first meeting in the 1970s and never would have guessed that this guy from Drumcondra with the long black hair would ever be Uachtarán Fhianna Fáil. The chairman was called Tom Houlihan. He was a real pro going back to the 1940s, very much an organisation man, whose father-in-law had been one of the key organisers in the O'Donovan Rossa Cumann in the 1920s. Tom soon became my mentor. In 1972 I was made cumann treasurer, and the following year, secretary. The year after that I became secretary of the organisation committee in the new Dublin Finglas constituency. Three years later I was selected as a Fianna Fáil candidate.

That makes it sound seamless, but the early 1970s was a turbulent time to join Fianna Fáil, not least for me. I had come from a strong political family, known for our Republican sympathies. Throughout the sixties I had done a bit of leafleting and postering at election time. We had been strong de Valera supporters and I had been greatly influenced by Seán Lemass. Although I came to respect him later, at this time I was not as sure about Jack Lynch. Dad admired him because he was 'Cork' and a GAA man. But politics in the South were being driven by events in the North. That drove a wedge into Fianna Fáil politics that would not be resolved until the mid-1990s. It also forced me to make hard choices about where my political priorities lay.

I had been up to the North a few times on school trips, but I only really got to know it at the end of the 1960s when my brother Maurice married Moira, a lovely woman from Ballynahinch, County Down. The wedding was around the time of the riots in Belfast in the summer of 1969, so some of us went up to look around. We went in early one morning when we thought it would be quiet. Bombay Street was a total wreck. Burnt out. Barricades everywhere. There was no tension, because nobody was around. The army were in control around the Falls Road by this stage, but we only saw a few soldiers. It was eerie. We started wandering about a bit. What hit me about Belfast was how close all the different areas were. You turned the corner and went from a Nationalist to a Loyalist street. In a Protestant area, I was there with my new Kodak when a couple of heavies came over and told us to stop taking photos. 'Give me your camera,' one said. 'Would you not just take the film?' I asked. 'I'm only after getting the camera.' So he did. Fair play, I thought.

But not much else up there seemed fair to me. Looking at all the destroyed houses and wrecked cars, I thought that here were all these Nationalist people just trying to get their civil rights and for their efforts they were getting burnt out of their homes. There was no protection, no support. On 13 August 1969, the Taoiseach, Jack Lynch, had said that the Republic 'can no longer stand by' while Nationalists were being attacked in Derry. I was happy when I heard that. The Irish Army mobilised to the border, setting up field hospitals to look after Nationalist refugees. We thought that was great. It looked like real action to protect these people. That was when the Loyalists had reacted by destroying Bombay Street. It was left to the British Army to rescue Catholics in Belfast and Derry. There was a lot of talk about lads getting together and going up to Dundalk with the trucks. Everyone was saying, 'We've got to do something.' The people

I was drinking with thought it should have been the Irish Army going in, not the Brits. We were shocked when we heard that Haughey had been sacked over the Arms Crisis, but I suppose we were glad that someone was trying to do something. God knows what really went on with the Arms Crisis, but I can understand now the kind of pressure that Lynch was under, even if back then I just wanted us to go in.

For me, the tipping point came on Bloody Sunday, 30 January 1972, when the paras killed thirteen unarmed civil rights protesters in Derry. It had been terrible weather in Dublin. I remember we played a match that afternoon on a snowy pitch with an orange ball. I had gone over to Church Avenue and then I heard it on the radio. I got really fired up. I was fuming. Dad was very upset, trying to calm me down. I went to the Ivy House with some of the lads, including Robin Booth and Dáithí Ó Broin. And you could feel it in the atmosphere. Something had changed for us all.

My immediate priority the next day was to support and encourage colleagues in the unions who were organising a protest march to the British Embassy in Merrion Square. Thirty thousand people turned up. The atmosphere was fierce. People were throwing petrol bombs and missiles. Union Jacks were burnt on mock coffins. The protests went on for almost three days, until on 2 February the embassy was burnt down. I was there for all three of those days and recognised some of the people who were involved in burning the embassy. The Gardaí hardly bothered to make an effort to stop them.

That was the moment when some people left Fianna Fáil. I wasn't interested in any splinter groups, even though ten members of my own cumann had left to join Kevin Boland's Aontacht Éireann in 1971. But I could understand how people had to decide between the constitutional road or the armed struggle. Some of the lads I knew had already joined the IRA, asking who the hell was going to protect the Nationalists in the North if we didn't. I remember talking with one of my closest Drumcondra friends, someone I really respected, an educated guy who had been Fianna Fáil all the way through, and him saying to me, 'Jesus, haven't we got nowhere just playing tiddlywinks with them? It's time for a real campaign.'

Bloody Friday, 21 July 1972, made a big impact on me as well. In seventy-five minutes the Provisional IRA detonated at least twenty bombs in Belfast that killed nine people and mutilated some 130 more. It was horrific. One of the victims was a fourteen-year-old schoolboy. Of the injured, seventy-seven were women or children out shopping in the city centre. Seeing the pictures on television of body parts being collected in black plastic bin bags was enough to make me see sense. I talked about it with Dad. He had seen some things in his time, but he was angry at what the Provos had done. He was an old school Republican. He could admire a border campaign. Even the deaths of British soldiers in the North left him unmoved. But targeting civilians was another matter. You could expect gun battles as a soldier, but putting bombs in cars or buses that killed innocent women and children was murder. It disgusted him. That had a big influence on me.

I remembered that conversation on 17 May 1974, the day of the Dublin and Monaghan bombings, which killed thirty-four civilians, including a pregnant woman and her unborn child. It was Friday night and a crowd from work had gone for a drink in Crowley's on Hill Street. It was not that far from where one of the bombs went off. We rushed around the corner to see what had happened and then went back to the Mater to do what we could. It was mayhem, everyone under incredible pressure, so I tried to help with the admissions, but I was only after working in the hospital a short time. Most of the time I just stood there consumed by the horror of it all. The carnage was terrible. Blood everywhere. Victims hanging on for life. The dead brought in and taken to the morgue. I had seen it on television, but nothing prepared me for the real thing. Anyone would feel revulsion at the violence that had caused this. There had to be another way, I kept telling myself.

That was when I started to think about politics really seriously, maybe even having a run for the Dáil. I had a long talk in the Mater with the the senior consultant, Bryan Alton, who was very encouraging. He was Dev's doctor and one of the most famous physicians of the day. In 1975 he saw an opportunity for me and passed my name on to another of his well-known patients, Charlie Haughey, who had just returned to the party's front bench as health spokesman. That got me on the committee to draw up the health manifesto for the next election. It also got me noticed in the party as the new guy from the Mater who had got a head for figures. Then Séamus Brennan, the general secretary, put me on another committee to do a statistical analysis of the potential FF vote under the 1974 Electoral Amendment Act. We prepared a report for the National Executive. It said that despite the 'Tullymander' being a partisan move by the Fine Gael/Labour coalition to keep them in office, just a 5 per cent swing could turn a general election to Fianna Fáil's advantage.

The executive didn't pay much attention, but Brennan did. He sent the report on to Lynch, who called us in for a short meeting. We brought him through the figures and he seemed impressed. It was my first proper meeting with him, and now I could see the steel behind the friendly manner. Clearly he saw something in me too, because soon I was invited to join a group from Ógra Fianna Fáil on RTÉ's 7 Days to show the youthful face of the party. Back then, there was not much choice about what we watched on television, so I got big exposure from the programme. It helped establish me as a coming man in the party, and reinforced my position in the local organisation.

The 'Tullymander' had created a new constituency, Dublin Finglas, which included the O'Donovan Rossa Cumann. The Comhairle Dáil Cheantair had already agreed on two candidates. Jim Tunney was the outgoing TD for the area, and nothing was going to stop him getting re-elected. He was a popular guy, who had played football for Dublin. He had a natty dress sense and was known as the Yellow Rose of

Finglas, because he always wore a rose in his buttonhole. The other candidate was Danny Bell, a local councillor since 1974. Danny was all right, but the problem was that he was from the same part of the constituency as Tunney. The constituency delegate on the National Executive, Ray Walsh, wanted us to run three candidates, using the third as a way of sweeping up votes for Tunney and Bell in the Drumcondra end of the constituency. It might also give a young hopeful a decent run-out in a general election. Once that prospect was raised there was never much doubt I would give it a go. I discussed it with my brothers, Maurice and Noel, and with Joe Burke. They all thought I should put my name forward. Noel was especially gung-ho. 'If you run,' he told me, 'you'll win.'

That didn't mean I wouldn't have to work for it. I was up against some tough local candidates for that third spot, including a future Master of the High Court, Edmund Honohan, and Michael Shortall, whose sister Róisín would later become a Labour TD and whose father was one of our party's leading lights in the area for many years. I canvassed all the cumainn in the constituency to put my case. Each cumann had three delegates at the constituency convention to select the ticket, and for most of the cumainn it was a question of going round to someone's house to make a direct pitch. I kept my appeal very simple. I was from an ordinary working family around here. I played for the local sporting and youth clubs. I'm at the Mater. I've done a decent job on the organisational side in the constituency. Give me a chance and I'll bring in votes in the Drumcondra end of the constituency.

Tunney, briefed by Walsh, was very supportive. Bell was more neutral. I think even then he could see the dangers. That became apparent at the convention in Beneavin College, Finglas, a month before the general election. Tunney was elected by a huge majority. Bell came second. I was third, but only four votes behind him. That definitely put the wind up Bell. His supporters moved that the party should only put two on the ticket to avoid splitting the vote. I was worried, but Walsh, presumably with Tunney's blessing, told me to wait for the National Executive to put me on. That was all right for him to say, but I knew that the likes of Honohan and Shortall were better known at headquarters than I was. Honohan was also close to Lynch and involved in writing the party manifesto, so he was an insider. But Walsh was as good as his word. He went to the National Executive and spoke up for me. With less than four weeks to go, my name was added to the ticket as a Fianna Fáil candidate for the Dublin Finglas constituency.

From the beginning I decided that I wasn't in this for a laugh. I was going to give it a right good go. Dáithí Ó Broin ran my campaign and he put in a Trojan amount of work. He's a really bright guy, phenomenally organised, and as hard as nails when it comes to campaigning. He also had a car, a brown Datsun, which helped. Miriam, my brothers and my sisters did their bit. Joe Burke was around and put up all the posters. Brian Bogle was out canvassing all hours and, with his wife Anna, would continue to do so until his death in 2003. Even better, he could sing the most wonderful rendition of 'Danny Boy' any of us had ever heard. There was also Paul Kiely and lots of the football crowd. It was a small group, but they gave everything to the campaign. We took over the front room in Church Avenue and used it as an office. The walls were covered with maps and lists of streets and voters. Names were crossed off and colour-coded after each canvass. Mam and Dad, bless them, never complained as their home was turned into a public thoroughfare. Mam fed and watered everyone, making sure that nobody canvassed on an empty stomach. Church Avenue would remain as HQ for election campaigns right up until 1989. Friends and family always rallied round and the craic was mighty. It was the foundation of a wonderful team spirit, which was always a key to my success.

One of the crucial figures in all this was Tony Kett, who over the next three decades until his untimely death in 2009 would be my closest friend. I can honestly say that I would have never made it to Dáil

Éireann without Tony's encouragement, dedication and organisational skills. He worked on that first election campaign and he was deeply involved in every other election I contested afterwards. He was a hugely committed political activist with a genius for electioneering. He even kept All Hampton going when I got elected. I had first met Tony in April 1974, when I was twenty-two years old and a new recruit in the Mater. Tony was already on the staff and a great friendship grew between us and later our two families. We had mutual interests in sport and politics, we both liked to be busy, and I suppose as young lads we also imagined that we worked and played hard. In those days, Tony and I were in each other's company all the time. We would see each other at work and later in the evenings at Fianna Fáil meetings and at the sports club, or out and about doing a spot of canvassing or having a drink. To start with, we were better known as footballers than as politicians. In fact, if truth be told, we only got really immersed in politics as frustrated footballers, when our legs started to go.

Tony loved canvassing and he loved meeting the different characters on the doorsteps. I remember one evening canvassing down in Vincent's Street – off Berkeley Road. Tony called at a door and was met by a tall woman we might diplomatically describe as being well endowed. You can imagine Tony's surprise when her opening words to him were 'What are you going to do about my knockers?' It wasn't often you saw Tony lost for words but we were all taken aback that day. The lady continued to repeat the question and became more irate when Tony started cracking up. Her closing line as Tony almost fell over the side wall laughing was 'All Fianna Fáil can do is laugh when me and my neighbours have had our Victorian brass knockers robbed!'

In 1977 we would have probably replaced her brass knockers ourselves if she had promised to vote for us. We were the rank outsiders and needed every vote we could get. But we did have a plan and it was a simple one. We needed to get enough votes in Drumcondra and Glasnevin to give me a chance of getting a good first preference vote. There was a vacuum there left by the retiring TD Celia Lynch and we were going to fill it.

The conventional wisdom at the time was that you had to have as wide a coverage in a constituency as possible. That meant going for high visibility in public areas, letting the voters come to you. If you went knocking on doors it was in a group, identifying your likely supporters, then getting your people to say, 'Would you like to meet the candidate?' My technique was different. I had identified a small local area to canvass. On the June bank holiday weekend I went door to door on my own. We made sure they had already got the leaflets. We knew which houses were ours, but I went to them all, including Fine Gael and Labour supporters. I needed their second preferences to knock out Brendan Halligan, the well-known Labour candidate. Everyone in my cumann area got to look me in the eye and to take the measure of me. If they were prepared to talk, I made my case. This was an important election for the country. We'd had a disastrous coalition government since 1973 that had doubled the debt. Here I was, a young man from the community, saying, 'Give me a chance to speak on your behalf.'

I was establishing a bond as a local candidate. Celia Lynch's supporters started to come on board, and we began to make a few raids into the Finglas area. I would turn up at supermarkets, to flirt with the housewives and joke about football with the husbands. That really gave Tunney and Bell the hump, made worse when party HQ put me on an election TV broadcast. This was also the start of a bit of aggravation between the campaigns. Bell we didn't care about, but Tunney was the sitting TD and trickier to deal with. He had warned us off his area, but was happy to muscle in on ours. And Dáithí was no shrinking violet. When Tunney's team turned up in Drumcondra to put the squeeze on us, they were informed, probably not very politely, that they might consider returning to Finglas at their earliest convenience. After all, he was the Yellow Rose of Finglas, not Drumcondra.

On the election morning, 16 June, we pulled off a great coup by leafleting at 5 a.m. Everyone in our small local area woke up to 'Good morning, voters!' The message was: 'We hope we haven't bothered you too much in the last few weeks, but please consider giving us your vote.' That campaign tactic hadn't been done before, so it would be much commented on afterwards. Then it was down to the polling stations, making sure we had someone at every place. Elections were a rough-and-tumble business back then. There were no rules about keeping a certain distance away from the polling station. Canvassers would jostle for space, which would often intimidate voters. It was important to have your own people there to ensure fair play.

When I went to bed that night I had no idea whether I would be elected. We had worked incredibly hard, really given it our best shot. Some of the papers were saying that the party was going to lose, but I was confident about our chances in the constituency and nationally. I could feel the goodwill towards the party on the doorstep, but would it be enough to put me in? I was confident Fianna Fáil would take Labour's seat. The question was whether it would be me or Bell.

The following day I left it as long as I could before going down to Bolton Street for the count. When I arrived in the early after-noon, there was great excitement. Everyone knew by this stage that Fianna Fáil were sweeping the country. I didn't go inside, but every so often one of my tally men – Paul Kiely, Tony Kett and Dáithí Ó Broin – would come out and tell me how it was going. On the first count Tunney was elected with 7,963 first preferences or 28.75 per cent of the vote. Luke Belton of Fine Gael was in second place with 3,896 first preferences. Halligan was on 3,055. Bell had 2,598. But on that first count, I was in third place with 3,729 first preferences. I think that was the moment when I thought it was going to happen for me.

Around 8.30 p.m. the returning officer went to the microphone to announce that Bartholomew Patrick Ahern had reached the quota to win the second seat and was duly elected. It was an incredible moment. Miriam gave me a huge kiss. The lads were all slapping me on the back. Eileen was emotional. Jim Tunney came over to me and was very warm in his congratulations. Ray Walsh was delighted. Bell on the other hand was bitterly disappointed, which I could well understand. I got to know him better later, but on this occasion he just said 'Well done' or something, and that was it.

My parents, who were getting on in age, hadn't come to the count, so the first thing I wanted to do was to go back to Church Avenue to see them. That turned out to be incredibly moving. Coming up the Drumcondra Road, cars were blaring their horns, everyone waving. There was a crowd gathered in the road. Now I knew a lot of these people were not Fianna Fáil voters, but there they all were, cheering and clapping me. That was about a sense of community and it was the only time I felt my emotions wobble. When I got up to the house, I could hardly get in the door. Typically the last people I managed to find were my mother and father. Mam hugged me and whispered, 'Well done.' Dad gave me the firm handshake and a look in the eye. He didn't say anything, but pride was written all over him. I never thought about it at the time, but the history of Fianna Fáil was in that grip – the Anti-Treaty Volunteer of the civil war congratulating his son, the newly elected Teachta Dála.

From the house I went to the Cat and Cage, which was heaving. People were spilling out onto the street, so they had to let me in through the back door. When I emerged behind the bar the place erupted. 'Bertie! Bertie!' I didn't know whether to feel delighted or embarrassed. I said a few words of thanks, had a couple of pints, and then went out to Santry Stadium, where my brother Maurice and more supporters had also gathered. It was only in the middle of the night, around four o'clock, that we finally got back to the house in Artane. I was asleep in five minutes.

3

MAN ABOUT THE HOUSE

School. It was just like going back to school.

Walking through the gates of Leinster House for the first time as a TD, I felt more nervous than excited, mainly because I didn't even know where to go or what to do. I had got a telegram from the Fianna Fáil whip's office telling me when the first meeting of the parliamentary party was to take place. Nothing more. No other communication or advice. Now, a few days after the election, I had wandered into the Dáil to see what needed to be done. The place was almost empty. There was certainly no anticipation about a 'new term'. The guy on the security desk told me that I had to register, so I went off to sign the book. There was no ceremonial. I didn't even get a photograph. Eventually I was told that I had an office on the fifth floor, next to the parliamentary party's meeting room. I went up to find it. There were plenty of desks, so I claimed one and went off in search of the stationery office to get some supplies. Then I went back to Drumcondra. I don't think a single person had said 'congratulations' or 'welcome' the whole time I was in the place. Anticlimactic doesn't even begin to sum it up.

I had to wait for the first day of business on 5 July 1977 to get any sense of occasion. I went to the chamber early that day to see the new Taoiseach being nominated. Although I had been into Leinster House for a few meetings, I had never even sat in the public gallery, so it was a thrill arriving for a debate, seeing the chamber for the first time. I looked around and took it all in. From behind, a laconic voice said, 'You sit on that side, lad.' It was Labour's Brendan Corish, the outgoing Tánaiste. That was a nice touch. I grinned sheepishly. Corish would be encouraging to me in that first term, congratulating me on speeches and the like. So too, on one occasion, did the former Taoiseach, Liam Cosgrave. It was my first induction into the oldest rule in politics: the other lot are the opposition but you actually find your enemies on your own side.

Up on the fifth floor, I found myself joining a colourful cast of other new boys, including P. J. Morley, Joe Walsh, Barry Cogan and Jim Fitzsimons. The loudest voice in the office was that of Pádraig Flynn, a new TD for Mayo West. He had attracted a bit of attention on the first day by turning up in a white suit. 'Would someone tell that feckin clown he's in the Dáil not the circus?' Charlie Haughey was overheard to say. In our office, Flynn was always bellowing down the phone or guffawing, so it would be hard to get any work done with him around the place. He was definitely confident, maybe too much so.

My own approach was the opposite of Flynn's. I would say that hardly anyone knew I was there in that first year. At twenty-five I was one of the youngest boys in the class. Just like in Church Avenue or in school, I gave myself plenty of time to get my bearings before I tried making my mark. I spent a lot of time studying the speeches of Seán Lemass and reading the proceedings of the Dáil that lined the shelves of our office. In the chamber, I listened more than I spoke. My maiden speech, on European Assembly elections, was on 26 October

1977. 'No fireworks, please, Bertie,' Jim Tunney advised me before-hand, so I kept it simple, making the point that 'Most people know very little about the European Parliament and it may be a difficult task to arouse sufficient interest in order to get a high percentage vote'. Some things never change.

In the office, I got on especially well with Cogan and Walsh through our Cork connections. I also struck up a good friendship with Dr Rory O'Hanlon, who I had come across at the Mater. But the government had a huge majority and seemed to think of us only as 'lobby fodder'. Paddy Lalor, the government Chief Whip, might have been a talented hurler, but with a big majority at his disposal he didn't need to develop much team spirit in the parliamentary party. There was certainly no communication with the leadership. In the whole time Jack Lynch was Taoiseach I don't think he spoke to me once. Sure, I was just a new backbencher, so I wasn't looking for private chats in his office. But I did expect to be brought in as part of a group to see what I had to say. After a while of not getting the call, you were afraid even to try. I remember once passing him in the corridor. I could see him coming a way off. Unusually he had no one with him, so I kept my head up, hoping I would get a quick word. But no, on he went. All I got was a half-smile. To be honest, a lot of us felt he didn't even know which constituency we were in. Years afterwards, when I became leader of the party, I made sure not to make the same mistake and I had every member of the parliamentary party out to my house.

Charlie Haughey couldn't have been more different. He was always careful to court the backbenchers. I had first met him as a boy at the polling station in Church Avenue in 1963 when 'Stan the Man' from St Patrick's National School lost the by-election. At the time, I would have rather met his brother, Jock, who had won an All-Ireland foot-ball medal with Dublin in 1958. He had seen me at closer quarters working on the committee to prepare the health manifesto for 1977. Now I was a TD in a neighbouring constituency, so he paid me even more attention. There were flowers for Miriam when Georgina was born and the trip to Inishvickillane. I was asked out to his home, which was a big thing for a backbencher. Occasionally he might invite me to receptions or conferences on health-related matters. It was nothing spectacular, but it made me feel that at least he, a senior minister, knew who I was. He never once said a disloyal word to me about Lynch. Quite the contrary. 'Don't worry about the old bullshit going on in Leinster House,' he said. 'Just concentrate on your constituency.'

There was a lot of bad feeling in the constituency after the 1977 election. I wasn't supposed to have won, so many of the calculations people would have made were suddenly turned on their heads. Bell's people were annoyed that he hadn't won the seat. Tunney was all right, but already he was thinking that having a second Fianna Fáil TD in the area was more of a threat than a blessing. After all, the 'Lynch tide' had brought us both in; if it went out, it might take me or him out with it. He was very nice to me on a personal level, but I soon got an insight into his more ruthless side. Lynch had appointed him a junior minister, which meant he had to give up his seat on the Dublin City Council. Once I declared my hand for that, there was no way the party wasn't going to co-opt me in his place. I was the TD for the area. I had precedence. That didn't stop Tunney from trying to block me. Obviously I got the seat, but when it came to fighting the local election in 1979, Tunney's people were noticeable by their absence. That was a really tough election, and it gave me a lot of satisfaction to top the poll after such a difficult campaign. In another ward, Tony Gregory, who had been in the Irish Republican Socialist Party, ran for the first time as an independent community activist.

I've heard the story that weeks after I was elected in 1977, a twenty-year plan was drawn up for me to be Taoiseach. There's no truth in it. From the moment I won in 1977 the only plotting I was doing was about how to hold on to the seat at the next election. I was still working full-time at the Mater. There was a new baby in the house. I was going into the city council to raise local issues. Tuesdays to Thursdays I was in the Dáil. But everything came back to the constituency. It was all about building up my local organisation, and getting ready for the big fight I knew was coming. To make the job harder, the government's popularity was in meltdown by 1979. A global oil shock was buffeting the economy. Fuel prices were going through the roof and queues outside the garages were growing by the day. That was a terrible year for industrial disputes. The post went undelivered for more than four months. Rubbish was piling up in the streets. Thousands of PAYE workers took to the streets to protest about the unfair taxation system. The only uplifting thing that year was the Pope's visit in September. Local and European elections in June were very disappointing for Fianna Fáil. In 1977, the party had won a general election by a landslide. Two years later we already looked to be heading for a hammering next time round.

Inevitably that raised the temperature in Leinster House. When we came back from the recess in the middle of October 1979, the atmosphere was horrendous. There were fellas from all sides talking in corridors, others watching who was talking to who, reporting back. In our office, Flynn was heavily involved on the anti-Lynch side. He was a tough character. At a meeting of the parliamentary party, Lynch challenged us all by saying, 'I heard there was a caucus meeting. Who was there?' Silence. Then Flynn stood up and said, 'I was there, Taoiseach.' I respected him for having the guts to say it.

The turning point came in two by-elections in Cork in November. The director of elections was Gene Fitzgerald, who had a voice like a foghorn. There had been great controversy about choosing the candidates in the two constituencies, so the atmosphere there was not great. But I love campaigning, getting out to meet the people, so I just got on with that and ignored the local politics. I spent a few days in the inner city, touring the shops to bang the drum for the party. This was also the time when I saw Tom Barry at his house in Cork be going. Even so, I was still surprised and disappointed when Lynch announced that he was standing down at a meeting of the parliamentary party on 5 December.

Haughey and Colley had been shadow-boxing for years, but now for forty-eight hours they went head to head for the leadership of the party. Afterwards, there would be reports of TDs being intimidated during the campaign, but nobody tried to bully or hassle me. I don't think I was even phoned. Des O'Malley, who was anti-Haughey, later said that this was because everyone knew I would be voting for Haughey, but in truth Des would hardly have known who I was at that stage. In fact, I didn't commit myself until after I had gone back to Drumcondra to gauge opinion. A few people said Colley, some of them said Haughey, but most said, 'You're a young fella in there, you have to call it as you see it.' The two candidates each asked me in person for my vote. I had told them the same thing: I need to talk to my people back in the constituency. Haughey seemed OK with that, but Colley was obviously annoyed. I wasn't surprised by that. Both of them had gone to school at 'Joey's' just up the road from me in Fairview. Somehow, though, when I talked to Colley I always had the feeling that he was looking down on me and thought I needed to show more respect to him as a Fianna Fáil diehard. On one level he had everything I admired. He was old Fianna Fáil. His father had been a veteran of the Easter Rising and the IRA. But Colley's record as minister didn't stand any comparison to Haughey's. In the end that was the decisive factor in my vote. Haughey seemed a man for the eighties.

On the day of the vote I went into the meeting not knowing who would win. There had been talk of bullying and dirty tricks by both sides. People were anxious. All the cabinet had been for Colley, but overnight the rumour started that Michael O'Kennedy had broken ranks for Haughey. That rattled the Colley team, but George himself still came in looking relaxed and confident. I had gone in early to get a good seat and ended up sitting close to Ray MacSharry, who was going to propose Haughey. When the result was announced – a Haughey win by 44 to 38 – it was like being on the Hill for the All-Ireland. People were jumping up, shouting, punching the air. MacSharry shook my hand. Colley's people on the other hand looked shell-shocked. I don't think George ever thought for one second that he would lose. There was a sense of entitlement. He had failed to understand that you can't disregard the backbenchers and then expect them to fall into line to vote for you. I looked over to Séamus Brennan, who was a senator and a Colley supporter. He looked like his best friend had died. I liked Séamus, so I gave him a rueful smile, but I don't think he even knew I was there.

Usually the Dáil debate to nominate a new Taoiseach is reasonably good-natured. Not in 1979. There were all kinds of rumours flying around beforehand that the leader of Fine Gael, Garret FitzGerald, was trying to get Colley's supporters to oppose Haughey's nomination. There was a weird background to this, with all three of them having known each other at UCD in the 1940s. There were class overtones to the relationship as well. When FitzGerald referred in his speech to Haughey's 'flawed pedigree', I couldn't believe it. Haughey's mother had had a very difficult life. Here she was sitting in the visitors' gallery having to hear that. It was mean-spirited and in really bad taste. It was also politically stupid. If Garret had wanted to entice a few disgruntled Colley supporters over, he lost them there and then. Even Martin O'Donoghue and Jim Gibbons, who detested Haughey, went through the lobby to vote for him. A few days afterwards, I ran into Luke Belton, the Fine Gael TD in my constituency. Belton came from a family with a long history in politics. He seemed embarrassed by the whole thing. 'What the hell was that about?' I asked him. He just shook his head sadly and said, 'It's just Garret.'

It was about a week after Haughey's election, I think, that I got the call from Pádraig Ó hAnnracháin, the new Taoiseach's unofficial Chief of Staff. Ó hAnnracháin was a tough character. He had that way in a meeting of not saying very much, so you would find yourself gabbling on, while he smirked out of the corner of his mouth. 'The Boss wants you in the whip's office,' he told me. I was delighted, although slightly taken aback to hear him call Haughey 'the Boss'. Soon everyone was referring to the Taoiseach that way, but on that day it was the first time I had heard it. Luckily, with Ó hAnnracháin being so terse, all I got time to say was 'Thanks', before he cut the line. It was a strange way to start my career as a government assistant whip.

The Chief Whip was the long-serving Dublin TD, Seán Moore. He was a quiet, reserved man, but you wouldn't want to underestimate him. The problem was that no sooner was I through the door than Moore became ill. With him being out, it often became my job, along with Ben Briscoe, to keep the parliamentary party in line. This was the first time I really got an adrenaline buzz from being in Leinster House. Suddenly I was being called to sit in on meetings with the Taoiseach. Members of cabinet were ringing me up to get the troops out for an important debate. I got the policy committees going again. I gave a report to the parliamentary party every week. That raised my profile. It also gave me leverage with ministers, because they knew if they didn't bother coming to meetings, I was going to stand up and say so. This all meant that I went from being low-key in Leinster House to everyone knowing who I was. Certainly Charlie had an eye on what I was doing. 'The name "whip" comes from hunting,' he told me. 'Keep the dogs in the pack.' He started referring to me as 'the kid', which kept me in my place, but also showed people that he thought I was all right. Not that he ever told me much about what was happening. The funny thing about being a whip is that everyone assumes you know everything. Anxious TDs would be sidling up to me outside the restaurant wanting to know when the election was going to be, or who was in and out of favour. I would just smile and say, 'Ah sure, what do I know.' That might have been the truth, but they always interpreted it as meaning the complete opposite.

A whip's job is about being around, making sure that people turn up for votes, listening out for any rumours or signs of trouble. Shouting or threatening people was never my way. I usually found if you asked someone politely to do something they would. The tricky bit was actually finding them in the first place. There were no mobile phones or pagers in those days. I always used to say that I divided my time between the deputies working at the bar and the others who were drinking in the bar. A whip never reveals his secrets, but I can tell you I sometimes ended up in fairly unusual places after getting various tip-offs. I would be running around for a few of them in the local bars and hotels near Leinster House to get them into the chamber for an important vote. Often I would be bumping into opposition TDs while I was there. 'No, don't worry, lads, it's just a Fianna Fáil meeting,' I would tell them.

I really enjoyed being whip, working to make the parliamentary party efficient and cooperative, but even as I was doing it, I was thinking, 'Enjoy it now, because it might not last long.' That was because I was already in a fight to hold on to my seat. After all the messing around with the 'Tullymander', there had been another review of the constituencies in 1980. Dublin Finglas was abolished. The Drumcondra end of the constituency went into a new five-seater, Dublin Central. The Finglas end went into a four-seater, Dublin North West. The easy option would have been to stay with Jim Tunney in Dublin North West. They knew I had worked hard for them. Now I was a whip, they could see I was on my way up. I wasn't much threat to Tunney, as Fianna Fáil looked set for two seats in the constituency. As it turned out, Tunney and a new candidate, Michael Barrett, would comfortably win two seats in 1981. But I wasn't from Finglas. I was a Drumcondra man. I wanted to win on my turf. Croke Park, the GPO, Phoenix Park, the 'Bots' and the zoo: this was home. If it had been a football team, Dublin Central would have been Man United. No one was going to say to you, 'Dublin Central? Which one's that?' And there was so much to do. We had the highest deprivation under every category that was listed, whether it was unemployment or drug addiction. This was a difficult time for people in many parts of the area. I had no intention of walking away from them.

Not that it was going to be an easy seat to win. The new constituency was made up of bits of old ones: Dublin North Central and Dublin Cabra as well as Finglas. Tunney was sorted. That left three other Fianna Fáil TDs besides me – Vivion de Valera, Vincent Brady and Tom Leonard – fighting for two seats. De Valera got sick and retired from politics. Brady decided to move out to a new Dublin North Central four-seater constituency as number two to Haughey. That made it more manageable. Then out of the blue, George Colley, who was out in Clontarf without a single house in the new constituency, decided he wanted to be in Dublin Central. He obviously saw it as an easy seat to win. Tom Leonard and myself were both new TDs. Colley had represented part of the area years earlier, so he felt entitled to it. Everyone, including George himself, thought that he would top the poll. Opposition from the other parties was stiff as well. Michael Keating was making a name for himself in Fine Gael. Alice Glenn from the city council also had a good reputation. Michael O'Leary would become Labour leader after the election. Tony Gregory was getting a lot of national attention as a community activist. So this was going to be tough. I got all the people close to me together and said, 'Right, are we up for this, or do we go with Tunney?' No one thought I would be the next Yellow Rose of Finglas, so we decided to stay put and fight it out.

There's been a lot of myths about the Drumcondra crowd. The truth is that I had a small group of people, including Tony Kett, Dáithí Ó Broin, Chris Wall, Paddy Duffy, Liam Cooper, Paul Kiely, Joe Burke and my brothers, who were prepared to bust a gut to get me re-elected. We knew the area. Most of our friends and family were there. And it was the same story as always: we worked, worked, worked. There were meetings almost every night, usually held under a lamp post wherever we were canvassing so as not to waste any time. If someone was on to us about broken lights, we would contact the lighting department that same day. Sometimes I would drop the letter in myself at eleven o'clock at night. I would be going to the city council to make speeches on local issues and raising awareness as best I could in the media. It was a very professional operation. Everyone had a job to do. We did our leaflets. We canvassed and re-canvassed. All the time, it was about establishing that this was our territory, our community. The message was simple: we are local, you can trust us to serve the community. As we headed into the 1981 Fianna Fáil Ard Fheis on Valentine's weekend, with Haughey widely tipped to announce the general election, we felt ready for a campaign.

Tragic events soon put politics out of our minds. I was driving home from the Ard Fheis late on Friday night. I was on the Malahide Road and as I got up to Griffith Avenue, all hell broke loose. Thirty, maybe forty fire engines, ambulances, Garda cars went hammering past me. I turned in to Kilmore Road, near my house in Pinebrook Road. That was when I saw the flames at the Stardust Ballroom. I parked the car and then sprinted – literally sprinted – towards the scene. Everything was happening at once. Flashing blue lights every-where. Cameramen and journalists were just starting to get there. I remember Denis Coghlan from the *Irish Times* arriving. After what seemed like an age, they finally forced open the locked doors and brought the first bodies out. It was horrendous. I realised that I was going to be more use at the Mater, so I rushed back to the house to tell Miriam what was going on. Suddenly I remembered that my neighbour, Joe Burke, sometimes worked at the Stardust, so I checked to see he was OK. When I got to the hospital, it was another terrible scene, and reminded me so much of the Dublin bombings in 1974. As I knew how things were done by now, I pitched in and worked the A & E desk right through the night and the following day, co-ordinating with the desk at the Richmond Hospital. At a time when everything that could have gone wrong did go wrong, we had one piece of luck. There was a party that had just started at the Boot Inn, near the airport, and a lot of the nurses and medics were at it. The hospital got the word out to them, 'get back now', so we actually had a big staff of incredibly dedicated people there.

In the end, forty-eight people died in the tragedy. The next morning the Taoiseach came to the Mater. The Stardust was in his constituency and he knew a lot of the dead and injured personally. Along with Sister Gemma, the sister administrator, and Gearóid Mac Gabhann, the secretary manager, I met him at the door and warned him about what he was going to see. He saw all the patients who wanted to talk. He spent time with the families and paid his respects to those who had lost loved ones. He was visibly upset.

Events at the Stardust had been a tragedy. And they also had a political impact. Haughey postponed the Ard Fheis. If he had been able to call a general election that weekend, as planned, I believe that Fianna Fáil would have won a comfortable majority. We'd had a strong win with Clem Coughlan in the by-election in Donegal the previous November. Haughey had seemed to make progress on the North at a summit with Margaret Thatcher in Dublin Castle. Even on the economy, which was still in rough water, the opinion polls showed that the recent budget had been popular. But by the time the Ard Fheis reconvened in April, the political world had changed. Bobby Sands and the hunger strike was a huge story around the world. A few days before the Ard Fheis, Sands had been elected MP for Fermanagh–South Tyrone in a heated by-election. There were rallies of support all around the country and in the constituency. Even people who had little interest in the Troubles got involved. Every night for months people gathered at the bridge in Drumcondra in solidarity with the hunger strikers. There was huge sympathy for the prisoners. No one thought it would end in deaths. Even Gerry Adams later said to me that it should never have happened. There should have been an accommodation. But there was no bending in Thatcher. And Haughey, conscious of not derailing recent progress with the British prime minister, refused to support the demands of the prisoners.

Sands died on 5 May. Nine others would follow in the coming months. The reaction was unbelievable. I remember talking to my dad about it. He had been on hunger strike during the civil war and understood what they were going through. He got very agitated about it. There were black flags around the constituency, hanging from houses and lamp posts. Some people felt let down by politicians and believed the parties in the South had not done enough to intervene. All of this meant that by the time Haughey went to Áras an Uachtaráin on 21 May to ask for the Dáil to be dissolved, the atmosphere was poison.

In Dublin Central, even without an H Block candidate on the ballot paper, we already had a very competitive election. Right from the start we went heavily after first preferences, wanting to maximise our vote. We kept expecting Colley's campaign to come after us. He had a lot of cumainn registered in the inner-city end of the constituency, and we were waiting for them to start canvassing. After a few days, it dawned on us. Most of these cumainn had nobody in them. They represented nobody. We would be standing outside churches on our own, canvassing door to door on our own. By this stage we had built up a huge team of volunteers to go into every part of the constituency. We went out into the highways and byways, finding places that had never been canvassed before. I remember one activist, Kathleen O'Neill, even found a small house in East Wall right in the middle of the dockyards. No other houses anywhere. There was a man living there and we made sure to get him registered.

Gregory was a challenge. He was a community activist, who had done some good work on local issues and through organising protests. But there would be no love lost between us by the end of this campaign. At the root of our disagreement were the posters that went up around the constituency saying, 'Vote for the H Block Candidate. Vote Gregory Number One!' Now I would have thought that would have been a plus for him, not a negative. Even voters who would normally run a mile from anything connected with the IRA were furious about what was going on in the Maze. But Tony went ballistic.

Seeing Miriam on the election morning, he went over to her and was very agitated. It was nasty stuff. He thought we had been behind the posters, but shouting at my wife crossed a line. The truth is that we had nothing to do with the H Block posters – we hardly had enough money to pay for own posters without doing his. I would be amazed if Colley or Leonard had done it either. My guess is that someone in his own campaign was behind it and that it was just a publicity stunt. Either way, it didn't make any difference. He only secured 6.77 per cent of the vote.

The day after the election I arrived at the count as late as I could. When the result came it was an amazing moment. I had topped the poll, with 18.78 per cent of first preferences. I had been up against heavyweights in Colley, Keating and O'Leary, and I took that result as an acknowledgement of our work rate in the constituency. I had put in long hours since I had been elected in 1977, not just canvassing, but dealing with real problems in people's lives, such as unemployment and training, housing, welfare, active age and youth issues. We had held constituency clinics on Saturdays and two or three evenings in the week. There was a genuine sense of energy and momentum. A lot of people had joined the campaign who would stay in the organisation.

Colley was shell-shocked by the result. He had finished a comfortable third, and although he was never in danger of losing his seat, it was another disappointment for him after losing the leadership election. He shook my hand and said, 'Well done.' He was too much of a pro to do anything else. But you could see the humiliation in his eyes.

While the election had been a success for me in Dublin Central, it had been a disaster for Fianna Fáil in the country at large. Even though we were still the biggest party, it was our worst election result for twenty years. Clearly the H Block candidates, who had won two seats, took votes away from Fianna Fáil. The economy had been important too. Although the most recent 'giveaway' budget had been popular in the short term, we had missed an opportunity to put our national finances back on track. In January 1980, Charlie had gone on television to deliver a state-of-the-nation speech, saying that 'As a community, we are living a way beyond our means'. Watching it on TV and for a while afterwards in the Dáil I thought he really wanted to get on top of public spending and pull the country together. Then you got all the PAYE marches. That meant he didn't follow it through. Everyone got pay rises instead. I saw the effect of this first hand with the increases to doctors and nurses, and the knock-on it had in the Mater Hospital. By June 1981, I think everyone realised we couldn't go on as we were. That election was like waking up with a hangover after a big night out.

Most observers expected Fine Gael and Labour to form a coalition with support from a number of independents. Not that pulling this off was quick or straightforward. Nothing ever was with Garret. The formation of the new coalition remained in doubt until the Dáil assembled on 30 June 1981. In the chamber, FitzGerald was frantic – scribbling notes, dashing up and down the steps. Charlie, meanwhile, stayed cool. The only moment of actual humour came when one of the independents, Seán Dublin Bay Loftus, suggested that perhaps Haughey and FitzGerald could serve as Taoiseach in alternate years.

Going back into opposition, Haughey asked me to act as spokesman for Youth and Sport. I was pleased enough, as I had taken over as chairman of Ógra Fianna Fáil during the previous year. Now I had an opportunity to bring more young people into the party. But debates in the Dáil and the country were dominated by the economy. The government introduced an austere supplementary budget within weeks of taking office, putting pressure on the coalition. Haughey's strategy during this period was unclear. He delayed appointing a front bench, and there seemed to be a sense of drift – it was like he was asleep. But he got a wake-up call from Charlie McCreevy. McCreevy had been one of the 1977 intake who had pushed for Haughey to replace Lynch. By 1981, his enthusiasm for Haughey was gone. Towards the end of December he gave an interview to Geraldine Kennedy at the *Sunday Tribune* where he questioned Haughey's leadership. He couldn't have been surprised when he lost the whip a few weeks later.

That was only the first move in a series of heaves that would dog the party throughout 1982 and 1983. In the short term, though, there were other fish to fry, with John Bruton putting his budget before the Dáil. I was in the chamber the night of the vote on 27 January 1982. Bruton had introduced a savage budget, including a tax on children's shoes. The independents propping up the coalition were not inclined to support it. Just before the vote took place, I remember seeing the Taoiseach squatting down in front of the Limerick socialist, Jim Kemmy, pleading with him not to pull the plug on the government. Kemmy sat there gloomily, barely able to look Garret in the face. Haughey as usual watched expressionless. After the vote was taken, our Chief Whip, Ray Burke, came bouncing down the steps waving the paper with the result. He shook hands with Charlie on his way to handing the paper to the Ceann Comhairle, John O'Connell. When the result was called – a government defeat by one vote – the Fianna Fáil benches went wild.

That was for public consumption. Back in the parliamentary party room it was a different story. There should have been euphoria. Instead there was only shock. Nobody had expected FitzGerald to make such a hash of keeping the coalition together. Now we had beaten them and everyone was thinking, 'Do we really want another election?' These were difficult times in the North. The economy was a mess. Personally, I'm thinking, 'Jesus, a winter election.' That snowy January had seen the coldest weather in Dublin for a century. That's terrible for campaigning, especially for someone like me who puts in the long hours. Winter elections are bad news.

Even so, I was in good shape going into the second campaign in a year. I had topped the poll last time round and the machine was well oiled by this stage. Since I had spent the last few months in opposition, there had been more time to concentrate on the constituency. I had built up the organisation in parts of the inner city that I had not represented in Dublin Finglas. Colley was more active this time round. He had been hurt by his experience in 1981. Now he based his campaign around being anti-Haughey Fianna Fáil. Inevitably that meant casting me in the role of Charlie's boy, and made the campaign a tough one. George canvassed more vigorously this time, but he still didn't understand that you couldn't just turn up at election time and expect people to fall into line. I looked after the constituency all year round. That's why I got more first preferences again in 1982, with Colley once again beaten into third place behind Michael Keating.

On a personal level I was delighted with the result, but the campaign itself gave me a real insight into how Haughey polarised people. I knew that there would be trouble ahead. I had read the opinion polls showing that FitzGerald beat Haughey hands down as the preferred candidate for Taoiseach. But opinion polls were not the same thing as public opinion. You only had to look back to the 1977 election to see how polls could end up being completely wrong. This time, though, they seemed to reflect the mood on the doorstep about Haughey. People were saying to me, 'We like you, Bertie, but would you not change your leader?' That became a regular comment at the doors. Obviously Fine Gael voters, sometimes pretending to be our supporters, complained about Haughey. You would expect that. But it was Fianna Fáil people as well. A lot of my own voters clearly wanted to see new leadership.

The heated debate about Haughey gave his opponents in the party just the chance they needed to attack him. Fianna Fáil had gained four seats and come within three of an overall majority on 18 February. We looked set to form the next government. But in the context of the times, it was a bad result. Many of the anti-Haughey people had done well. Jim Gibbons, who Haughey had sacked from the cabinet in 1979, did very well in Carlow–Kilkenny. Charlie McCreevy headed the poll in Kildare. As it turned out, he had been out of the Fianna

Fáil parliamentary party for just a week. The government had fallen seven days after his expulsion and the Dáil was dissolved. When the new parliamentary party met, he was back in the fold. That must be some kind of record for time in the 'sin bin'.

As the parliamentary party prepared for its first meeting, the anti-Haughey people began to gather around Dessie O'Malley as a challenger for the leadership. I thought that was crazy. Dessie was a bright guy even if he didn't have much charm. Undoubtedly he looked like a future leader of the party. But this was the wrong time. We were close to going back into government. That should have been the focus. Eventually the rebels just ended up looking like characters in a panto. Martin O'Donoghue, one of the leading anti-Haughey TDs, couldn't make up his mind whether he wanted a contest or not. McCreevy gave a confusing interview to RTÉ in which he went backwards and forwards. In contrast, Haughey's team, led by Ray MacSharry, was ruthless in dealing with the rebels. MacSharry's message was simple and clear: anyone who got in the way of us forming a government would not be forgiven. The parliamentary party met at 11.30 a.m. on Thursday 25 February. Haughey made a grand entrance to enthusiastic applause, including mine. O'Malley was sitting almost on his own. Pádraig Faulkner made a plea for party unity. Then O'Donoghue stood up and urged O'Malley to withdraw. Dessie's jaw dropped. Clearly Martin hadn't told him what he was going to say. George Colley was shaking his head and trying to catch Dessie's eye to urge him on. But it was too late. Dessie got up to say he was withdrawing in the name of party unity. Charlie replied that he looked forward to talking to Dessie about the formation of the new government. We all knew it was just a pause in the conflict.

Forming that new government allowed Haughey to re-establish his authority over the party. Despite a complex relationship with Neil Blaney over their roles in the 1970 Arms Crisis, Haughey was confident of winning the support of the Donegal North East TD. He started negotiations with the Workers' Party, which had three TDs.

And he also began personal talks with the new independent TD who had won the fifth seat in my own constituency of Dublin Central. Having another election so soon after his 1981 defeat had suited Tony Gregory. He had kept his momentum up after the '81 election and remained very active in the community. Relations between us were still tense, but I could see a lot of merit in his constituency work. Two days after this election, Haughey phoned me to ask about Gregory. 'Can we do a deal with him?' he asked. I said I thought we could. Partly it would be a matter of priorities. More significantly, it was also a question of personalities. Gregory was a Northsider. I just didn't see him cosying up to Garret, who would have been too Dublin 4 for Tony's tastes. Haughey had the handmade suits and the big estate in Kinsealy, but he was also a Northside boy who had grown up in difficult circumstances. He knew the area and its problems. And what he didn't know, I could tell him. He wanted briefing on all the local issues, projects that were being held back by a lack of money, what the pressure points were. I went to see the city manager and asked him to prepare a book of estimates on outstanding projects. That got everything itemised and costed. Afterwards, the city manager asked whether Gregory could see it. 'Why not?' I told him.

Gregory had requested a meeting with Haughey on his own turf in Summerhill. To avoid attracting too much attention I drove Charlie there myself in my battered Ford Escort. I wasn't sure if he had dressed down to make Gregory more comfortable, or because he was worried about the state of the Escort. 'We'll have to do something about getting you a new car,' he said at one stage. I thought I knew what that meant, but I just smiled. On the way into Summerhill, I took him through the main points of the brief. I waited outside as the two men negotiated. Afterwards, Charlie got into the car and said, 'You're going to get your plan, Bertie, but he's going to get the credit.' Fair enough. When it came to the fundamentals, Tony's strategic assessment was like my own. These things needed to be done and in the long run it would save money by investing in the area to break the cycle of disadvantage. Communities in the city centre were so far behind in terms of facilities and chances for employment that a huge investment package was needed to help them to catch up. That was a national imperative, not just a local one. To be fair, Garret recognised this as well. Tony told me later that during their talks he had found the Fine Gael leader sincere in wanting to get something done.

In the end, after several more meetings, Tony decided to throw his lot in with Fianna Fáil because he was convinced that Charlie had a better grasp of the issues and a commitment to delivering for the inner city. I like to think that in this respect, whatever our personal difficulties, Tony and myself worked together as a good double act. Maybe his priorities wouldn't have been exactly the same as mine, but that didn't matter. These were educational, housing and employment projects, developed by Dublin Corporation, that would not have got out of the blocks without the 'Gregory Deal'. Even if this made life a bit trickier on the ground for me politically, so what? It didn't matter, because the people of the constituency were going to benefit. Ironically, the figure who would kick up the most fuss was George Colley. He was really agitated. He should have been delighted – the projects were helping the area that he represented.

In parallel with the Gregory talks, Haughey was also negotiating with the Workers' Party. Because I had links with the Workers' Party from my union days, my role was to chat up one of their deputies, Joe Sherlock. A Cork man like my father, Sherlock had been active in the IRA border campaign in the 1950s. I liked him, because you sensed right away that he was in politics for the people he represented, not for himself. We got on easily and built up a good relationship. At the end of the talks with Haughey, the Workers' Party gave no indication about whether we had been successful. They held a meeting of the Ard Comhairle the night before the Dáil assembled to decide who to nominate as Taoiseach. Afterwards, there was no announcement, other than to say that Joe Sherlock would speak during the debate the following day. Most people were predicting they would

4
HEAVES

The cardinal rule of being Chief Whip is always to expect the unexpected. I learnt that on my first day.

The 23rd Dáil assembled on Tuesday 9 March 1982. Garret FitzGerald had spent the night trying to get enough votes to stay in power. The Workers' Party were refusing to say how they would vote. So was Tony Gregory. Labour was deeply divided about whether it would join any type of coalition. Everything was on a knife edge. So when TDs took their places in the chamber, there was a real sense of unfolding drama. Not for me though. I knew we had the numbers. It was one of my first experiences of being on the inside track, knowing what others in the House did not. 'You're looking very calm, Bertie,' a few of the fellas said to me on the way in. 'Ah sure, what can I do about it now?' I replied, giving nothing away.

Everything went smoothly to begin with. John O'Connell was nominated again as Ceann Comhairle. That got one independent off the books. Then Brian Lenihan and Ray MacSharry proposed and seconded Charlie Haughey as Taoiseach. Michael O'Leary and Peter Barry followed suit for FitzGerald. Then there was a pause that seemed to go on forever. All eyes were looking at the independents to see

who would speak first. Gregory, minus his tie, shifted in his seat. Neil
Blaney smirked. Jim Kemmy looked grumpy. After what seemed an
age, Joe Sherlock stood up. 'On behalf of my party, Sinn Féin the
Workers' Party,' he announced to the House, 'I wish to say that my
party decided to support the nomination of Deputy Charles J. Haughey.
The factors considered by us in arriving at that decision are that it
appears to us to be the choice of the voters that there should be a
Fianna Fáil government, and that the proposals put forward in the
economic and industrial package by Fianna Fáil seem to be what the
country needs at this time.' That released the tension in the House.
Blaney was up next, adding his support. Kemmy said he couldn't
support Haughey. Then Gregory rose to give his maiden speech,
outlining the deal he had made with Haughey. The Fine Gael benches
went beserk, heckling Gregory and telling Haughey that he had
bought the independent TD's vote. Haughey, as usual, remained
expressionless. When the Ceann Comhairle called for a division to
vote, Haughey's supporters swarmed around him to shake hands and
offer congratulations. 'Job done,' I thought.

Not quite, as it turned out. After the division bell had rung, the
Ceann Comhairle ordered the doors of the chamber to be locked.
TDs moved up the steps to vote. Then the opposition whip, Seán
Barrett, said to me, 'Have your socialist friends left already?' I looked
around the chamber. No Workers' Party deputies. I nearly got a heart
attack. I began frantically asking anyone if they had seen Sherlock or
the others anywhere. They had vanished. Suddenly there was a
commotion from the distinguished visitors' box, where Charlie's wife,
Maureen, was sitting. Sherlock, Proinsias De Rossa and Paddy Gallagher
came vaulting into the chamber like special forces and ran up the
steps to vote. 'Their method of entry to the House was somewhat
unorthodox,' Michael O'Leary later acidly remarked, 'but their
eagerness cannot be in doubt.' As it turned out, they had nipped
out for a minute. Mark Killilea, the recently defeated Galway West
TD, had saved the day. To gales of laughter from the press, he had

Charlie himself described as 'bizarre . . . unprecedented . . . grotesque and unbelievable'. A murder suspect ended up in the apartment of the Attorney General, Patrick Connolly. I was on the way down to Kerry at the time and I had to contact Charlie on Inishvickillane from Ballyferriter on the Dingle Peninsula. In those days the switchboard knocked off around six in the evening, so when I arrived I had a job convincing them that this was a matter of national importance. I finally got hold of Charlie and told him: 'Sorry about interfering with your holiday, but there's been an incident with the Attorney General.' Predictably, he was not best pleased. Then there was the 'Dowra affair', when the brother-in-law of the Justice Minister, Seán Doherty, walked away from an assault charge after the RUC had detained a key prosecution witness hours before the trial, although there was no suggestion that Seán Doherty himself was involved. Conor Cruise O'Brien rearranged Haughey's words to coin 'GUBU', which for him described the Haughey era. It was a tag that Charlie would find difficult to shake off. It also gave the anti-Haughey faction in the party the excuse they needed to mount another heave.

On Friday 1 October I was staying late in the whip's office when I received a motion of no confidence in the leader signed by Charlie McCreevy. The House was not in session and a lot of deputies were on holidays. That would usually give me more time in the constituency, but not that week. There had been rumours of plots, rumours about rumours, plots about rumours, stories of secret meetings and cabals, so I had decided it was best to be around. Everyone knew something was going on, and now here it was out in the open. As soon as I received the motion, I phoned Haughey to tell him. He was notorious for his short temper, but I wasn't worried about making the call, because in my experience he was never one to shoot the messenger. This time he was even calmer than usual. McCreevy had made sure that a copy of the motion had been delivered to Haughey at the same time that the original was being dropped into me in Leinster House. I heard afterwards that a messenger had turned up at Kinsealy in a bright yellow Mercedes. When I had spoken to Haughey, I started ringing around to activate people. Over the next few days, MacSharry would often call me with the names of waverers who might want some reassurance. A lot of these conversations were listening to complaints along the lines of 'Gregory can get millions, what about my constituency?' or 'Why can I never get in to see the Boss when the Workers' Party walk in whenever they like?'

These conversations were never easy. I had to trade on a lot of the goodwill I had built up over the previous months. It was a tricky business. No one could have been in any doubt that I was supporting Haughey. But I was the party whip. That meant I had certain obligations. I had to tell everyone what was happening. I had to make arrangements for the meeting of the parliamentary party that would consider the motion. I had to inform the press, explaining what was going on. And all the time my phone would be ringing with calls from supporters of both sides making demands about the procedure or urging me to put pressure on one side or the other. I had already heard the arguments from Haughey about his leadership in cabinet, and at meetings of the ministers of state and the National Executive. I knew the parliamentary party meeting was going to be messy. When it came to the day of the vote, Wednesday 6 October, I was sitting at the top table taking the minutes and watching the carnage. As whip, I decided not to make a contribution to the debate, which lasted twelve hours. Tempers were lost. The room was stuffy and uncomfortable, filled with cigarette smoke. At the end, a roll call was taken. The first name called was Bertie Ahern. I voted against the motion of no confidence. The motion was defeated by 58 votes to 22.

I was glad that Haughey had won, but what happened afterwards was shameful. There were chaotic scenes outside in the lobby. Those who had voted against Haughey were jostled and jeered by overzealous supporters of the Taoiseach. Jim Gibbons was physically attacked. The stress of events that night can't have been good for his health – a few weeks later, he suffered two heart attacks. Not that there wasn't fault on the other side too. McCreevy's courage is one of the things I've always admired about him, but the Gardai had advised him that walking out of the front door of Leinster House would only inflame an already volatile situation. In the middle of all this, I was there trying to brief the press, giving an explanation of what had gone on at the meeting. It was one of the nastiest days I've witnessed in all my political career.

Two cabinet ministers, Des O'Malley and Martin O'Donoghue, had resigned to support the motion of no confidence. There were real doubts about whether TDs in the 'club of 22' who had voted against Haughey would support the government in the Dáil. By the time the House sat again on 27 October, Gibbons was in hospital, and Dr Bill Loughnane, the popular Clare TD, had unexpectedly died. All this weakened the government's position in the Dáil. We relied more than ever on the independents, and especially on the the Workers' Party, who were on a direct collision course with the Minister for Finance, Ray MacSharry.

The stress on everyone was unbelievable during this time. I remember Miriam asking me one week how many hours I had spent in Leinster House. I sat down and totted the time up. It came to well over a hundred hours. The strain on me as Chief Whip may have been greater than most, but to be honest almost every deputy would have been putting in similar hours in the House or in their constituencies. This led sometimes to medical emergencies and even deaths. A few months after Bill Loughnane had passed away, Clem Coughlan, who drove backwards and forwards to his Donegal constituency every week, was killed in a car crash on his way to the Dáil. Liam Hyland suffered a heart attack in the lobby of Leinster House when he heard that news. Paddy Power collapsed after a Fianna Fáil parliamentary party meeting. Jim Fitzsimons got an ulcer. Paddy Lalor needed a pacemaker fitted. Within the year, George Colley would die of a heart attack, aged fifty-seven. Ber Cowen, Brian's father, died of a heart attack at just fifty-one. You would convince nobody that these were not in some way related to the pressures of political life in the 1980s. People were exhausted. Tempers were short. The stakes were high. That made it a dangerous lifestyle, and hardly any wonder when colleagues paid the ultimate price.

Despite Noel Treacy, helped by Patsy Geraghty, winning the by-election in Galway East over the summer, the government was still on the skids by the time the Dáil met on 27 October. The previous week, MacSharry had launched our new economic plan, 'The Way Forward'. This was a bold move, because for the first time it set out the steps the government needed to get the state finances under control. Joe Sherlock immediately communicated his reservations to me about the plan, especially the proposed cuts in health spending. I knew from other sources in his party that they had already decided to defeat the government. In June, we had had the numbers to get round that problem. Now, with one TD dead and another in hospital, the situation looked irretrievable. To compound our difficulties, Garret FitzGerald announced that he was putting down a motion of no confidence in the government.

That led to a number of last-ditch efforts on my part to keep us in power. The Chief Whip's job is to win the vote, never mind what knots you tie yourself into to get it done. That was certainly the case with my efforts to 'pair' Jim Gibbons. Pairing is one of those practical aspects of parliamentary business that keeps the place running smoothly. If someone has a personal matter to attend to, the whips on both sides usually agree to 'pair' him with a TD from the other side. As a result, their votes cancel each other out. We all do it, because we know that one day it will be us looking for the favour. That was never going to happen in a confidence motion, even with a man in hospital down the country. The only chance we had was if an opposition TD was prepared to go 'rogue'. Our target was Oliver J. Flanagan, the Father of the House, who didn't get on with FitzGerald. The government was committed to holding a constitutional referendum on abortion. FitzGerald was opposed to the referendum. That gave us an opening with Flanagan, who was a keen supporter of an early referendum on the issue. My proposal to him was this: if we could get Gibbons to leave the hospital in an ambulance (before immediately turning back) would he pair with him? Flanagan would earn a rebuke from his party, but he could just about say that there had been a misunderstanding. When I met him, I brought in Brendan Shortall from the pro-life campaign to help make the case. After a bit of toing and froing, Flanagan agreed that he would probably do it. That meant I could get on to Gregory to tell him what was about to happen: he had said that his vote would never be the single one that brought down the government, so now he had the excuse not to vote with the opposition. The final piece in the jigsaw was Jim Gibbons. I never spoke to him in person, but I did have a telephone conversation with one of his sons, who made it clear that his father would not be travelling anywhere to save Charlie Haughey's bacon. 'All he has to do is get in the ambulance,' I implored him, 'and then get right back out again.' The answer was no. That was the end of that.

Just before the no-confidence vote, I made a few noises to Mervyn Taylor, the Labour whip, about the possibility of them voting with us. Labour had just elected a new leader, Dick Spring, and wanted more time to prepare for a general election. I don't know if Taylor took it to his parliamentary party, but there was definitely no enthusiasm to help Haughey. Supporters of O'Malley were suggesting that Labour might bite if Haughey stepped down. Haughey would have rather shot himself than agree to that one. So the government was defeated by 82 votes to 80 on 4 November. There was no great sense of triumph on the opposition benches, no whoops of joy or cheering. To be honest, I believe we were all thinking, 'Please, not another election.'

The general election campaign ended in a satisfying result for me personally if not the party at large. I increased my first preferences with 23 per cent of the vote. The real loser of the election in Dublin Central was George Colley. He kept his seat, but he secured fewer first preferences than Gregory. Colley had known going into the election that he was under pressure. He did not have a high profile in the constituency. I'm not sure whether he had ever talked to me about an issue in the area. When he sent his leaflets round, they even admitted that he would not 'sail in' and that 'George Colley needs every vote he can get'. Colley was definitely bruised by not topping the poll last time round. This time he wanted to make a fight of it. His supporters felt they had been pushed around at the previous election. Now they were mad. They went door to door urging people to vote for Colley as the alternative to what they called the 'Haughey camp'. On election day, they prowled around polling stations, making sure there was 'no funny business'. Inevitably, that led to a bit of handbag stuff between various sets of supporters. Later they would complain about 'massive intimidation' from us. The reality was that a lot of outsiders came to canvass the area determined to be seen standing up to us. That was never going to happen. Anyhow, the people of the area made their choice clearly enough. I was elected on the first count with double the number of Colley's first preferences. He got in after my surplus was redistributed. That was the reality of Fianna Fáil politics in Dublin Central.

The general election gave no party an overall majority. Fianna Fáil was down six seats, Fine Gael up seven. Labour was up one, the Workers' Party down one. Independent socialist Jim Kemmy lost his seat. The net result: a Fine Gael/Labour coalition with Fianna Fáil sent into opposition. While I was disappointed, the only strategy for the last year had been to stay in office. Now at last we would have time to regroup and develop our ideas. But the question was whether that would be done under Charlie's leadership.

In late January, the new Minister for Justice, Michael Noonan, made a number of disclosures about the previous government. Seán Doherty, Noonan's predecessor in Justice, had authorised phone taps on two prominent journalists, Geraldine Kennedy and Bruce Arnold. Ray MacSharry had used surveillance equipment to record telephone conversations with his cabinet colleague, Martin O'Donoghue. Stories about bugging journalists had been in the papers since before Christmas. There was also gossip doing the rounds that people were beholden to Haughey because they were in financial difficulties. As whip I got to hear most of those rumours. O'Donoghue seemed to be hinting that there were other people who would be happy to help those who needed it.

Noonan's revelations threw us into turmoil. A bad-tempered meeting of the parliamentary party resolved nothing, but momentum was building for Charlie to go. Chief Whip is an odd position. Your job is to keep the troops in line for the leadership, but it is also to listen to what those troops are telling you. By Wednesday 26 January, the clear message I was getting was that it was 'time for a change'. These weren't just the usual suspects, such as the 'club of 22'. Plenty of others were telling me that the party needed a fresh start. George Colley came to see me and told me it was my duty to go out to Kinsealy to tell Haughey that the game was up. Funnily enough, it was one of the friendlier chats I had with George. Meanwhile, I knew that senior members of the party had already activated their campaign teams ready for a leadership contest. That was the message I took to Kinsealy on 26 January.

When I got there, Haughey hadn't arrived back at the house. He was at the Olympia with his family watching *Bottler and the Beanstalk* – a panto with his friend Brendan Grace. His opponents in the parliamentary party would soon find out that whatever Charlie was, he certainly wasn't a bottler. When he got back, I had a nice exchange with the family, who must have known that I was there with bad news. Eventually I went to the office to talk to Haughey alone. He was friendly enough, because I had only been acting on his request to take a private tally of likely votes in the contest. 'Come on then, Bertie, where are we?' he asked me. I told him that I had done a tally of the parliamentary party. 'If there was a vote today,' I said, 'you would lose.' I also told him that if he decided to go, Michael O'Kennedy would have a clear victory. I had the figures. I knew what people were telling me: a Haughey defeat, followed by an O'Kennedy win. Usually when I told Charlie something, it was hard to read him. There would be almost no reaction. This time was different. I suppose I expected either acceptance of his fate, or to see that famous temper of his. Sure, the press had been predicting his downfall all week. Now, though, here I was there telling him that many of his parliamentary colleagues wanted him to go.

'Well, they can do what they like,' Haughey said quietly. 'I'm staying.' In that case, I told him, there was only one option. 'Play for time.' He had been looking away from me until then, but when he turned towards me I could see in his eyes that his mind was already focusing on how to fight back. We had a brief chat about the logistics, how the matter would go to a vote, a vote he was confident that he would win. 'You can tell everyone there'll be no resigning,' he told me as I left. That was the message I took back to Leinster House. The next day the *Irish Press* published Haughey's political obituary on its front page.

In the end tragedy intervened. The party was due to meet on 2 February to decide the matter, but then Clem Coughlan died. It would be usual in the circumstances to adjourn the meeting as a mark of respect. But I had heard the night before that some of Haughey's opponents were planning to call for the meeting to go ahead. Common decency said that had to be wrong. I agreed with Jim Tunney, the chairman of the parliamentary party, that he would come into the meeting and adjourn it after saying some brief words of respect. I then planned to have RTÉ waiting on the line in an adjacent office and to announce immediately what had happened. In the end, that is exactly what we did. Vincent Brady opened the door. I was out of the parliamentary party room as soon as Jim finished speaking and while I was talking live on air to John Bowman, I could hear fellas shouting in the background that the meeting must still take place. It was disgraceful. The atmosphere around Leinster House over the next few days was grim. Colley organised a petition wanting another meeting that week to consider the leadership, which was signed by forty other deputies and seven senators. A meeting was called for 7 February. Everything was chaotic. Colley dropped into my office with a motion that 'the Fianna Fáil members of Dáil Éireann request the resignation of Mr Charles J. Haughey as party leader now'. There was a problem, however, as the motion wasn't signed. I got Colley back in. He was a bit iritated, like I was making a fuss over nothing. But he couldn't sign it himself, because the motion was in the name of Ben Briscoe. Eventually I got hold of Briscoe on the phone. 'You're after forgetting to sign the thing,' I told him. 'You need to come in.' He wasn't happy about it.

With so much gossip and speculation about Haughey's future flying around the place, the Committee of Inquiry into the question of the bugging was a bit overlooked. The committee was chaired by Jim Tunney. The other members were David Andrews and Michael O'Kennedy – both barristers – and myself as Chief Whip. There was tension right from the start between Tunney and Andrews. O'Kennedy said very little. It was left to me to stop the bickering and get the thing done. Tunney stormed out at one point. Then there was an incident that predictably gave everyone a great laugh. We had agreed to tape all the interviews, but the machine broke. If only that had been the case earlier, maybe we would have avoided all this trouble in the first place. We had everyone in, including Charlie, but at the end of the day the inquiry had very little status. No one gave evidence under oath, and we were basing our findings on what people told us. It was a report of what had been said, rather than an investigation. Those who wanted to believe it was a whitewash thought exactly that. It really came down to a question of whether or not you trusted the word of parliamentary colleagues.

We had agreed right from the start that there could be dissenting opinions in the final report. David being David wanted his own say. He's always had his opinions, strongly given, but he's straight. You always knew where you were with him. Admittedly he could sometimes be a bit pompous, but most of the time he was a good guy and we seemed to get on well. When it came to the final report, he put in two paragraphs of 'minority' opinion, saying that although 'Mr Haughey while in office was not aware of the telephone tapping of the journalists, it seems to me, however, that on the principle of ultimate responsibility, he should have been so aware'. To my mind that only seemed to confirm that we didn't have the evidence to say that Haughey was involved, even if I believed that David thought it was a whitewash.

The report was the first item of business taken at the meeting of the parliamentary party on 7 February. We didn't want the press to get hold of it, so I read the complete report to the meeting. Perhaps that's why some people asked if they could read it for themselves in the anteroom. Then we moved on to the main issue: Briscoe's motion of no confidence. The mood was different to the bad-tempered marathon meeting the previous October. Everyone seemed fed up with it all now, keen to decide one way or the other. The vote was by secret ballot. Few seemed to bother showing their votes publicly. I voted for Haughey out of loyalty and because I thought he was better than the alternatives. Had the motion passed, I would have voted for O'Kennedy, who I genuinely respected. The other person I would happily have voted for if he had stood was Ray MacSharry. He was a class apart.

When the result of the vote was announced – 40 to 33 in favour of Haughey – the room was subdued. I shook Charlie's hand and he thanked me for everything I had done to hold the party together. People gathered round him, speaking in quiet tones. Even when a great roar came from outside, where a crowd of his supporters had gathered, most people ignored it. I think we all had a sense that last time round everything had got out of hand. No one wanted a repeat of the incident with Jim Gibbons. Later I slipped away back to Drumcondra. Everyone was amazed but pleased that Haughey had survived. In fairness, this third and final heave of the eighties would stabilise things for Haughey. He would get another nine years as leader. Funnily enough, this was the moment I had my first real run-in with him.

When I heard the news of George Colley's death on 17 September, I was really shocked. He had always had that look of a 'party elder' about him, but even though he had been in hospital, his death still came as a surprise to me. It just confirmed my view that the stresses of political life were putting us all under a terrible strain. George was another victim. We had never been particularly close, and at election times in the constituency there had been a fair amount of tension between our two teams. But I have to say that in all my dealings with him, even when he identified me as a supporter of Haughey, he always maintained an old-fashioned professional courtesy. George was a gentleman in politics, with a great respect for the Republican traditions of the party going back to the Easter Rising. We didn't agree about everything, but I did admire him. He had made an enormous contribution to Fianna Fáil over many decades.

Following Colley's death, emotions in the party were running high for the resulting by-election. I was now a leading figure in the constituency, regularly topping the poll at election time, so I was made director of elections. The problem was, who would be our candidate? Dessie O'Malley immediately began to push for George's widow, Mary, to stand to protect the Colley legacy. Haughey, meanwhile, was making claims for his friend John Stafford, a local undertaker. I liked both Stafford and Mrs Colley, but running either of them meant choosing between the two competing wings of the party. My strong view was that if we were to win the seat, we had to pick a candidate who both sides would be prepared to campaign for. That meant taking charge of the process. Shortly before the convention, Charlie came to see me to discuss Stafford. He didn't say outright that I had to run his man, but he made it pretty clear that he wanted it. I told him that I thought Stafford would be a good candidate in a general election, but that the view of my team in the constituency was that he was the wrong man for the job this time. 'Come and meet them to talk about it,' I suggested.

Charlie came to Drumcondra for a meeting in the constituency office above Fagan's pub. I think he was a bit taken aback. There were around eighteen people in the room. And it quickly became clear that these were not just hired suits for the night. These people knew their areas, street by street, house by house. They could tell him in precise detail which TDs needed to campaign in which areas to win the seat, including getting people like Des O'Malley out to Marino to woo the Colley supporters. Without a combined effort, they told him, we would lose the election. I took a back seat during the discussions, letting Paul Kiely lead the meeting. Towards the end, Paul put it starkly to Charlie: 'Is the issue about winning the seat for Fianna Fáil,' he said, 'or running John Stafford?' Charlie told him it was about winning the seat. 'Well, if you leave the candidate to us, I promise we'll win you the seat,' Paul said. Afterwards, Haughey said that I should do whatever I liked. 'But you had better win the seat,' he added, giving me the familiar look.

We had to play cute to get what we wanted at the convention. We put Paul Kiely's name in as a potential candidate, and everyone assumed he was 'my' man. But just before the vote was taken, we withdrew Paul and threw our weight behind Tom Leonard. I had campaigned with him before. He was a decent man, with few enemies, and was exactly the safe pair of hands we needed for a by-election such as this. No one was going to say they wouldn't canvass for good old Tom. Mary Colley was eliminated in the first round, and that left her supporters with the choice of backing Leonard or Stafford. Obviously they weren't going to back Haughey's man, so Leonard romped home in the second count. It seemed the best way to get round internal friction in the party. Stafford was livid and blamed me. That would be an issue later on, but for now I was delighted that we had a candidate I knew we could get elected. I probably put that in an unfortunate way on the night. 'Tom has had more than his fair share of failures,' I said. 'He has been a three-time loser, but as director of elections I will ensure that he will be a first-time winner.' I apologised to him afterwards, not least because he had actually won a seat in Dublin Cabra in 1977. What I had meant to say was that I was determined to get him elected in Dublin Central.

Tom understood that as soon as we went out campaigning together. The contrast in styles was noticeable. Despite his background in fruit and veg, he wasn't much of an outdoors man. Tom was slight, with a bit of a stoop. His campaigning was polite rather than energetic. He was almost apologetic about calling at houses, always saying sorry for disturbing people's dinner. He would only knock on doors once. There was not much banter. Gates were always opened and closed quietly. 'Never mind that, Tom,' I joked with him, 'jump over the gates!' Soon he knew how we had been winning all these years. The Fianna Fáil party, as predicted, turned out in full. I remember one Saturday afternoon during the campaign looking down a street in Cabra East, seeing Des O'Malley, Mary Harney, Ray Burke and Michael O'Kennedy all canvassing together. Any differences in the party were not on show in Dublin Central.

Charlie had told me he would let me have my way as long as I won the seat. At the by-election in November, Leonard was comfortably elected with a 5 per cent increase in the Fianna Fáil vote. That was a real achievement in the poorest constituency in the country. It was the first piece of good news for the party in a while, ending 1983 on a high note after so many traumatic events. I had shown what could be done if factions were put to one side and we all campaigned as Fianna Fáil. That reinforced my position in the party. We had stood out for uniting the party, getting people to work together. We had won victories in the three previous elections, but those were to get me elected. By-elections are always a bit more like a national campaign. If we had lost, Haughey and the party would have been at our throats. Instead, I heard soon afterwards that he was cumainn. 'We're not having any of that nonsense,' I remember him saying. 'We need real cumainn, with real people in them.' Predictably there was a big fight about it, but to be honest those in paper cumainn showed their weakness, because they couldn't even muster enough support to keep themselves going. Joe Burke called it 'the slaughter of the innocents', but to be honest it was more like the slaughter of the guilty. I was strongly of the view that they had been using Fianna Fáil for their own electoral purposes rather than for the greater good of the party or the areas they served. To those who said this was just about me reinforcing my control over Dublin Central, my immediate response was that I was already running an efficient organisation in my own constituency. I had topped the poll three times and had just run a successful by-election campaign. Nobody likes to get complacent, but 'Operation Dublin' was never about me. It was about helping Fianna Fáil win back the city. When it came to my own prospects, I decided against the easy ride. Looking at the various seats for the locals in 1985, I decided that despite already having a safe seat I would put myself up as a candidate in the North Inner City.

Throughout the eighties, the inner city was a tough place. It had the highest unemployment in the country. Deprivation was every-where. I was at meetings almost every night, seeing the problems first hand. Drug-related crime was a massive problem. An IMS survey showed that Dublin had higher crime rates than any large US city. I had already courted some controversy with my views on what needed to be done with drug dealers in the area. When vigilantes knee-capped two young lads in the constituency, I had to make the point that many in the area I had spoken to had little sympathy for these 'known criminals'. People were regularly approaching me asking for advice about whether they should start policing their own areas. I always said the same thing: I took the Garda line about it being very dangerous. But a few months later many of them would come back and say that they had cut down crime where there were vigilantes. That made it hard to keep saying to them, 'Well, that's not a good idea.' I made that point to John Bowman on RTÉ radio. 'In my own area they've taken various actions, some of them I'm totally opposed to. But unfortunately I must say they are also quite effective. In one particular part of the constituency, very severe action was taken against known criminals and the area has almost cleaned itself up since.' That got me a rebuke from the Association of Garda Sergeants and Inspectors. In private many Gardaí told me I was right.

I was so busy with the organisation in the city that for once I took my eye off things locally. I nearly got a taste of my own medicine, I suppose, when John Stafford managed to get the nomination for the North Inner City, but I ended up on the ticket anyway. To be honest, Stafford was not really a factor in 1985. Our real head-to-head was with Gregory. Time and again he had said that I only got my huge vote in the general elections because of the size of the constituency. In the inner city though, Tony said he was king. I knew that was wrong. The way to prove it was to take him on in his own ward. Our rivalry would become the source of much banter in the coming years, but the contest in June 1985 was a fierce one. It was as simple as me against him on his own turf. It was a real battle with both of us wanting to win outright. It might have been just a local election, but it created great interest in the area. In the end, I easily got more first preferences than Tony and he admitted that I had 'wiped the floor' with him. That said, we continued to work very effectively together on the council on important issues. I helped get him on the board of Dublin Port, which was important to him because his father had worked on the docks. We were never personal friends, but we knew how to cooperate to get things done.

Although I took great satisfaction from the result in the North Inner City, the overall result for Fianna Fáil was more important. For almost two decades Fine Gael and Labour had had a stranglehold on local politics in the Dublin area. We broke that in 1985. There were spectacular performances by Fianna Fáil candidates everywhere. My brother Noel was elected. Charlie Haughey's son, Seán, who was

only a young fella, was elected in Dublin Artane. A huge number of
people were elected who would be the backbone of the Fianna Fáil
organisation for the next twenty-five years. I became leader of the
Fianna Fáil group on the city council. It was a great moment when
we elected Jim Tunney as Lord Mayor in July. Everyone liked and
respected Jim. He had been kind to me early in my career when we
were both TDs for Dublin Finglas. The year before he had been
bitterly disappointed to lose in the European elections. Now he would
be Lord Mayor. It was nice for him and for us.

'Operation Dublin' had succeeded. For the first time in years
Fianna Fáil had a mandate to rejuvenate the city.

5

PARTNERSHIPS

I've had many interesting and important jobs throughout my career, but the one I enjoyed most was Lord Mayor of Dublin.

I succeeded Jim Tunney as Lord Mayor in the summer of 1986. The day I took office was a proud one for the Ahern family. Both my parents were thrilled to see me accept the chain of office. Coming from Cork, where the office of Lord Mayor had a great historical significance in the Republican tradition, I think it meant more to them even than me being a TD. To see their son as the Lord Mayor of Dublin: that was something that made them extremely happy. It was an emotion that I shared. I'm Drumcondra man and boy. But I am also a proud Dub. To represent the city where I was born gave me real satisfaction.

That said, it was a huge job and required a lot of energy. I had the opportunity to get out to every part of the city. What immediately struck me was the level of commitment and activism that there is in our communities. There were charity workers, community workers, support groups, residents' associations. They were dealing with all kinds of illnesses, misfortunes and deprivation, trying to help make life better in their areas. It left me with an enormous feeling of just how many good people are out there. We don't always hear about them, but these are the people who keep our communities going. One of the nice aspects of the job was that I was able to bring them to the Mansion House to recognise the work they were doing. They never asked for any reward, but it was good to be able to say thank you to people who were giving so much to the life of Dublin.

My year as Lord Mayor also gave me a sense of the potential that Dublin had as a city. I went to cities in Britain and America to build links and look at the kind of regeneration schemes they had in the run-down areas. We twinned with San Jose in California, which in time would reap great rewards for IT investment, including bringing the likes of Intel to Ireland. In London, the Docklands scheme was just beginning and when I saw those plans, I knew that we had to be as ambitious for Dublin. A few months after I took office, the FitzGerald government, in conjunction with the city, gave me the opportunity to launch a major initiative to encourage private developers to help regenerate the inner city. Dublin Corporation had been criticised for a low-key approach to attracting investors. I had the developers, auctioneers and architects into the Mansion House to promote a new initiative, 'Inner City Development, New Incentives for Designated Areas'. I told them that there were few other cities in the EEC and America that had as many sites waiting to be developed. The success of redevelopment in those areas would depend on money coming from the private sector. It wouldn't be enough to 'keep the show on the road with the resources we have', I told them. 'It is our city and it is up to us to take on the challenge to redevelop it.' I was delighted at the reaction we got. It went down well that I was trying to imbue a spirit of enterprise and leadership, as nothing much was happening in Dublin at the time.

Over the next two decades, the regeneration would transform Dublin into one of the most vibrant cities in the world. That is one of the reasons why I support plans for a directly elected mayor in

Dublin. We need a mayor with the authority and the proper powers to effect real change in the city. At the end of the day, local people always know what's best for their local area rather than national politicians – and I say that as someone who has served at both levels.

My role as Lord Mayor gave me my first experience of implementing executive government. It was sobering. As Chief Whip in Leinster House I had had my fair share of battles to sort out, but that was a question of trying to facilitate parliamentary colleagues. In the council, I worked with some good officials. Later I would get on extremely well with John Fitzgerald, the Dublin city manager. In 1986, the manager was Frank Feely. We would work successfully together on the Dublin Millennium Project. He always did his best to promote Dublin during a difficult time economically, but he wanted to run the city in his own way. In 1985, when I became Majority Leader on the council, I had insisted that councillors, not officials, would take control over the preparation and presentation of the budget. That meant extra work for us, but it was the only way to avoid the introduction of the service charges that were being proposed by officials. I quickly learnt how to make sure that measures voted through had money earmarked for specific projects. That stopped the practice of money being approved for a particular scheme and then being used for something else. Predictably this led to disagreements. I don't remember the incident myself, but Ruairi Quinn reminded me years later that after one disagreement with Feely, I hung my chain of office round his neck, saying, 'You've behaved all day as if you were the Lord Mayor, so you might as well wear the chain!' Whether or not that's a myth, it was certainly how I felt often enough.

Being Lord Mayor was a full-time job. The problem was that it was just one of many for me. In addition to my role on the council, I was also Fianna Fáil's spokesman on Labour and Public Service. That was a recognition from Haughey, he told me, that I had done a good job as Chief Whip. Now I was shadowing John Boland at

Public Service and Ruairi Quinn at Labour. Boland was a good minister and I worked well with him debating his White Paper on public sector reform, but I did not know him especially well. Quinn I knew much better. He was one of the brightest ministers in the Dáil. We didn't always agree on things – although actually we did agree on quite a lot – but you always knew that he was coming at issues in a serious way. We developed a mutual respect over the coming years. I learnt how to recognise the little smile he would give if I caught him out on something. There was an appreciation on both sides that, in the cut and thrust of debate, your opponent might actually have something helpful to say. Of course, it gave me a misleading impression of what frontbench politics was really like. Not everyone would turn out to be as interesting to spar with.

Alongside my city council duties and those as an opposition front-bench spokesperson, I was also a vice-president of the party and a member of the National Executive. Plus there was the constituency to look after. I was actively involved in the regeneration of the city and in planning for Dublin's millennium celebrations. In addition to all these political activities, until around the time I became Lord Mayor, I was still working part-time in the Mater, because I needed the money. Being a TD was prestigious, but it was not a career that made you rich. I had made that point a few years earlier in 1983 when the Oireachtas Committee on Procedure and Privileges looked into the matter. 'It is no secret that many deputies have been forced out of public life because they could not face the financial strain of it,' I had said. Without my post at the Mater, where they were very good to me, I might have been in that position too.

When I moved into the Mansion House in 1986, it very quickly became apparent that my marriage to Miriam had reached its breaking point. For years I had been doing all these jobs, had been out all hours, and was never getting back to the family. I left home at six thirty every weekday morning and got back when I got back. I could never plan it, and it was never early. If I was home at midnight I was doing well. Then I was gone again first thing. Saturdays there were all-day clinics starting at ten in the morning, followed by constituency walkarounds, which in the summer did not finish until ten at night. There was more time on Sundays, but even then I would need to catch up on paperwork and read up for the next week. So I was doing so much politically, as well as working at the Mater, not getting enough sleep and never seeing Miriam or the kids. The truth is that as a politician, your life is not really your own. And it is not your family's either. I'm not complaining, because no one forces you into public life. But I don't think anyone starting out really understands what the commitment is until you're there. Looking back on it now, I can see that I should have been around more. I neglected Miriam and the girls. They knew I loved them. They just didn't see me.

In truth, even when the work was done, I was spending more time socialising than I did with my family. Hindsight is always clear and I now recognise that I was more than a little selfish in this period. I was working hard and felt entitled to spend any spare time I had out enjoying myself. I was still only in my early thirties, having got married at the young age of twenty-four. I wanted to blow off steam and the pressures of the job. But I was behaving as if I was young, free and single instead of facing up to my responsibilities as a married man. I had a beautiful wife and two great kids. Now I realise that I should have been at home with them, not out on the town with others. I was being careless and I put our relationship under strain. I know how much I must have hurt Miriam and that is one of the greatest regrets of my life.

At the end of the day, it was my fault. I knew Miriam was deeply disappointed in me and I can't say that I blamed her. I ended up staying in the Mansion House while Miriam lived in our family home in Malahide. I had messed up, but I had become set in my ways and now Miriam wanted out. This was an awful time. It was traumatic for me. It was traumatic for Miriam. It was traumatic for everyone we loved. My parents were absolutely shattered. They loved

Miriam and took the separation very hard. My sisters were extremely upset.

Of course mine and Miriam's biggest worry was the girls. We both sat down with Georgina and Cecelia to discuss what was happening. It is never easy for kids when their parents break up, but ours were very calm about everything, though I know they must have been churned up inside. In fairness to Miriam, when she could have tried to cut me out, she said right from the start that whatever happened, we had to make sure the girls didn't suffer. To start off, they would come to stay over in the Mansion House every week. Later I would have them for weekends, with Sundays in particular always being the day they spent with their dad. We would still celebrate birthdays or special occasions as a family. I would call to the house regularly, and Miriam would come into Church Avenue. And that was how Georgina and Cecelia grew up: Miriam and I both kept tight to them. We're both still very close to the girls, which means that although we got a lot wrong, we must also have got something right as we muddled through.

I don't know if things at home could have been different. I should hardly have been surprised, but at the time I was still stunned when Miriam told me it was over. In hindsight, I don't know how she put up with my behaviour for so long. Miriam had been left to run the house with two small children with no help from me. And even when the split happened, I was so busy that I didn't have time to put things right. Life as Lord Mayor was frantic. A few months afterwards, there would be a general election. Then I would be thrown into the life of a cabinet minister in a minority government, dealing with endless strike negotiations that would run and run, usually into the early hours of the morning.

I sometimes look back and ask if politics was worth it. What I know now, but what I didn't see then, was that there had been one opportunity six years earlier to change everything and live a normal life. A TD's salary in the autumn of 1980 was just under IR£9,000.

The boundaries of the constituency had been changed for the forth-coming election. That would involve a massive campaign effort on my part to get re-elected. That year I was headhunted by the Mater private. I had done a good job in the Mater public. Now they wanted me as chief executive of the private hospital. I went through the inter-view process with the recruitment consultants. In the end I was offered IR£20,000 a year and a car. If I wanted to do some tax consultancy in addition to my role in the hospital, that was fine. But I would have to give up politics. Obviously I could not act as a chief exec-utive and be a TD at the same time.

As I turned down that offer, I committed my life to politics rather than my family. Not that it seemed like that at the time. I knew I was giving up the chance to earn a lot of money. The position at the Mater and the tax consultancy would have made me well off. Plenty of money, big house, smart car, regular hours: these were the rewards on offer. But that would have meant giving up politics and the chance to make a difference in national life. And I would have been letting people down. I had motivated the organisation in the constituency. People were giving up time every week to go out canvassing. They had faith in me. It would have been hard to say, 'That's it, lads, I'm off to make some money.' And I would have been bored. There was so much to be done in the constituency, parts of which remained among the most deprived areas in Ireland. So I decided to stay with politics. By the time my marriage was on the rocks, I couldn't go back and remake that decision about the Mater. When I made the choice I thought it was really between money and politics. Only at the end of my marriage did I realise it was more fateful than that. I remember the day I made the choice, thinking, 'Jesus, what decision do I make?' If I had known then what I know now, I really don't know what I would have done. It was the crossroads moment for myself and my family.

As well as all the turmoil in my private life in 1987, there was a lot going on in the country. We were facing a general election and

Fianna Fáil was going into that campaign without some high-profile TDs. At the end of 1985, Dessie O'Malley and Mary Harney had left to set up the Progressive Democrats. That was a big blow to Fianna Fáil. I remember talking to Brian Lenihan about it over a few jars in a Donnybrook pub after we had been on RTÉ's *Saturday View* before Christmas. Brian was normally such a positive guy, always looking on the bright side, but I remember him saying to me that this was bad. 'They'll hold the balance of power next time round,' he said. 'They'll want Charlie's head on a plate.'

I couldn't understand why they wanted to go. Throughout my years in Fianna Fáil I had stuck to the principle of loyalty to the leader. I had not plotted against Lynch, and had supported Haughey in the three heaves against him. O'Malley was a sharp guy. He should have seen that he would be the leader of Fianna Fáil if he only bided his time. He wasn't always the most popular, but people respected his abilities. A bit of humility and some patience would have seen him Taoiseach. Being a persuasive fellow, he took some good people with him, and I would say tempted a few others. I was especially sorry to see Mary Harney go, because I rated her highly. Pearse Wyse, Lynch's friend and running mate in Cork City, soon followed Mary into the new party. Then there was talk that Joe Walsh might join them. Rumours were also flying around about Charlie McCreevy, David Andrews and Séamus Brennan. Councillors around the country, including the Mayor of Galway, Bridie O'Flaherty, defected from Fianna Fáil. There was even speculation that Jack Lynch was backing the new party. So this looked as if it would be a formidable organisation. They seemed to be having big launches almost every night. Huge crowds turned out. They were gaining momentum and money, and we had no idea how many votes they would take away from us.

I thought the ones who stayed to fight their corner were the brave ones. People like Charlie McCreevy and David Andrews were anti-Haughey. Here was an opportunity for them to go, but they stayed with the party. That got my respect. The biggest shock to me was when Bobby Molloy went. That really knocked me back. Bobby could often seem impatient and a bit touchy, but we always got along fine together. Obviously I hadn't known him as well as I had thought. One night the week before he joined the Progressive Democrats, we were both in Leinster House together. He was going down to the bar to convince Wyse not to leave Fianna Fáil. When he came back, not only had he failed to convince him, he seemed to have had a change of heart himself. I was amazed. 'Why would you go, Bobby?' I asked him. 'If you stay, you'll be a minister in a year.' One thing was clear: he didn't want to talk about it. The following week Molloy left. I have to say I was surprised by the way he did it. He travelled down to Galway, stopping along the way to phone his secretary in Leinster House to say there was a letter in the filing cabinet he wanted delivered immediately to Haughey. That letter informed the leader that Molloy was resigning from Fianna Fáil and the parliamentary party. I think Bobby owed it to himself and to Charlie to have done that face to face. A few hours later he was on a platform beside Des O'Malley announcing that he had joined the Progressive Democrats. It seemed a sad way to end more than twenty years as a Fianna Fáil deputy.

The worst of the situation was that it came at a time when the country was crying out for firm leadership, not division. By 1986, the Irish economy was in free fall. When the *Economist* magazine ran that infamous special report about Ireland being 'The Poorest of the Rich', it was scathing about the performance of the disastrous FitzGerald administration. Ireland, the *Economist* said, was 'on the skids'. In four years our national debt had doubled to IR£25 billion. That was IR£28,000 for every Irish household. As a proportion of GDP, Ireland's debt was the biggest in Europe. The unemployment rate hit 17 per cent. Inflation was a roller coaster. Rising taxes put pressure on pay. Emigration from our shores reached its highest level since the 1950s. The national debt per capita was higher than that of Ethiopa. Having seen the official papers, I know people will get a shock when those files are released after thirty years to see just how close the IMF were to coming in.

Many commentators and a few politicians argued that Thatcherite solutions had worked well in Britain. Happily, the idea that there is no such thing as society didn't find too many takers here. In fact, my view was that society would actually get us out of the hole we had found ourselves in. When Haughey appointed me as Fianna Fáil spokesman on Labour Affairs, he told me he knew it was going to be a challenge. 'Kid, you've done a good job as whip,' he said. 'Now it's time for you get into a full brief, bring yourself on and really get up there.' I don't know whether he thought I was bright or stupid, but he definitely wanted to give me a tough assignment. That meant a lot of hard work. I started by doing a huge amount of reading to get myself into the subject. That was when I got very interested in the Austrian model for social partnership. This put the emphasis on 'tripartitism', which saw the political parties, the employers and the workers agree a consensus approach on pay and the economy to keep inflation and unemployment low. The result was a competitive economy rising from the ashes of a world war to rank well above the OECD average on most indices.

As spokesman on labour, I knew the role I could play would be to engage the trade union movement. That started even when we were in opposition. Things had been nurtured slowly in 1984 and 1985, but by 1986 I was developing strong links with the unions. In particular I forged a productive relationship with Billy Attlee, general secretary of my old union, the Federated Workers' Union of Ireland, as well as with Phil Flynn and Christy Kirwan. The unions produced a thoughtful document on the jobs crisis, which was their response to where we were economically. I put together a working group to shadow what they were doing. We would meet over Fagan's to discuss the issues. There were people from all walks of life: former civil servants, academics and some trades unionists. I also formed good links with the Employers and the Chamber of Commerce movement, working closely with Dan McAuley and later John Dunne. From 1987, Pádraig Ó hUiginn, chairman of the National Economic and Social Council, would also be hugely influential in encouraging the development of the new approach. So was P. J. Mara from the start. We were looking at everything, including training and retraining, skills generation, certification and various aspects of employment cycles. That meant when the unions issued their paper on the jobs crisis, we had our response ready.

I took our paper to Haughey. He could see that a lot of work had gone into it. He also liked the fact that we were stealing a march on the FitzGerald coalition, including the 'comrades' in the Labour Party, whose relationship with the unions was difficult. In fact, he liked it so much that later he would be claiming credit for the idea – a leader's prerogative, I suppose. Haughey told me to make formal contact about opening talks with the Irish Congress of Trade Unions. A meeting was arranged at ICTU headquarters in Raglan Road. That was a big deal. There had been a decent relationship between Fianna Fáil and the unions during the Lemass era, which had later broken down. For the leader of the party to take his frontbench team to Raglan Road to meet the likes of Attlee and John Carroll, president of the Irish Transport and General Workers' Union, was a major development. It signalled unambiguously to the unions that Fianna Fáil was committed to a new approach based on partnership. After Charlie came in and gave the whole thing his blessing, the unions knew that they could deal with us, and with me.

Over the winter of 1986–7, working under MacSharry, we hammered out in opposition an embryonic economic strategy that took the 1982 'Way Forward' White Paper to the next level. It formed the outline of the 'Plan for National Recovery', which we would later negotiate in government during the summer of 1987. I had devoted hours to agreeing the broad outlines of that before the election in February of that year. After the election, it became the basis of negotiations with the social partners.

That's the aspect of politics most people never see. There's no glamour in sitting in an airless room, poring over the detail of financial information. There would be plenty of rows, but everyone wanted to keep the process going, inching the thing along line by line. Everyone knew what was at stake. This was a battle for our economic survival. The enormity of the struggle we faced in the 1980s was massive. Debt, inflation, unemployment, hopelessness, emigration. I think it's a credit to the unions that they wanted to find a way forward. We did that by tackling the problems in a creative fashion, determined to find consensus. Discipline and patience. That's what I learnt even before I became a minister. Dialogue had to mean exactly that: talking to people. If it took a long time, fair enough. It would be worth putting in the hours if we could get a result. Of course, everyone had their own agenda, but in those early meetings, we got a bond of trust and shared a real sense of what was best for the country as a whole. That might sound a bit pious, but it's what happened. Representatives from all sectors pulled together for the good of the people. That's a valuable lesson from our recent history which is as relevant today as it was in the dark days of the 1980s.

Going into the 1987 election, I had been confident that we could do a deal as a government with the unions, but first we had to get elected. In Dublin Central we pulled out all the stops, getting three Fianna Fáil deputies in the five-seater constituency. Neither of the coalition parties got a TD. Michael Keating, who had defected from Fine Gael to the Progressive Democrats, and Tony Gregory both held their seats. We got three seats for Fianna Fáil through really tight vote management. My surplus split almost evenly, bringing in the other two candidates. You could only do that if you were running a smooth operation in your constituency. Throughout the eighties I had developed a ward system to stay on top of constituency affairs and to canvass all year round. I made sure there was an active group in every ward. Each had a ward boss. There were around forty in total. Our aim was to make sure that we had active and hard-working groups to respond to issues on the ground. I would meet the ward bosses on at least a monthly basis in the Gresham Hotel on O'Connell Street. They would report on what was going on in their area, telling us what people were saying on the doorstep. I would chair those meetings, but there was no real hierarchy. Once you were a ward boss, you had your own team and were there with equal status in discussing the constituency. Then I had my team of elected constituency officials who provided advice and office support. These included Chris Wall, Des Garvin, Paul Kiely, Mary O'Donnell, Paddy Reilly, Liam Cooper and Ray Brady. They kept me up to date with issues as they developed in the constituency, making sure I knew what was happening in the area.

We all knew our success was built on the work of the regular activists. We would ask for a commitment from them of two hours a week. Many gave more. At any given time, there would be around two hundred real activists involved, out in all weathers. It was pure grass-roots stuff. Meeting ordinary constituents who were not 'polit-ical' people. Gathering cases, listening to the issues of concern. We would get to know the organisations, clubs and residents' associations to see what we could do to help. A lot of the time, it was dealing with people who didn't know where else to turn. We would arrange to get the relevant councillor or TD onto particular cases. So we were visible around the place. People sometimes wonder how I've always managed to get such huge first preferences in all my elections from 1981 onwards. The answer to that is simple. Anyone can see that we're committed to the constituency full-time. I don't just come round looking for a vote on election day. I'm there all year round.

I hoped getting that extra seat in 1987 might be part of a swing towards Fianna Fáil throughout the country. There's no doubt we had gone into the campaign thinking we could get an overall majority. FitzGerald said we were 'petrified' going into the election on 17 February 1987. Well, we certainly weren't worried about them. Fine Gael and Labour were at each other's throats, and the economy was in dire straits. The real killer for us was the Progressive Democrats. They were organised and ran some well-known candidates, such as Geraldine Kennedy and Pat O'Malley, who had a good chance of winning seats. They also had a clear strategy, focused on privatisation and lower taxes, to deal with the economic mess the country was in. They argued that MacSharry had put together a good plan with 'The Way Forward', but that was 1982 and he couldn't get it through the Dáil. Trust the PDs now to do the job five years on, they said. It was a popular argument. The PDs exceeded their own expectations and ours by winning fourteen seats. If they had had greater self-belief, I think they could have got more.

The frustration for us was that around two-thirds of those seats would have been 'ours' on a normal day. In the event, it left Haughey three seats short of an overall majority. That was a missed opportunity. The country had been turning our way. Without the PDs, we would have held a decisive majority. Instead we had come up short. Haughey wasn't interested in dealing with them, knowing that the price would be far too high for him. A few days before the 25th Dáil met, Ray Burke went on the radio to warn off anyone who was thinking of using the situation to oust Haughey. 'Let nobody outside Fianna Fáil have any feeling that since they've left the party they can influence our leadership,' he said. 'They tried that when they were on the inside and they're not going to do it from the outside.'

But it was nail-biting stuff. Haughey's view was that it was a Fianna Fáil minority government or nothing. There was no repeat of the 'Gregory deal'. Neil Blaney was not given the reassurances that he was looking for on the North. If either Blaney or Gregory had voted against him when the Dáil met on 10 March, Haughey would not have had the votes to be Taoiseach. With FitzGerald falling short as well, that would have been the start of a constitutional crisis. In the end, Gregory abstained, leaving the vote tied at 82–82. The Ceann Comhairle, Seán Treacy, gave his casting vote in favour. Haughey was 'the Boss' again. And I was a cabinet minister.

Haughey had phoned me the night before to tell me that, if elected, he would make me Minister for Labour. 'Time to be a serious politician, with a serious job,' he said. I thanked him for giving me the opportunity and promised that I would give it everything I had. When I got off the phone, I called the girls, who were excited even if they were too young to understand what it meant. Then I went back to Church Avenue. Everyone was thrilled. I organised tickets for the family to come and watch as I was nominated in the Dáil. Everything that day seemed to pass in a blur. I remember the new cabinet gathering beforehand. Everyone seemed happy enough with their portfolios. I had a chat with Ray MacSharry, who was going to be Minister for Finance. He told me that securing the support of the unions was going to be vital in sorting the country's finances. 'You and me have got to keep tight on this,' he said. I replied that there was no point being in politics, no good being a minister, if we didn't get these things right for the country. It was that sort of a day.

Parading into the House was a strange moment, both humbling and a bit embarrassing. Most people seemed pleased for me, although no doubt there must have been a few thinking, 'Who does this guy think he is, just thirty-five and a minister.' Then it was up to Áras an Uachtaráin to receive the seal of office from President Hillery. I think some of us were interested to see how Hillery and Haughey would get along, but it was all very good-humoured and friendly. I felt very conscious that I was the young kid on the block, but Hillery went out of his way to welcome me. Looking back at the photograph, there I am the young fella with the long black hair surrounded by a lot of these very senior people who had seen it all before. I had attended cabinet as Chief Whip. Now, for the first time, I was a full member in my own right. That felt like a real step up.

MacSharry was the minister I would be working most closely with. He was also the one I watched to see how the job was done. He seemed happy to take me under his wing, and I probably learnt as much about government from him as any politician. He was tough, very precise and gave his life to politics at this time. He would get an absolute hammering from some quarters for his financial policy – 'Mac the Knife' – but history proved him right. He was determined to go in and get the job done. He had wanted to do it five years earlier. He was not going to miss this second chance. MacSharry was not a drinker, so we would meet for a cup of tea several times a week in his office. Sometimes I thought I spent more time in Finance than I did in my own department. He used to make sure he involved me in talking about what needed to be done with the finances, so I got to know him very well. There were plenty of little tricks he passed along to me, especially about how to listen to officials or colleagues without committing yourself. The oldest trick, though, wasn't a trick at all. 'Just know more than they do,' he advised me. That meant studying your parliamentary questions – not just the oral ones but the written ones too. Read your papers thoroughly so that you're on top of your brief. Putting in the effort gets you a long way in politics. It always amazes me how few people realise that.

We had a huge economic and fiscal challenge in front of us. 'The Way Forward' document was still the blueprint, now updated and ready to implement. There were long, long meetings, poring over the estimates of revenue and public expenditure, looking for ways to cut, cut, cut. There were all kinds of rumblings from the unions, but the first real dramatic challenge came from workers at the ESB in May. When it was announced there would be no increase in the current pay round, they threatened to go on strike. My job was to hold the government line that the country could not afford pay increases. MacSharry was totally with me on this. Haughey was 100 per cent behind me. Then the strike began on 5 May and all hell broke loose. By midday, I had Haughey calling me into an emergency meeting after a tense phone call with the Federated Union of Employers (later IBEC). 'The Employers have bottled it,' he told me. 'They're saying we can't have the ESB out, because industry will close down.' I was furious. I told Haughey that we had to stand firm. 'If we back down,

I'll have no authority left with the unions.' Up until the strike the Employers had been saying we needed strong government. Then, at the first sign of trouble, they were caving in. Haughey agreed that we had to face the strike down, but I could feel people in Leinster House, in the unions and in the Employers saying that this was a test of a young minister, that this will see if he's going anywhere.

Perhaps officials in my own department were trying to be protective, but the general advice to me was 'Minister, don't get too personally involved.' There was definitely a feeling that the strike was a matter for the ESB management and that the unions should sort it out for themselves. I ended up operating out of the Mansion House during the dispute because my own department didn't seem that pushed about getting a resolution. There was one official though, Kevin Bonner, who took a different approach. An expert in industrial relations, he was superb during this strike and later. I told him that I had to hold the government line. Having come in with a pay policy, we couldn't back down from a challenge after just a couple of months in office. 'I need to be hands-on,' I told him, 'otherwise I'll have no credibility with these guys.' Bonner agreed and helped me find a way to be involved without being seen to interfere or take sides. The talks took place in secret at the National College of Industrial Relations. I kept close to both sides in the negotiations, helping to bang heads together or to bind the wounds when necessary. I didn't mind the discussions throughout the dispute, but the cigarettes were a nightmare. Whatever about hammering out deals in smoke-filled rooms, some of these talks were enough to ruin your lungs forever.

When I wasn't in meetings with one side or the other, I would get an update by phone every thirty minutes. No-one in those negotiations could have been in any doubt that I was involved. I liaised privately with Joe La Cumbre, who was the ESB worker director and a friend of Mary O'Rourke's from Athlone. The industrial action lasted from 5 to 7 May. At the end of it, the power went back on and there was no increase in the pay award that had triggered the strike. The government's pay guidelines remained intact. That was a victory for us and for the country.

There was a cabinet meeting the day after the dispute had ended. Everyone was in great high spirits, saying, 'Fantastic! We held the line!' And to be honest I felt a bit bemused, because some of them had been keeping their heads down over the last few days. Only Haughey and MacSharry had been telling me to stick with it. But on the Friday morning, everyone was saying that we had won. I was just the young fella in the room, so I smiled and agreed that it was a great day for all of us. That was collective responsibility. To be fair though, I heard later that members of cabinet like John Wilson and Gerry Collins were going around telling people that I was bright and handling things well. That gave me confidence when facing up to the series of industrial disputes, including CIÉ, RTÉ and Irish Steel, that were a feature of that summer. Some of these ended up in strike action, others didn't. By the time we got to the Sugar Company in September, I had decided to change tack. We would let them go out on strike and then leave them to it. 'I'm not going to solve this one,' I told my officials, who were amazed. Having been initially sceptical, the department now seemed to be enjoying its new high profile. They had got used to being a governmental backwater. Now they were front-page news. When the sugar workers went on strike on 21 September, I let it be. That dispute was never settled before they came back to work. The reality was that we couldn't have unions in every industry challenging us one by one, especially going into the winter. A line had to be drawn somewhere and this was it.

I was determined that we would try to create a new era of industrial peace, and this came about in the 'Programme for National Recovery' agreed in October 1987. Strikes and fractured labour relations between employers and trade unions were destroying any chance of making economic progress. This was the beginning of a major period of reform in Irish industrial relations. I got legislation through the Dáil to establish a new Labour Relations Commission and a

Health and Safety Authority. There was legislation on part-time workers and on the payment of wages. A new Industrial Relations Act was passed that restricted secondary picketing and provided for secret ballots before strike action. It was the first major reform of that Act since the beginning of the twentieth century.

The unions seemed to like the fact that I wanted to be a reforming minister. In return, the intense negotiations I had over this time confirmed my deep respect for them. I had been a union man myself and I could see how genuine their leaders were in trying to do the best for their people. Obviously there was a certain amount of rhetoric for the troops, but most of the time I felt they were serious and genuine. Once they realised that I wasn't going to lie to them or go out of my way to be unfair to them, they were always prepared to listen on issues. If you played games you were gone. But if you were straight, that gave you credibility with them. That didn't mean you would always agree. But it did mean you could talk. That would be vital in playing my part to get the deal that paved the way for the country's future economic success.

I have always said that social partnership was one of the great foundation stones on which Ireland's economic transformation was built. I was deeply involved in the negotiations for the first ever national agreement in 1987. Over the two decades that followed, I would play my role in the negotiation or implementation of a further six agreements. The size of our problems was huge. We knew that the country wouldn't get out of this mess by divine right or good luck. We understood that we had to be proactive in building consensus between government and the different sectors of Irish society to establish a model of economic progress. Of course, all the participants in the partnership process had their own agendas, but I think we all shared a strong sense of what was right, not just for our constituencies but for the country. It would be poor form not to recognise the role played by Alan Dukes, the new leader of Fine Gael, and his 'Tallaght Strategy'. It gave us the breathing space we needed to implement tough fiscal action.

I was already working closely with MacSharry, but the partnership talks were the first time I was really brought inside the tent by Haughey. Obviously as whip I would have had plenty of dealings with 'the Boss', but as a cabinet colleague during tense negotiations, I was in another league. He was impressive in those big meetings. Watching him, I wondered if I would ever have it in me to do that job so well. On the same day he might be talking to employers, farmers, unions, this or that delegation. He had to be up to speed on everything. If the farmers wanted to talk about beef and lamb, he had to know about beef and lamb. If the dockers wanted to talk about roll-on roll-off, he had to be on top of that. And so it went on. One thing I learnt from him during those talks was how to get the tone right for a meeting. I might see him beforehand when he was furious about something or other. Then he would go into those big meetings smiling. He knew how to create a good atmosphere. In public he rarely appeared grumpy or hassled. He might have been thinking, as he joked with me one day, that 'the country's fucked and youse all fucked it up'. But it never showed.

The 'Programme for National Recovery' was published on 9 October 1987. The results were almost immediate. The national debt peaked that year and the new partnership agreement, with strong trade union support, undoubtedly facilitated the difficult political and financial decisions made to put the economy back on track. Public expenditure and borrowing were cut dramatically. Confidence in our economy began to return and a rapid fall in interest rates followed. A sign of its success was that initially zero growth was forecast for 1987. In fact, almost 5 per cent was achieved.

It had been a long time coming, but at last Ireland was embarking on a period of sustained economic growth.

6

ELECTION BLUES

Life in politics involves putting in the hours. And you quickly learn that it's just when you take your eye off the ball that it smacks you right in the face. I found that out the night Charlie Haughey returned from an official visit to Japan on 26 April 1989.

I was in Scruffy Murphy's having a few pints with my friends Des Richardson and Gerry Brennan. That afternoon Ireland had beaten Spain in a World Cup qualifier to put the Boys in Green on target for Italia 90. It would be the first time that Ireland qualified for the World Cup Finals. The good fortunes of the economy and the soccer team seemed to be going hand in hand. Ireland was giving it a lash. The mood in Scruffy's that night was high-spirited to say the least. I had a 'pair' for the Dáil, which meant I didn't have to attend the vote. I was busy enjoying myself when I got the message from the government whip, Vincent Brady: 'Get back, the Taoiseach's coming in.'

When I got to Leinster House it was buzzing. Deputies from all sides of the House were charging around trying to find out was going on. In all my years in the Dáil, I think it was the only time I saw Vincent actually running. I could sympathise. I had done that job myself and knew what it was like when an ordinary night turned into an extraordinary one. What I heard amazed me. 'Charlie's going to call an election,' one backbench TD told me. I thought that unlikely. A bit later, when I saw the Taoiseach come in, I wasn't so sure.

I had never seen Charlie so determined. He came marching down the corridor in a rage. Officials and a couple of ministers were walking a few steps behind him with their eyes fixed on the carpet. That night a vote was taken on a private member's motion to provide a higher level of compensation for haemophiliacs infected with the HIV virus by blood supplied by the state. Obviously it was a highly important and sensitive issue, but in strictly parliamentary terms it really didn't matter if the government was defeated as we weren't losing legislation. The Taoiseach thought otherwise. Against his better judgement, during a minority administration, he had been persuaded to go to Japan. Now he was back to find the government losing votes. He made it clear that this was a challenge to his authority and that of the government. Vincent Brady, in alerting the opposition whips, made it clear that Haughey could well call an election if he lost the vote.

The atmosphere in the chamber was at fever pitch. The Taoiseach brought in almost the entire cabinet for the vote. I sat there with my serious face on, but thinking, 'What the hell is going on?' At the top of the front bench, I could see Albert Reynolds getting agitated as he talked to Haughey, who made it plain that he didn't want to listen. When the government lost the vote, there was cheering from the opposition benches and the public gallery. Out of nowhere, we seemed to be going into a general election. The government spokesman, P. J. Mara, was around the corridors afterwards trying to tell the political correspondents that this was not inevitable. But it seemed obvious to everyone that Charlie, having marched us all to the top of the hill, wasn't going to march us back down again.

I was despondent when I left Leinster House that night. My first thought was 'if only MacSharry were here'. He had been appointed European Commissioner for Agriculture and Rural Development in

January. Europe's gain was our loss. He was probably the only one to whom Haughey would have listened. Ray would have calmed him down, got him to see the bigger picture. As it was, a rush of blood to the head ruined everything. Some in the cabinet wanted an early election, but I wasn't one of them. The government was not under threat. The Tallaght Strategy was working. There was no popular demand for an election. The economy was coming right. 'There's a time and a season,' as my dad used to say. Had we waited, it would have been obvious that the economic situation was turning for the good. More to the point, it would have been clear that it was our policies that had done it. A minority government had to expect to lose a few votes along the way. That wasn't the end of the world. We were less than two and a half years in government. Stay in for as long as we can, I thought, and if we're good the voters will reward us for it.

That was the line I took when the cabinet met to discuss options. Albert Reynolds, who had replaced MacSharry as Minister for Finance, was against an early election. He knew the economy was improving and thought we should wait. Others were more bullish. Pádraig Flynn was his usual loud self in demanding that the party take advantage of good poll numbers. Ray Burke argued the same. That seemed short-sighted to me. Everyone knows that you can't rely on opinion polls once a campaign starts, and I knew there was no appetite in the country for an election. That was certainly the case on the doorstep in Dublin Central. If people are not up for an election, they usually punish the ones who've brought it about. That was why later on I always took my governments to their full term. Do what you're elected to do, then ask the people to put you back in. I think that in the end Haughey just found it a personal affront to his dignity that he had to rely on the goodwill of the opposition to keep him Taoiseach. In 1989 he had read the polls, thought he had a chance for the elusive overall majority, and went for it. The election took place on 15 June. Turnout was down. Fianna Fáil lost four seats. Far from improving our position, we were looking like a party that would never get an overall majority again.

The next few weeks were frustrating. The 26th Dáil assembled on 29 June. Another constitutional impasse loomed. No one was sure who would form the next government. It was not clear whether there would be a second election, or if there would be a coalition government, which for the first time in its history might even see Fianna Fáil governing alongside another party. It was a farce, that day in Leinster House. Haughey, Alan Dukes and Dick Spring were all nominated and none of them elected. Haughey then said that he would not resign as Taoiseach until a new one had been chosen. There was uproar. It may have been the right position under the law, but it would never stand politically. Charlie seemed to be losing his touch. By the end of the day, he was just 'acting Taoiseach'.

The real question for Fianna Fáil was whether we could stomach dealing with the PDs. After a bit of soul-searching, Haughey agreed to talks on 30 June and nominated myself and Albert Reynolds as the Fianna Fáil negotiators. The Progressive Democrats' representatives were Pat Cox and Bobby Molloy. Cox was a smooth operator, whose experience in television meant he knew how to ask the killer question. As for Molloy, I had shared an office with him and respected the work that he put into his Galway West constituency, going out to the islands and taking their concerns seriously even though there were only a few votes in it. He had been Fianna Fáil through and through. That dedication made up for his abrupt personality. When he left to join the PDs, the personality issues came to the fore. Privately we got on all right. In the negotiating arena we did not. Looking back, I'm amazed that I was even prepared to say that in public. Usually I prefer to keep my thoughts on individuals to myself. It seems I was prepared to make an exception with Bobby. 'I am sure he has his nice points,' I said in a radio interview when it was all over, 'but they don't easily come across, and they didn't in the negotiations.'

The first round of talks broke down almost as soon as they started, and Charlie came out publicly saying that coalition was completely ruled out. At the weekend, I retreated to the grounds of All Hallows to write a short position paper on the options available to the party. These were fairly straightforward if unappealing: call an election; do a 'Tallaght Strategy' to let Dukes lead a minority government; or go into coalition with the PDs. While I was in the college I got talking to a priest called Father Conlon. He was a very learned man, who had written on the early history of the college. I explained to him what I was doing and talked it through. At the end, he said, 'It sounds to me like you need to get away from it for a bit,' so he took me off to the college kitchens for a bowl of strawberries. By the time I went back to my paper, I had concluded that we would be mad to go into opposition just as we were turning the country's finances around. It was time to go into coalition.

The next day, Sunday 2 July, I went to see Haughey at Kinsealy with P. J. Mara. I told them what I had done the previous day and presented the paper that explained my thinking. Beforehand, I had thought I would probably get thrown out of the window. In fact, Haughey's reaction was almost non-existent. When I finished giving my analysis of the situation, he just grunted. I didn't know whether it was in agreement or disagreement. I found out soon enough, because that afternoon Charlie went on *This Week* to rule out coalition yet again. I realised as well that he wasn't pleased with me. Perhaps he thought I had been too presumptuous. This was the beginning of a period of tense relations more generally between Charlie and myself. You can't be 'the kid' forever.

It took another twenty-four hours for Charlie to see that if he were to remain as Taoiseach he had no choice but to negotiate a coalition. By the time the Dáil met the next afternoon, it looked like he had made his mind up, even though many in the party were unconvinced. On 5 July, acting on Charlie's instructions, I did a groundbreaking interview on the *News at One*, saying for the first time that we were prepared to consider a coalition. The negotiations began the following day in the Berkeley Court Hotel. 'Let us never negotiate out of fear,' I said on the way in, quoting Kennedy, 'but let us never fear to negotiate.' Fear or not, it was not always plain sailing. A few days into the talks, I was waiting there with Albert for the PD delegation to arrive. It was a scorching hot day, when everyone would have rather been outside in the sunshine. I watched a bit of the coverage of Boris Becker beating Stefan Edberg in the men's final at Wimbledon – my brother Noel was a keen tennis player, as were most of my family, so I had always had a bit of an interest. Patience, it would be fair to say, is not one of Albert's virtues, and he was getting more and more annoyed. 'Where the hell are they?' he would say every two minutes, each outburst sounding angrier than the previous one. Suddenly he shouted out, 'What the . . . ?' I jumped up to join him at the window. There across the way, looking out of another window, was Bobby Molloy, apparently without a care in the world. His expression soon changed when he saw us watching him. Five minutes later Molloy and Cox were in our suite, full of apologies. 'It's just a misunderstanding,' they kept saying. Me and Albert went through them for a short cut.

But our annoyance was nothing in comparison to the anger we felt at the treatment by our party leader. I had got on very well with Albert during the negotiations. We felt we were making real progress in getting a good deal for Fianna Fáil. That's why we were so aggrieved when it became obvious that Haughey had gone behind our backs in dealing directly with the PD leader, Des O'Malley. Talking to O'Malley was Haughey's prerogative as leader. Failing to tell us was not. Albert and I only learnt that Haughey was prepared to concede two cabinet places to the PDs when we heard it on the radio. Both of us were as annoyed as hell. 'What are we wasting our time for here then?' I asked him. We had been negotiating the real detail of a coalition, and all the time Haughey had been going behind our backs. We were out of the loop. All that would have been required was for Haughey to send a message saying, 'Lads, I'm going to talk to Dessie about it.' Instead he made us look like complete eejits.

That evening, 11 July, we confronted Haughey. I told him that I thought he was wrong to give the PDs – a party of just six TDs – two seats at the cabinet table. 'The party won't buy it,' I warned him. 'They'll do as they're feckin told,' he fired back. When I left with Albert afterwards, we were even angrier than when we went in. As we were doorstepped on the way out by Kathleen O'Meara of RTÉ, we showed our defiance. 'There was a clear message from the parliamentary party and the National Executive that the mandate they've given the Taoiseach is to talk about one seat at the cabinet table,' I told her. 'Nobody likes the idea of an arrangement, a pact [but] we can try to sell it to the organisation on the basis of one seat at the cabinet table. That's what our Taoiseach is, I'm sure, conveying at the meeting of the leaders.' Albert then repeated the mantra. 'I don't know anybody in Fianna Fáil who likes going into partnership,' he said, but the party would be 'reluctantly prepared to tolerate what they believe is a fair and reasonable distribution of cabinet seats on a proportionality basis, which is one seat in cabinet'.

The interview was broadcast the next day on *Morning Ireland* in the prime ten past eight spot. Predictably, Haughey was livid. Immediately afterwards I got called in to see him. It was one of the worst rows we ever had. We argued it out and I stood my ground. The issue was very simple. I was not disputing his right to give away two cabinet seats. He was the leader, so he had to negotiate the best deal he could with O'Malley. What I would not accept was the suggestion to the parliamentary party that Albert and I had tied his hands. The calmer I remained, the angrier he got. He had wanted us to be the fall guys, but by the end of the meeting he knew that I wasn't standing for it.

Later that day, Haughey and O'Malley shook hands on a deal to go into government together. The Progressive Democrats got their two seats at cabinet – O'Malley at Industry and Commerce, and Molloy at Energy – along with a junior ministry for Mary Harney.

That set an unfortunate precedent. From that day to this, even the smallest party feels entitled to two places at the cabinet table when entering a coalition, although I drew the line with the PDs in 2007 with their two TDs. There is no doubt that O'Malley outmanoeuvred Haughey, calling it right that Haughey would give him the two ministries to do the deal. Albert and I were very annoyed. I would get over it. Albert on the other hand never really did.

After such a difficult and tense period, I was glad to get back to the Department of Labour. By now I had the advantage that I was there long enough to know how to get things done. That gave me the confidence to tackle a major piece of legislation: the 1990 Industrial Relations Act. A new Act had been in preparation since Paddy Hillery was minister in the 1960s, but it was never brought to completion. Before the election I had convinced Haughey that new legislation was essential if we were going to build on social partnership. There had been revisions in 1946, 1969 and 1976, but to all intents and purposes Irish industrial relations were still working within a framework that had been set out by the British in the Trades Disputes Act of 1906. That might have been all right for the workers lighting the gas lamps in earlier times. Now we needed a rethink. The bill that I introduced in 1989 provided a mechanism for the improved conduct of industrial relations and for the resolution of strikes. The aim was to maintain a stable and orderly industrial relations climate. It came after an exhaustive consultation process with the Employers and ICTU.

The main provisions were to reform trade union dispute law, introduce pre-strike ballots, restrict the use of court injunctions in disputes and facilitate the further rationalisation of the trade union movement. A new Labour Relations Commission would ensure that potential disputes could be examined in a cool and coherent fashion, with the commission establishing a code of practice and offering a conciliation service. Getting that legislation through the Oireachtas was rewarding but exhausting. I had no minister of state, so I was left to steer the bill through every stage myself. Pat Rabbitte, Ruairi Quinn and Jim Mitchell took the lead on the opposition side. They took a constructive attitude to the process and at the end I was genuinely able to thank them for their cooperation. We had all spent a lot of time on the floor of the House going through the complicated detail. The result was a new landscape for industrial relations essential in building the prosperity that would follow.

There were some good moments that summer of 1990. The Industrial Relations Act passed in July, which left me tired but thrilled. Ireland had done brilliantly in the World Cup. After all the drama of the penalty shoot-out against Romania, we played Italy in the quarter finals. Ireland handed over the EU presidency to the Italians in Rome just before the match and then we all headed to the Olympic Stadium. Ireland lost 1–0 to a goal by Toto Schillaci, but the overwhelming feeling was pride in the performance of Jack Charlton's team. At the end of the game, I watched from the stands as Charlie took to the field to acknowledge the Irish supporters who had been great ambassadors for our country throughout that World Cup. Italia 90 was a great occasion. So was the GAA that year. Cork did something tremendous by winning the All-Ireland at both football and hurling. Those were bitter-sweet weeks for us as a family. Dad was quite sick by this stage and I think we all knew he was nearing the end. The GAA kept him alive. We watched a lot of those matches together on the television that summer, and you could see the boost it gave him. When the Cork footballers beat Meath in September to complete the double, the look on his face is something I'll always remember. If anyone could pick their time to go, I think that would have been his.

The day after Cork's victory, the Fianna Fáil parliamentary party met to decide on its candidate for the upcoming presidential election. I proposed Brian Lenihan, who won easily against John Wilson. My most important contribution had been to talk Albert Reynolds, the Minister for Finance, out of backing Wilson. Immediately after getting the nomination, Brian asked me to be his director of elections. I was delighted, as this was my first national campaign and I admired Brian hugely. I had got to know him well during 'Operation Dublin' and on the National Executive. It was always fun to be in his company. I remember on an official visit to New York in 1983 being told that the limousine to take us to our meeting was waiting outside the hotel. We jumped in and Brian immediately poured us two drinks. The problem was we were in the wrong car. 'We'll finish our drinks anyway,' Brian said before we got into a smaller car.

The Labour Party candidate, Mary Robinson, had already declared that the presidency should not be a retirement job, so it was clear which direction they were going in. Lenihan was an influential politician in the government. He carried more weight with Haughey than anyone else. He was also brilliant at pouring oil on troubled political waters. He was a really decent man, and one I had always admired. What did cause concern was his health. He had undergone a liver transplant in the Mayo Clinic, Minnesota. At one stage it had looked as though that might fail, but by September he was able to produce a doctor's report, read out to a meeting of the parliamentary party, that said he was completely fit to campaign and take up office. When I saw the full report, I realised that actually he would only be able to undertake less intensive campaigning. We had to factor in his medication, diet and need to rest each day. I thought we could overcome those with a clever campaign.

My plan was to use the four European constituencies as the basis for campaigning, with keynote speeches at big events. I was confident that Brian's cheerful personality would play well in the intimate surroundings of the television studio, but I also wanted him to give major speeches to show that as president he would speak for all the people of Ireland. Because these events would be limited, he could keep his strength up, with plenty of time for recuperation. If each night we could see pictures on the news of Brian in full health delivering measured and dignified words, I believed this would attract floating voters. We already had a lock on the Fianna Fáil faithful. What we needed to offer was reassurance to traditional values voters outside the party who were worried by Mary Robinson's positions on some social issues. That would help us sweep up transfers from Austin Currie, the Fine Gael candidate.

Brian wasn't having any of it. 'No, Bertie,' he told me decisively, 'I want to tour the country just like the old days. I need to show them that I can still do it.' I tried to warn him that this would not make the most of the media, who needed set-piece occasions that they could fit into a two-minute package for the news. And it would be exhausting. I discussed it with Ann, his wife, who I knew was worried about the impact on his health, but there was no moving Brian. So off we went, touring the country by bus. Our campaign theme tune was Tina Turner's 'Simply the Best', and it's no disrespect to Tina to say that I listened to that song so many times, I'll be happy if I never hear it again in my life. Everywhere we went, the numbers was terrific. We would go to places like the Temperance Hall in Ballinasloe, where huge crowds of well-wishers would turn out. There was an incredible torchlight procession in Kerry led by Jackie Healy-Rae. This was real grass-roots stuff and it was fantastic. I was still worried that we were preaching to the converted, but maybe that didn't matter. There was so much affection for Brian, it was difficult to see how he could lose. The polls and the feeling on the ground all seemed to point in the same direction – a Lenihan victory.

Then Brian went on *Questions and Answers* on Monday 22 October and got asked 'that question' by a member of the studio audience. That exchange altered the course of the election.

– I want to ask Mr Lenihan directly about the events of 27 January 1982. He's commented on it, but I want a straight answer. Did he make a phone call, or phone calls, to Áras an Uachtaráin in that period, when the Taoiseach Garret FitzGerald was seeking a dissolution of the Dáil?
– No. I didn't at all. That never happened. I want to assure you that it never happened.

I was in the hospitality room watching, having gone along to support the candidate. To be honest I was more bemused than worried. The question in the audience had been a plant from a former chair of Young Fine Gael, but Brian dealt firmly with it, suggesting he wasn't bothered. The media, notably the *Irish Press*, had been sniffing around the issue of what happened that night in 1982, but there was no reason to think it was going anywhere. It was a niggle, nothing more. There were rumours, but then there always were.

Late the next day, Tuesday 23 October, I got a call from Denis Coghlan of the *Irish Times*. 'We've got evidence that Brian Lenihan phoned the President that night,' he told me. 'Got a comment?' I liked Denis, had been with him that night of the Stardust tragedy and knew that he was straight. 'What evidence?' I asked him, playing for time. 'You know I can't tell you that,' he replied, 'but it's there.' I told him I would get back to him.

I phoned P. J. Mara. 'There's a tape with a UCD student,' he told me. 'Ask Brian what's on it.' When I spoke to Lenihan on Wednesday morning, he was adamant that there was no student, no interview and nothing that would implicate him in the events of that night. That was a relief, but I still couldn't understand where Coghlan, a good journalist, was coming from. Quietly I got on to Lenihan's private secretary, Brian Spain. 'Would you ever find out if the Tánaiste met this student?' I asked him. I knew Lenihan was always generous with his time to anybody who wanted to talk to him. Soon afterwards he got back to me to confirm there had been a meeting with an MA student called Jim Duffy. When I spoke to Lenihan about it again at lunchtime, he acknowledged that the meeting must have taken place, but he still couldn't remember the student. A few minutes later I was in the Dáil studio being interviewed for the *News at One*. The best I could do was kick for touch. Afterwards, I bumped into Garret FitzGerald. I liked Garret and he had always been helpful to me. This occasion was no different. 'Be careful, Bertie,' he said. He meant it kindly I think, trying to warn me that there was trouble ahead. But when I pressed him about the tape, he just shook his head and wandered off.

More than ever I needed to know what was on that tape, and I pushed Brian hard about what he may or may not have said. 'If you said something, let's get it out there now before they play that tape,' I urged him. He was absolutely certain he would not have implicated himself in any way, but he still could not remember anything about the interview. Slowly I was beginning to realise that this was the problem. Even when prompted, Brian remembered nothing about the encounter. He never would. It was a complete blank. In the end, I asked Brian Spain for a copy of the letter from the MA student confirming the meeting.

The next day, Thursday 25 October, Duffy held a press conference in the Westbury Hotel to play the tape. When I heard it, I almost died. 'You made a phone call?' Duffy was heard asking Lenihan. 'Oh yeah, I did,' Lenihan replied. '. . . I got through to him. I remember talking to him . . .'

It was a disaster. We had walked right into it. Brian got hold of Mara on the phone. 'I want to do an interview now,' he apparently told him. 'All right,' Mara said, 'but you've only got one shot at this. Remember, you're talking to the Irish people, so look them straight in the eye and just tell them what happened.' Brian would take that advice literally.

I met Brian at Montrose. After all the frantic chasing around, with the candidate besieged by reporters, the television centre was bedlam. Brian was nervous and upset. I tried to reassure him, but he was visibly shaken when they came to take him into the studio. The interview was a horror show. Seán Duignan was one of the best in the business. He had got Brian on the ropes and he wouldn't stop hitting. Brian's defence that 'on mature reflection in the last few days, I did not ring President Hillery' sounded weak. The indication that he would be phoning Hillery to ask if he remembered anything seemed disrespectful of the office. And when he turned away from

Duignan to look directly into the camera to address the people of Ireland, he looked pathetic. It was one of the saddest things I've ever witnessed in politics – a fine man's reputation so badly damaged over the course of a short interview. By the end, Duignan was more or less saying that Lenihan was not competent to be president. After that performance, it was hard to disagree. He looked all wrong on that programme; everything looked wrong. I bet every politician in the land made a note to themselves never, ever to turn round and talk right into the camera. The ridiculous point about it is that Brian had always been a real pro on the television. But he was rattled on the day. He just couldn't remember. Perhaps he shouldn't have done the interview at all, but there were fifty journalists outside his door and Charlie Bird up at the Park Gates trying to get a comment from the President. Hiding away wasn't an option, and anyway that was never Brian's style.

The problem for Brian was that he wasn't sure in his own mind. He was talking about two events – the phone calls and the Duffy interview – neither of which he recalled. Interviews with Duignan were hard enough at the best of times. Brian was defending what he thought was the correct position but still he could not be sure. In fact, he had no idea. Around this time I got a phone call from a medical friend in the Mater. 'Bertie, would you not just look at the dates for that student's interview,' he implored me. 'Look at the dates.' That made sense. Brian had been very sick in the Mater just beforehand when it looked like his transplanted liver was rejecting. He must have been completely out of it, heavily drugged up. But that was as much a problem as it was a solution. How the hell do you go out and say, 'Sorry, my candidate was so out of it on his medication that he can't remember a thing.'

Brian was really upset, almost tearful, after the *Six-One* interview. The next morning I could see that his family were distressed. They were shell-shocked. To make a bad situation worse, the opposition had put down a motion of no confidence in the government. The

Progressive Democrats, who saw this as the kind of 'GUBU' issue that had caused many of them to leave Fianna Fáil in the first place, were also jumping up and down, threatening to pull the plug on the government unless Haughey sacked Lenihan. The party grass roots were angry and confused. Everything was a mess. Everyone was looking for cover. At times I felt completely alone. Sleep did not come easily and some mornings I picked up the early editions of the newpapers, dreading what might come next.

Early the next week, Charlie called an informal meeting at Kinsealy involving cabinet ministers who were around, namely myself, Ray Burke, Gerry Collins, Michael Woods, Rory O'Hanlon and Séamus Brennan. The atmosphere was very solemn as we discussed whether there were any options other than Brian resigning from the government. The plausible alternatives – either a general election or a dismissal from cabinet – were too horrible to think about. In the end it was agreed that I would bring Brian to Kinsealy to talk it out with Charlie. When I started to tell Brian why Charlie wanted to meet, he cut me off with a small wave of the hand, saying quietly, 'OK, we'll go . . .'

We broke from our canvass schedule to go to Kinsealy by helicopter early on Tuesday morning. Brian brought some of his family with him, so there were a few awkward niceties together before Charlie took Brian into his office to talk. He asked me to join them. I was really uncomfortable. I would rather have been anywhere else than in that room. These two men had been friends and allies for decades. They knew each other's strengths and weaknesses to a fault. Even now the banter between them was easy. But nothing could disguise the tension. The strain was apparent on both of them. And no wonder. Charlie needed Brian to resign from the government in order to avoid a general election. It was obvious that Brian thought he had done nothing wrong and didn't want to go. Even if he had made those phone calls to the President – a fact he was unclear about – the tapes suggested he had done so at Haughey's insistence. Brian certainly wasn't going to take the fall for Charlie in the middle of the campaign. None of this was actually said. Charlie did not ask Brian to resign. He only wanted him to 'reflect on the situation'. Brian promised to do that. Stalemate. I hardly said a word throughout the entire meeting. Apparently there was another meeting later that day in Government Buildings when Charlie took the gloves off and presented Brian with a draft resignation statement.

With pressure mounting, Brian headed off, with me to follow, for his next campaign rally in his boyhood town of Athlone. I got reports that at stops along the way he was being greeted by crowds of emotional and excited well-wishers. That must have buoyed his spirits, but it also hardened his resolve not to resign. When I got down to Athlone, I was greeted by Mary O'Rourke, Brian's sister. Mary was Minister for Education at the time, and we got on at cabinet, but she was never one to pull her punches. Contrary to public appearances, she would not have been seen inside Leinster House as being particularly close to Brian, and certainly was not part of his political loop. Despite this it was clear that Mary, on her own territory, was now determined to show Brian that she was his No. 1 supporter. She confronted me, as she later briefed any journalist who would listen, asking me whether I was there as friend or foe – if the latter, then I wasn't welcome. It was done in such a theatrical, public way that I almost laughed. For all the hostility it was just grandstanding. She was in her own back yard and wanted to be seen playing tough. Brian was friendly enough, though, and just rolled his eyes. The last thing any of us needed was Mary going around being aggressive. Brian had to clear his mind and not have people agitating him. We were getting hammered. If ever there was a time for cool heads rather than hot ones to prevail then this was it.

I wasn't the only one to see Mary in full flight. Pádraig Flynn also got an earbashing for his troubles. The day after the meeting in Athlone, Mary and her supporters were needling people to 'stand up for Brian' in the lead-up to a meeting of the parliamentary party.

That meeting was to take place on the morning of a vote of no confidence, which the government was going to lose if the PDs walked. The meeting left it in the Taoiseach's hands, and at 6 p.m. Charlie phoned Brian with the bad news. No one felt good about it, least of all Charlie, who told me afterwards that it was the worst day in his political career. Their relationship went back thirty years. In later years I felt that Haughey often wondered whether he should have just stood by Lenihan and taken the consequences. It was no coincidence that Charlie in the instructions for his own funeral in 2006 asked that Brian Lenihan Jnr should be invited to do the reading. This was a gesture of reconciliation.

The night Haughey announced Brian's dismissal to the House was very emotional. Mary O'Rourke was still agitated, shooing people away who wanted to offer their commiserations. Her face was like thunder as she went through the Tá lobby to vote for the government on the confidence motion. Brian on the other hand was calm and dignified. He was deeply hurt by what had happened, but he had been in politics long enough to know that there's nothing to be gained by throwing a wobbly. I think he was glad it was settled. For the first time in days, he seemed focused on the election. Immediately afterwards, he gave an accomplished press conference in Kildare House. When it was over, he pulled me to one side and said, 'You can't win every day, but make sure we win the big one.' Even in adversity, he was ever the statesman.

It can't have been easy, but Brian could see that being sacked might actually help the campaign. No one likes to see anyone being kicked when they're down. Brian was a popular guy not just with the Fianna Fáil grass roots, but with voters generally. A lot of people thought Mary Robinson was a bit high and mighty. While Brian might not have appealed to Dublin 4 intellectual types, ordinary people throughout the country liked him and a lot of them thought he had been badly treated. I saw that for myself in O'Connell Street the day after he left the government. He got a huge reception, with hundreds of people pushing towards him to sympathise and wish him well in the election. Time and again over the next few days I would hear people saying how it was disgusting that a sick man had been hounded. While all the controversy over the tape was going on, Robinson's campaign built up a real momentum. But I knew they were terrified about a sympathy vote for Brian. Now I really believed we could turn goodwill towards Brian into votes. And there was a good chance we might win. What we really needed was a straight run, no more dramas. What we absolutely didn't need was Pádraig Flynn putting his foot in his mouth.

The Saturday after Lenihan had been sacked, with the election less than a week away, we were out campaigning together in the West. We were getting a fantastic reaction from people who were flocking to see Brian and to wish him luck. He was like a new man. A load had been lifted and the goodwill of the people was raising his spirits. The previous night he had put in a fantastic performance on the *Late Late* demonstrating what a great television performer he really could be. We did a rally in Ballina, County Mayo, which was attended by thousands. Later that day I was grabbed by the coat in Shop Street in Galway. When I turned round I was given an earful by a woman who was absolutely furious. At first I thought she must be supporting another candidate. But no, she told me that she was Fianna Fáil through and through, and that her father had supported de Valera. 'Would you ever do something with that bastard Pádraig Flynn?' she hissed at me. 'Why's he even allowed go on the radio?' I was completely bemused. 'Sure, Pee's a nice fella,' I hedged. 'What's the problem?' Then she told me. Apparently he had got into some spat with Michael McDowell on the *Saturday View* programme, saying terrible things about Mary Robinson and her family.

When I eventually got hold of the recording, I couldn't believe my ears. Flynn had accused Robinson of 'having a new-found interest in the family, being a mother and all that kind of thing, but none of us, you know, none of us who knew Mary Robinson very well in previous incarnations, ever heard her claiming to be a great wife and mother'. As soon as I heard those words, I knew the election was over. Later, Robinson was gracious about the whole thing, which contrasted with the stupidity of the original remarks. All told it was a disaster. I was left touring the radio stations and turning up on *Questions and Answers* to try and explain that Flynn had not meant it the way his comments came out. I did my best, but it was defending the indefensible. The campaign had been back on track. Even Fergus Finlay, who was working on the Robinson campaign, admitted later on that 'the tide of public opinion' had swung Brian's way. And after everything, we still got Brian up to 44 per cent of first preferences, well clear of Robinson's 39 per cent and Currie's 17 per cent. And only for Flynn, we would have got him a few more. I don't know if we would have won the election, but there is no doubt in my mind that Flynn's outburst killed us.

I felt very sorry for Brian. In a short space of time he had lost his job as Tánaiste and Minister for Defence, and then a presidential election. He couldn't work out what had happened or why everything had gone so disastrously wrong. Afterwards he thanked me. I think he always knew I had done my best for him. Later on, he encouraged me to run for leader, so I know there were no hard feelings. I was pleased that so many people bothered to get in touch with me over those few days. Whatever the circumstances, no one likes losing an election, and, if you're looking for a scapegoat, the first target is often the director of elections. But everyone was saying to me that they were amazed it hadn't been worse. Our numbers had been down in the 20s at one stage. To get that up to 44 per cent had meant squeezing every vote. People understood that we had made a decent fist of a terrible situation.

In the end I came to the conclusion that between the tapes and the attacks on Robinson, too many people had been alienated. Afterwards, I went out on behalf of the campaign to say that whatever the ups and downs of the election, President Robinson must have our full loyalty and support. And as it turned out she served our country with great distinction. A few years later I would have the opportunity to make good on my promise to give her my full support. In 1993 she took a lot of stick for her decision to shake hands with Gerry Adams during a visit to West Belfast. The media were all over the story. The British government were unhappy. Even Dick Spring, the Labour Party leader and Tánaiste, had a crack at her. I had been in Cork that day, but I made a special trip back to Dublin to go out to the airport to meet her on her return. I knew the press were going to give her a hard time and I wanted to make sure somebody defended her. It was hostile stuff, but I made it clear that I totally supported what she had done. There were some people in the government, especially Spring, who were miffed that I had supported her so publicly. They knew I was making a point. But Mary Robinson had acted courageously and she had been right. The handshake was a small but important step in winning the trust of the Nationalist community in the North.

That was in the future. The night after the election in 1990 I gave a speech to party members, repeating my line about loyalty and support. I got huge applause for saying that. It seemed obvious to me that a lot of the Fianna Fáil audience that night had in fact voted for Mary Robinson.

There was a wind of change blowing through the country. Ireland was changing, and changing fast.

Dad's passing hit me hard, and my personal circumstances made things even worse. By this stage I was often putting my head down in the new Fianna Fáil constituency office on the Drumcondra Road, opposite Fagan's pub. For all the attention that St Luke's has had, you would think we had taken over a palace rather than a very ordinary red-brick two-up two-down. It had been a doctor's surgery, and it was ideal for constituency clinics. Downstairs there were a couple of rooms for offices and a reception area. Upstairs there was a sitting room and a small bedroom. A single-storey extension went up at the back to give a bit of space for office equipment. It was a very modest premises and a bit run-down when we took it over, but Des Richardson had done a brilliant job, as he did so many times for me, turning it into a real working environment where we could help constituents with their problems.

I really just fell into living in St Luke's. After the split with Miriam, she had the house in Malahide for bringing up the girls. I wasn't getting my own house, so I spent a lot of time back in Church Avenue. I also stayed with friends, especially Joe Burke, and when St Luke's opened at Easter in 1990, I sometimes stayed there for the odd night. As time went on it sort of became a permanent arrangement. I was in there all the time anyway, so why not get my head down for a few hours as well? Most of the time I was too busy even to notice. That Christmas of 1990, though, was not the best. I remember just as I was going over to Eileen's for my dinner on St Stephen's Day picking up the phone and talking to a constituent about some problem they were having with a visa. I was happy to help, but even I could see that I was in a strange situation. Years later I had a wry smile to myself when Tony Blair was on to me about living 'above the shop' in Downing Street. Civil servants always coming in with problems, everyone knowing where to get hold of you, the line between your public and private life almost non-existent. I think that was why Tony liked Chequers so much, because at least he could get away to the country for a bit of peace and quiet. 'Tell me about it!'

I thought to myself, remembering those days. Difficult though it was subsequently, I would have been amazed if you had told me then that where I was living would become a political football as well as a personal issue for me.

If 1990 had not been the best of years, 1991 didn't start much better. There was still a bad feeling in the party about the way Brian Lenihan had been treated. People were very upset about it. More to the point they were worried about their own seats. The PDs had overplayed their hand during the presidential election and their threats had shown everyone how precarious the government really was. A general election could happen at any time. After the presidential campaign, the feeling was that Fianna Fáil was not that well got with people. That left everyone with the sense that the government was shaky. Over the Christmas period there were all kinds of rumours circulating about another heave against Haughey in the new year.

Charlie did not help himself by adding to the instability in the government. He delayed reshuffling the cabinet, which had a vacancy after Brian had gone. I had made it clear that I wanted to move from Labour. I had been in the department longer than any of my predecessors. I had done everything I could and was ready to move on. The next social partnership agreement – the Programme for Economic and Social Progress (PESP) – was being wrapped up that January, so the timing could hardly have been better for me to go. I just needed another challenge. There was a lot in the newspapers about me going to Environment, but it just dragged on and on. In the end I just wanted to know one way or the other.

Eventually I phoned P. J. Mara. 'Will I be going to Environment or not?' I asked. 'Because the papers are making us all look like eejits.' I told him that if my moving was a problem, I would be prepared to stay on in Labour. I just wanted an end to the speculation. I certainly would have preferred to move, but I was sick of reading about myself day after day. A lot of the gossip must have come from friends of the current minister, Pádraig Flynn, because the message was that he was not for going. The papers added another line that this was a battle between two cabinet rivals. Mara was vague when I talked to him. I don't think he knew what was going on either, which didn't happen often. But I knew that he would get the message to Charlie that I was letting everyone off the hook. Sure enough, the reshuffle was announced a couple of days later. Flynn stayed where he was. So did I. 'You're stuck with me till the election now,' I told Freda Nolan, my excellent private secretary, when I got back to Labour.

Haughey's opponents were betting that my disappointment would turn me against him. My own belief was that he wouldn't be hanging around long and that he should be allowed to go in his own time. Reynolds was waiting in the wings. He had already said that he would be a candidate for the leadership when a vacancy occurred. I felt Albert needed to slow down, but around him was a group of senior people who wanted to hurry the process along. They worked hard to recruit me onto their side throughout 1991. I would be invited to meetings in private homes, including Albert's in Ballsbridge, to discuss the state of the party. The full cast list for these would change, but usually the same faces would keep cropping up, including Máire Geoghegan-Quinn, Michael Smith, Noel Treacy and Flynn. They knew better than to try to involve me in a plot to oust Haughey. I liked Albert, had worked well with him during the negotiations with the PDs and as Minister for Finance, and had even been racing with him in Galway. But I told them I was never going to be part of a coup. I hadn't plotted against Lynch in the 1970s. I had supported Haughey through three heaves in the 1980s. I wasn't going to change my tune in the 1990s. 'No, no, of course not, Bertie,' they would say. 'We're just looking to the future, planning for the transition.' Obviously I took that with a massive pinch of salt. 'Just wait, Albert,' I told him, 'and it will happen.' I think he accepted that. Some of his supporters, however, were more edgy. For the first time, my name was in the press as a possible future leader of the party. Increasingly, I think

Albert's people came to recognise that I might be a potential rival as much as a friend. As I was the younger man, time was clearly on my side. He was obviously thinking he might miss the boat. That led him into making mistakes that would cost him in the long run.

Over the course of the summer, we got hit by a series of controversies in the press, involving Michael Smurfit and the Telecom Éireann site in Ballsbridge, Larry Goodman and the Irish beef industry, the sale of the Carysfort campus in Blackrock, and the privatisation of the Sugar Company. Taken together these caused a great deal of friction in the government, not least because they fed the idea that the Progressive Democrats had about the links between Fianna Fáil and business interests. Haughey had set up the Beef Tribunal to keep the PDs happy before a review of the Programme for Government.

This was all bad news for us. The review had looked like a fairly straightforward process. The same crew of Cox, Molloy, Reynolds and myself was reassembled to hammer the thing out. Papers were circulated before the summer recess. No one thought the result would be anything other than positive. Then the controversies started to get traction over the holiday, which rattled the PDs. By the time we entered talks in October they were wound up really tight. Molloy and Cox seemed to be getting on each other's nerves. I got the sense that O'Malley was sending them contradictory instructions. That might sound good when you're sitting on the opposite side of the table, but the last thing you need is not knowing where you stand or who in the other delegation has authority. These deals are always about detail and if you can't pin down specifics, you're really in trouble. The funny thing was that we agreed on most things, but what really had to be worked out was policy on taxation. The PDs wanted to reform the tax system by abolishing the various tax shelters, tax allowances and tax breaks. The savings from that would be used to reduce the standard and top rates of income tax. I supported that because it was transparent and fairer. Everyone got the benefit of the lower taxes.

In effect, that's what we ended up doing, but it was a devil of a them all.' I just looked at the journalists – Sam Smyth, Stephen Collins and Gerry Barry. Each of them was scribbling away, getting that very quotable quote down in their notebooks. 'Jesus, that's all I need,' I said after Haughey left. I think I asked if there was any chance they might forget that one. They just laughed. It's dogged me ever since. The problem, of course, was that it referred to a very specific time. Haughey was thrilled that the Programme for Government had been agreed. The negotiations had almost gone down a few times. Talks were tense. We were all trying to use a bit of guile and brink-manship to get the thing sorted. So it was all about context, but of course it then gets taken out of context and repeated so many times that the original meaning is lost. Maybe Haughey meant to be helpful, or perhaps he was just winding us up.

At the end of the summer Haughey had brought me up to Kinsealy for a talk. That was when I got my first hint that he was thinking about going. As I listened to him talking, all the plans were about what would happen between then and the following Easter. There might be jokes along the way about emulating some of the Chinese leaders who hung on to power into their eighties. But I am convinced Charlie had made his mind up to get out. The problem was that Albert wouldn't wait. All through the autumn his supporters kept pushing him to make a move against Haughey. I urged patience. 'Just wait,' I told him, 'Charlie's going soon.' He wanted specifics.

'When?'

'Early next year.'

'He told you that?'

'No, but that's when he'll go. He's near the end now.'

That wasn't enough for Albert. Soon enough, the Kildare TD Seán Power put down a motion of no confidence in the leader. Reynolds announced that he would be supporting it. Haughey asked him to resign. When Reynolds refused, Haughey fired him. The party met on Saturday 9 November to vote on the motion. The motion was defeated. The rebels only managed to drum up twenty-two TDs. In the past, I had helped rally around the leader, but the principal role in organising had been taken by more senior guys like Brian Lenihan. This time I was the senior guy. Haughey came to me, told me again that he would be going soon, but that he would not be pushed out by Reynolds. I think a lot of TDs had expected Charlie to go without a fight. They misjudged him. I supported and helped him, and believed him when he said it would not be long before he went.

Much more importantly, I believed that heaves were bad for the party. They always left too much mess to clear up. There had been all the hassle with Lynch. Then the battles between Haughey and Colley. After that it was Haughey and O'Malley. Now it was Reynolds. None of this did the party any good. Ordinary members in the party hated it. Voters were bemused by it. Only the media were happy, because a party at war makes good copy. Haughey had said after the heave in 1983 that he wouldn't be around forever. But he was only three years leader at that stage. Now after more than a decade in the job, nobody thought he would be going on and on. So there was no need for this. That last heave was completely unnecessary. It didn't make him go any quicker. All it did was make Albert's life harder when he actually did become leader not long afterwards.

In the reshuffle that had come when Reynolds and Flynn left the government, Haughey had made me Minister for Finance. That was a great honour, because really it's the second most important job in government after the Taoiseach. That said, I had been thrown in at the worst possible time. Ideally you would want to go in around March, just on the other side of the Budget, so that you would have time to get your feet under the table. Instead, I had two months to prepare the Budget, and at a time when the economy was going through a rough patch. The European Exchange Rate Mechanism (ERM) was beginning to come under pressure, the global economy was in recession, and we had problems of our own – so there was plenty to be done. I went to see Albert to talk to him about it, and in fairness he could not have been more helpful. He made the changeover very smooth, talking me through plans for the Budget. I repeated that I thought Haughey would be going soon.

That Christmas, Charlie confirmed it to me. 'I'm going next year,' he said, 'and you need to be ready.' That was the first time he had said that he thought I should have a crack at the leadership. I told him that I thought Reynolds would get it and that he had the numbers. Charlie wasn't so sure. 'Albert's not a vote winner,' he said, and he reminded me about a recent MRBI poll that said I would be the popular choice for leader. I told him I thought I should get more experience in Finance and that it would be Reynolds.

In the end it was a face from the past that brought the Haughey era to a close. I remember hearing a rumour sometime around the middle of January that Seán Doherty was planning to go on television to make allegations about his time as Minister of Justice under Haughey. Sure enough, he turned up late one evening on *Nighthawks* making some vague comments that 'people knew what I was doing' when he had the phones of two journalists tapped in 1982. A week later Doherty rolled up again with a more straightforward claim that Haughey knew about the tappings and that he had at no point expressed any reservations about them. It was nearly ten years since I had spent all that time looking into this when I was on the Tunney Inquiry, and now here was Doherty saying that Haughey had lied about it in 1982 when he was Taoiseach, and that he was lying to everyone again now. Doherty also seemed to be admitting that he had been economical with the truth himself in 1982. We will never know whether Doherty was telling the truth on this occasion or in his initial account. What's certain is that only one of his versions can be correct. Years afterwards, I would make an official apology as Taoiseach to Bruce Arnold and Geraldine Kennedy, the journalists who had been bugged. Some people were annoyed at me for that, including Doherty, but I believed strongly it was important to demonstrate that there are some things the state cannot and should not do, and that this was one of them.

I knew the game was up for Charlie this time. I had expected he would go around St Patrick's Day or possibly Easter. Initially, he thought the Doherty revelations were part of a plot by Reynolds to oust him. In fact, the real threat came from the Progressive Democrats, who immediately began pressing him to consider his position. Eventually Bobby Molloy came to see me. It was the usual story. 'Listen, this is a problem for us,' he said. 'It will put us in a difficult position if it goes to a confidence motion.' I went out to Kinsealy afterwards to see Haughey. I told him about the rumblings in the PDs. He just shook his head. They weren't going to make any difference to him. I knew immediately that he had made up his mind. All the fight had gone out of him. This was one battle too many. Normally he would have talked about arranging briefings with the press to get his message out there, asking whose spine needed stiffening, who we could rely on. This time he didn't ask any of those things. There would be no more arguing. He had already made the decision last Christmas that he would go. It was only a question of what day or on what issue. This seemed as good a time as any. 'I've had my nine lives,' he said as I was leaving.

An era was drawing to a close. Haughey would announce on 30 January his intention to resign as Taoiseach. I was proud to have served with him and to call him my friend. I could remember, as a teenager, canvassing for Charlie at election time. That's what we called him, that's what everyone called him, because we felt he was one of us – and he was larger than life. Charlie had brought to the office of Taoiseach an array of talents perhaps unmatched in the modern era. He was a consummate politician. He had an incisive mind and superb parliamentary skills. Even his enemies admitted that he had natural charisma and a driving spirit. These had helped make him the dominant public figure of late twentieth-century Ireland. He may have been, to say the least, controversial, but in part that was because he was someone who did not ride the winds and the tides, but sought to change them.

I do have one personal regret about the circumstances of his going.

A boy from Drumcondra. In the garden
at Church Avenue

Young republican.
My father, Con Ahern, in the 1920s

My First Communion Day, with my sister Eileen.
I got an apple and an orange

Confirmation Day. Outside St Patrick's
National School, Drumcondra

The School athletic
team with our coach,
the great Brother Clarke

St. Aidan's Athletes 1964 – 1965

A. Hanna, M. Molloy, D. Foran,
M. Treacy, D. Foley,
B. Ahern, M. Gaffney, A. Clarke,
T. Kelly.
Br. T. Clarke – Coach

The Committee, All Hampton Sports and Social Club, 1971. Pat Byrne, Fintan Diggins, Michael Lenihan, Paddy Dalton, Noel Kennelly (Amateur Football League) and BA

With Miriam in the early 1970s

Mam and Dad with the
new Lord Mayor, 1986

Christmas 1986. Santa and the girls

The Minister for Labour, after settling the ESB strike in 1987

Outlining Fianna Fáil's policy on Social Partnership in 1986

Honouring The Dubliners in the Mansion House. With Ronnie Drew and Christy Moore

Budget Day 1992

With Charles J. Haughey
and Albert Reynolds, my
immediate predecessors
as Leader of Fianna Fáil.

On the threshold. With Mam in Church Avenue on the night I became Uachtarán Fhianna Fáil

'Eight steps down.'
Canal End, Croke Park on the last day before demolition to make way for a new stand. With my brother Maurice.

Sharing a joke with Charlie McCreevy and Brian Cowen at a European Council Meeting

With my coalition partner Mary Harney

On the day that he announced his resignation, Haughey held a meeting of Fianna Fáil ministers to inform us what was about to happen. I know he was hurt that none of us stayed around to show our support. I had a meeting to go to about the Budget, but I should have cancelled it to be with Charlie. I know how much it meant to me when the cabinet accompanied me to the press conference when I announced my resignation in 2008. I had been proud to stand next to Charlie all my political career and I wish that I had done more for him on such a difficult day.

I think the ultimate judgement of history will be positive on Charlie, but there's no doubt he also let himself down and the country as well. When the Moriarty Tribunal reported in December 2006 that Haughey had received or misapplied several millions in private donations between 1979 and 1996, the sums of money involved saddened me. To those of us who had worked with Haughey over the years, the details of the report came as a huge disappointment. Even now, as someone who thought of him as a friend as well as a colleague, I find it difficult to understand the complexity of the man and the other life he led.

I've been criticised for the way in which I signed blank cheques for Haughey, giving him access to the Fianna Fáil Leader's Account. From when I was government whip in 1982 and then opposition whip the following year, I was co-signatory on the chequebook. Using pre-signed cheques was not an uncommon feature of political life at the time. It was done for convenience and to save time. There was no reason for me to believe that any unusual use was being made of these cheques, and thank God the vast majority of them were put to proper use. But a small number were used otherwise. Later I would introduce reforms, first within the Fianna Fáil system and then through legislation, to make sure this practice could not be repeated. Haughey had a particular lifestyle – the flash house, the island, the horses – so that was an extravagant way of living. He obviously had to fund it somehow. We all thought he had made his money through clever investment. It made me angry when I found out the party was helping to finance it. At the Ard Fheis in 1997 I would condemn that kind of behaviour. It was a painful speech for me to make, and I really had to drag it out of myself, because the old reflexes for Haughey remained. But it needed to be said and I stand by it.

That was to come. The question that everyone was asking me in January 1992 was whether I would throw my hat into the ring for the leadership. When I left the meeting with Haughey at Kinsealy there was no doubt in my mind that he was going. 'Jesus, this is too early for me,' I thought. 'I need a few more years in Finance.' But the papers were already saying that I was the candidate to challenge Reynolds. Colleagues seemed to think that too. During the heave against Haughey the previous year, a number of TDs had told me that by voting for Charlie, they were voting for me. Now I was getting phone calls from TDs, including cabinet ministers, saying not only that they would support me, but they thought I could win. Time and again I kept hearing 'Albert's not the right man'. In fairness, I had always had friendly enough relations with him and had found him very competent when he was Minister for Finance. We had been on opposite sides during the heave against Haughey before Christmas, but we had managed not to fall out over it. I was never in his clique but we got on all right.

All this was going on as I was putting the final touches to my first Budget. That's always a busy time, and not one when you want to be thinking about leadership bids. I was happy in my own mind that I had only been Minister for Finance for a couple of months, wanted to get into the job properly, and needed to deliver a good first Budget the following week. But all the time guys were appearing at my door saying, 'Bertie, you have to run.' My response to all of them was that I was working on the Budget and didn't have time for anything else. 'Do your Budget on Wednesday, become leader the next week,' they would say. It was all good-natured. They obviously thought I was being 'cunning' to hide my leadership ambitions so well. The truth was I was just too busy to think about it. I was looking at the estimates with the civil servants and advisers. We were all working on the speech. Mess that up and no-one would have been wanting me as leader of the party anyway.

That didn't stop some people playing games. My own marital situation was well known by this stage. One of the rituals of being Minister for Finance was the public appearance on the plinth at Leinster House with your family. Miriam and I could have played happy families for the photographers, but neither of us wanted that. The best thing, we decided, was to tell the truth. So on 11 January 1992, before the leadership was even on the agenda, I went on TV with Pat Kenny to talk about my marriage difficulties. I had a brief chat with Pat beforehand to tell him what I was going to say. He's a straight guy, so he handled it fairly, didn't try to sensationalise it. It wasn't easy though. I am a very private person and don't feel comfortable talking about my family in public. So I decided to grit my teeth and say it as it was. The next morning, the Sunday papers had changed their front pages to cover it. We knew that journalists would be writing some pretty awful stuff, but we accepted it. And it was rough for us, but once it was done, we could get on with our lives. The girls were coming to the Budget with me. Miriam was going away for a few days. Difficult for all of us, but done with.

Then a mate of Albert's, Michael Smith, a TD from Tipperary North, went shooting his mouth off. I never had much to do with Smith, and he wasn't a friend of mine. I wouldn't agree with Pat Rabbitte that often, but he was good with one-liners, and got it about right when he described Smith as 'droning on like a Monsignor on a bad line from Medjugorje'. In an interview with the *Tipperary Star*, Smith observed that Reynolds was the envy of politicians in terms of his family life. That seemed an obvious go at me. It was a stupid remark and it irritated many people, including me. A lot of us thought, 'Hang on, is this the way these "country and western" people are going to behave?' A few months earlier, we had Flynn dissing Mary

Robinson during the presidential campaign, alienating even Fianna Fáil people. Now here was Smith trying to use my personal circumstances to damage me politically. There were also other comments attributed to Albert, but denied by him, about people wanting to know where the Taoiseach of the day lived. These kinds of remarks did not sit well with anyone.

People thought when I didn't declare that I was playing a game. I was even called a ditherer and a poor man's Machiavelli. But there was no plan and no campaign, just people coming to me asking me to run. It was only once the Budget debate was well under way that I began talking to my own people. I met the gang in St Luke's on Friday night. Chris Wall had done the figures based on chat coming out of Leinster House and was predicting a win for me in the parliamentary party of two or three votes. We kicked it about for a bit, but in the end they accepted my view that it was the wrong time for me. I also had a talk with Brian Lenihan. I thought he would be supporting his sister, Mary O'Rourke, but he believed she hadn't a snowball's chance in hell. Brian told me I had to run, that he would do everything he could to help a campaign, and that he thought I would win. He had been asking his people to sound out TDs and get the tallies. I was popular in the party. I had got most of the cabinet. There were a lot that didn't like Albert's group, especially after Smith's recent remarks. Brian was someone I was still very close to and whose advice I respected. But in the end I told him that I wanted to stay at Finance. 'For Christ's sake don't say that in public,' he warned me. There was still some negotiating to be done with Albert about my position. As I left, he told me to think again about running.

I had agreed to meet Albert that weekend. We didn't want the press watching us arrive, so each of us came up in a service lift from the basement of the hotel. He was already in the room when I arrived, sitting at a table doing some work. It was a very friendly, courteous meeting. I was pleased when he started out with an apology. 'I'm sorry for all that nonsense with Smith,' he told me. He said that it had been nothing to do with him, and that he had spoken to Smith about it. Smith had protested that he had meant nothing by it. 'He meant it all right,' I replied. Albert didn't disagree. He also made it clear that the comments attributed to him about my living arrangements had come from another source. I accepted that. We then had a conversation about the leadership. He indicated to me that he did not see himself in the job for the long haul. I don't think he meant as short as it would eventually turn out, but he made it clear that he only expected to do one full term as leader and then would be looking to hand over. I asked him outright if he wanted me to remain as Minister for Finance. He said he did. Once he had told me this, I was able to reveal my hand. I reminded him that I had said the previous year I would support him. We had disagreed on the heave against Haughey, but on everything else we had worked well together. To be honest, I said, my numbers were showing that it would be a very tight vote and the last thing I wanted was another divisive contest. A story did the rounds afterwards that we had compared lists, but neither of us would have been so naive. At the end of the day I was happy. If Albert planned being around for a term and a half, that would give me the opportunity to master Finance and plan for the day when, taking nothing for granted, I might put myself forward to lead the party. We shook hands on it. Albert seemed relieved to have my support. 'You know they're calling us the Dream Team!' he laughed.

In fact, it didn't take long before it turned into a nightmare.

8

SLASH AND BURN

Life was different in Albert Reynolds's government from the start. That first day was like the St Valentine's Day Massacre.

Albert came back to Government Buildings after he'd been presented with his seal of office at the Áras. He had about half an hour before he was due to lead his new government into the Dáil. When it came to style we would do things very differently, but even then I was taken aback by what came next. Within those thirty minutes he had sacked or demoted more than half the outgoing cabinet, including around two-thirds of the Fianna Fáil ministers: Gerry Collins, Michael O'Kennedy, Ray Burke, Mary O'Rourke, Rory O'Hanlon, Vincent Brady, Noel Davern, Brendan Daly. All gone, just like that. The junior ministers weren't safe either. A dozen were fired. By the time Albert had finished there, only three of them were left in place. Dermot Ahern was axed as Chief Whip because he 'didn't come on board for Albert early enough'. It was predictable that some of the replacement ministers would be from the 'country and western' set – Pádraig Flynn, Michael Smith, Máire Geoghegan-Quinn – and there were a few new faces at the cabinet table too with David Andrews, Charlie McCreevy and Brian Cowen. Noel Dempsey was made Chief

Whip. I was the only Fianna Fáil minister to stay in the same post. When we walked down the steps to the front bench, there was a real sense of shock in the Dáil. Personally, I felt it was disaster. I wanted to put the divisions of the Haughey years behind us. Instead, Albert had made them worse. I was especially sorry to see Gerry Collins go. I had been working closely with him right to the last on the Maastricht Treaty. Now suddenly he had gone. That was a real loss.

Not being part of Albert's circle did not bother me particularly, because I had never really been a clique man in Leinster House. Even though I would have been close to Charlie, I wasn't part of his group in the way that Ray Burke or even Pádraig Flynn had been at one time or another. When Charlie needed to see me, he might ask me out to Kinsealy, but I didn't go to Le Coq Hardi for long boozy lunches to shoot the breeze. That was never my scene. So I most definitely wasn't part of Albert's group, but that did not affect me too much as I hadn't been used to it with Charlie. Instead, I kept myself to myself in cabinet. Albert was extremely courteous, inviting me in regularly to discuss legislation and financial matters, although we rarely socialised. That was the nature of our relationship: formal, polite and professional.

It wasn't just the personnel that changed when Albert became Taoiseach. He brought a different style as well. Meetings with Charlie were quite clipped, but Albert loves conversation and the meetings were definitely longer. He didn't work as hard at keeping in with the PDs. Albert seemed not to like his coalition partners, but I think his difficulty in dealing with them may have been down to his business background. He was used to giving orders and people following them. He might just have got away with that in a single-party government, but a coalition, where you had to be more diplomatic, did not play to Albert's political strengths. For all their differences, Charlie Haughey and Dessie O'Malley had actually got on extremely well on a personal level in government. When we were abolishing the tax breaks in 1991, I remember the amused look between the two of them when we got to the exemption for stallions. I've never seen two men agree on something so quickly as when they decided we should keep that one. So they had their shared interests. And they knew how to work with each other. Charlie never sprung anything on O'Malley in a meeting. He had always smoothed everything over beforehand.

I sensed that Albert didn't bother with that. He had a gut dislike for the PDs, thought the coalition was temporary, and so didn't seem to make much of a play with Dessie. I think he was getting wound up by a lot of his supporters, including Brian Cowen, who was in my old job at Labour. 'The PDs have already seen off a Fianna Fáil Taoiseach, Tánaiste and Minister for Defence,' Cowen would say. 'They're now trying to bring down Albert. Well, they can shag off.' That made cabinet meetings more fraught than they had been. I remember during the summer with O'Malley giving evidence at the Beef Tribunal, when the atmosphere was terrible around the cabinet table, thinking to myself, 'This isn't going to last long.'

Right from the start, the new government got thrown into controversy over the 'X case', when the Attorney General, Harry Whelehan, got an injunction from the High Court to prevent a fourteen-year-old rape victim travelling to England for an abortion. This was a legal and ethical minefield, one that got a massive postbag in the constituency. To be honest, my first thought was, 'Jesus, what a nightmare.' What that poor girl must have been going through, I don't know. She was not far off the same age as my own girls. The government was under a lot of scrutiny on the matter, and rightly so. There were big issues involved, not to mention the welfare of a vulnerable fourteen-year-old. None of us were especially comfortable dealing with the subject, and Albert especially never seemed to get to grips with the issues involved. His skill was business. He was good at policy on investment and job creation. But being Taoiseach means you have to deal with the issues of the day no matter what they are. The X case pulled him away from what he was good at into areas that he wasn't as comfortable with. He got deeper and deeper into the legal and political details, until eventually there was a sense of panic that never really went away.

Life for me in the Department of Finance was challenging. Ireland had hit a really rough patch economically, as we found ourselves buffeted by storms in the international markets. I lost more sleep during this period than at any other time in my political life. I was up all hours following the financial markets in different time zones. The summer was dominated by the fallout from Denmark voting 'No' in a referendum on the Maastricht Treaty. By the time of the EU Economic and Financial Affairs (Ecofin) meeting in Bath in September, endless meetings in Brussels during the previous weeks had failed to come up with an adequate response to the turbulence of the markets or to re-establish confidence in the future of the European Monetary Union and Exchange Rate Mechanism. It seemed to me that Norman Lamont, the British Chancellor of the Exchequer, who chaired the meeting, was out of his depth and appeared very casual about taking measures to settle things down. I made my annoyance clear and it was a very acrimonious meeting. Lamont was unwilling or unable to get to grips with the system and didn't have the first idea about how to get consensus on reforming the monetary system. Later, I would work with Kenneth Clarke, who was more engaged and better company. But Lamont wasn't a guy you could get close to. His inflexibility and lack of leadership were deeply frustrating. I was working an eighteen-hour day and losing sleep about the future of the punt. Lamont didn't seem bothered. The meeting in Bath was a real missed opportunity to try and get a grip on the system. Instead we got 'Black Wednesday', which came ten days after Bath and forced Britain out of the ERM.

At least that wiped the smirk off Lamont's face. For us, though, it was a catastrophe. The collapse of sterling saw the value of the punt rise to unsustainable levels, putting pressure on me to devalue. Every week we were worried about hits against the punt by speculators. I remember coming in one morning to discover that overnight someone in Tokyo had made a IR£50 million bet against our currency. These were frightening times.

Luckily, I had very experienced people working with me during the currency crisis. Seán Cromien, the Secretary of the Department, was a venerable and knowledgeable official, who always managed to keep calm whatever was going on. 'You know, minister,' he said to me one time, 'some of your predecessors have come in and gone out of here in my forty years without ever having to understand the currency markets. I'm afraid you've had to become rather an expert on it.' I took that as a compliment. Second Secretary Maurice O'Connell, the Governor of the Central Bank Maurice Doyle, and Dr Michael Somers from the National Treasury Management Agency were all extremely able as well. Together we made up the currency 'war' cabinet. The five of us would meet, often early in the morning or late at night, to assess the situation and make decisions. These were tough, tense days, but their combined experience and ability to keep their heads made these top class people to work with. I was also glad to get advice during the crisis from my friend Padraic O'Connor at NCB Stockbrokers, and from Peter Sutherland. They gave me a real sense from the 'sharp end' of how the markets were behaving.

To begin with, we tried to defend the punt. We were hopeful that the markets would recognise that our economy was essentially sound, with the right policies to deliver low inflation, reduced borrowing and a low GDP/debt ratio. Obviously economic difficulties in the UK were going to have a major knock-on effect here. Thirty per cent of Irish exports went to Britain. When sterling fell below the punt, there was an inevitable cost to Irish exporters, with implications in terms of employment. What we did not anticipate was the position of the German Bundesbank. While the bankers in Frankfurt were happy to defend the French franc, they barely lifted a finger to help us. That was a painful lesson in EU politics – all economies are partners, but some partners are more equal than others.

In the end we had no alternative but to devalue, a step taken on

30 January 1993. By the end of that month alone we had borrowed IR£1 billion in foreign currencies to support the old exchange rate. Ordinary people could not be asked to suffer any more. But the trick was to devalue without the markets getting a whiff of it, allowing speculators to cash in at the last minute. Very few people in cabinet or in the department knew what we were going to do. The previous weekend I had loaded the car up with boxes of papers and gone down to Cork to get away from everything and everyone. I needed time to think and to assess. I remember the weather was shocking, so I sat in for two days, reading solidly. By the time I had finished I knew we had to devalue. When I got back to the department on the Tuesday, I asked Seán Cromien to come in and see me. 'We have to devalue,' I told him simply. 'I agree,' he replied. Seán had come to the same conclusion over the weekend. When we heard that Britain had reduced its interest rates, putting more pressure on the punt, we knew we had come to the right conclusion.

When the 'war' cabinet met the following day, Michael Somers suggested one last go with the Germans. That was thrown back in our faces on Thursday, when the president of the Bundesbank ruled out an interest rate cut. That was the end of the debate. Peter Sutherland wanted us to continue defending the punt, but that argument had become unsustainable. On Friday afternoon, very quietly, I asked Maurice O'Connell to contact Jean-Claude Trichet, the chair of the EU Monetary Committee and a future president of the European Central Bank, to arrange a meeting for the next day. I phoned the Taoiseach to tell him what we had decided. 'Bertie, are you sure?' he asked. I replied that I believed we had no choice. He was a former Minister for Finance and knew how complex these decisions were. He would not have wanted to interfere at the last minute. I also talked to Dick Spring, who had become Tánaiste by this stage. Later I spoke to both of them together and we all agreed that we had to devalue. But I knew that if the decision was the wrong one it would be my head on the block.

As soon as the market closed at 4 p.m. on Friday evening, we started to put our plan into action. The logistics sound funny now, but they were no joke at the time. O'Connell led the delegation to Brussels to inform the Monetary Committee of our decision. They were booked onto scheduled flights, as to organise an official plane would have aroused suspicion. I had an engagement in Cahirciveen, Co. Kerry, that night, so I kept it to give the impression of business as usual. The next day, I was back in Drumcondra, but was on the phone the whole time with the department in Merrion Street. The meeting in Brussels began at 3.30 p.m. and quickly sanctioned the 10 per cent devaluation of the punt. Finally the cat was out of the bag. In the end it had been the right thing to do. We lost money, and it was money we had to pay back over a long time. But we weren't bullied out of the system – unlike the UK – and I think that gave us a lot of credibility. On the other hand, I felt we had been badly let down by Germany. We went to the Bundesbank for multilateral aid, but the Germans only helped the French. I said as much to the media. I wasn't usually so undiplomatic, but I was furious at the way we had been treated. There clearly wasn't equal help for all member states in the ERM, and if you were a small country you could whistle.

In some ways, the devaluation crisis was the making of me. Most analysts, such as Pat McArdle, were supportive of the approach we had taken in the face of neglect and even hostility from some of our European partners. We had fought off the speculators during the first wave of the crisis in September and November 1992. Then a substantial devaluation of 10 per cent in January effectively stabilised our position. This was a competitive devaluation, big enough to make a difference. Interest rates came down immediately. Those two factors gave us the impetus for a take-off in the economy. Within a year, international commentators started talking about the 'Celtic Tiger' for the first time.

The autumn and winter of 1992–93 had seen financial instability and turmoil. It had also been a time of political upheaval, resulting in a change of government. Albert had made no secret of his contempt for the 'temporary little arrangement' we had with the Progressive Democrats. At the 1992 Ard Fheis he had told delegates that Fianna Fáil had 'no need of another party to keep it on the right track or act as its conscience', and Brian Cowen went even further. 'What about the PDs?' he asked delegates. 'When in doubt, leave them out.' I think many of us felt that way by this stage. Every time the PDs came into government, they were either leaving or about to leave or had left or were threatening to think about leaving. This happened so many times during the period 1989–92 that tension had become the norm. So when yet another crisis hit in the autumn of 1992, it was a case of 'here we go again . . .'

Albert was not a man who could rise above personal dislikes. O'Malley irritated him and he let that show. It would often become clear during cabinet meetings that Albert had not briefed Dessie on matters coming up for decision. There was no trust there at all. Unfortunately, their personal dislike became very public. O'Malley had given his evidence to the Beef Tribunal that summer, when he described decisions made by Reynolds as 'grossly unwise, reckless and foolish'. Albert was furious, but he wasn't due to give evidence before the tribunal until the autumn. He was hardly five minutes in the witness box before he raised the stakes by describing O'Malley's evidence as 'reckless, irresponsible and dishonest'. Once the word 'dishonest' was out, there seemed no going back. As soon as I heard what Albert had said, I went straight back to St Luke's and told them, 'Get ready for an election.'

The opposition put down a motion of no confidence in the government for 5 November. The night before, Dessie said he was pulling out of the government on the grounds of 'non-consultation and exploitation of loyalty', whatever that meant. Everyone knew the real reason was Albert's charge of 'dishonesty'. Before the debate, Albert came to me and said, 'We can't let these fellas off the hook, we've really got to hit them hard.' I was happy to help. I could cope with the PDs always playing the 'holier than thou' card. What bothered me was that they were putting party before national interest. These guys needed to hear some home truths. 'Politics is about triumphs and setbacks, achievements and defeats, swings and round-abouts,' I reminded them in the Dáil:

> Every politician, at some stage, has to make a choice based on the following question: do I sit down and whinge for the rest of my life and complain about other people and about circumstances, or do I get up, move on and try to learn from the experience? Clearly, the Progressive Democrats have chosen to take the first of those options. They are addicted to outrage, to annoyance and are hooked on a high moral tone. Consequently, at a time of international economic instability they are prepared to halt progress and stability to pay homage to the outraged feelings of their leader. They do not care about the damage this will do to the country, to Ireland's image overseas, or about the negative effect it will have on our currency. Clearly economic considerations do not matter as much to the Progressive Democrats as does their own status.

The general election was set for 25 November, the same day as the three referendums that came out of the X case. It was obvious early on that we weren't prepared for the campaign. There didn't seem to be any clear strategy. Someone seemed to decide we should be fighting the election around the Taoiseach's personality. But you only had to be out on the streets for five minutes with Albert to see that this kind of campaign didn't play to his strengths. He was a business-man. He might have a background in the showbands scene, but he wasn't one for putting on a performance. He would talk away all right, but there was no sense of excitement or razzmatazz surrounding him. He just never seemed to catch light. A poll during the election showed that his personal rating had dropped to just 28 per cent.

I threw myself into the campaign for Albert, but a lot of the people who were supposed to be close to him disappeared into thin air. It was left to people like myself and even Mary O'Rourke, who he had demoted, to put our shoulder to the wheel, travelling around the country, in and out of RTÉ studios, trying to whip up a bit of enthusiasm. Mary's commitment during this election was one of the reasons why in later years I asked her to be deputy leader. I could see for myself how she always put the party first. She more than lived up to that as deputy from 1994 until she lost her seat at the 2002 general election. Her commitment to the cause in that period was tireless and she would phone me every week with ideas and suggestions. That was an important factor in our success during those years. I was delighted when she won her seat back in 2007. It was typical Mary. She's a fighter.

In the election of 1992, Albert seemed to go downhill during the campaign. I remember phoning him the night of the leaders' debate to congratulate him. He said no one else had bothered, which amazed me. He sounded very low. After a difficult enough campaign, we managed to rally the troops in the last week and got our own core vote close to 40 per cent, even if we struggled with transfers.

Putting so much effort into the national campaign made life difficult in Dublin Central. The constituency had been changed from a five- to a four-seater. We ended up taking 39 per cent of first preferences, which should have been enough to deliver two Fianna Fáil seats. Against the advice of Dermot Fitzpatrick and myself, headquarters decided to run three candidates. This time it split the vote for Fitzpatrick and Olga Bennett. If we had dropped Olga, then Dermot Fitzpatrick's vote would have been higher and he would have got most of my transfers. This would be the only campaign since the constituency was created in 1981 in which we didn't win two seats or more. That really annoyed me, because we had actually polled a better vote than we had thought in a fierce campaign. At the next election we only ran two candidates and walked both seats.

In a difficult election, there was a piece of good news for the

Aherns. My brother Noel, who had been such a support to me going right back, was elected in Dublin North West. That included parts of the old Dublin Finglas constituency that had been my first seat, so it was familiar territory for us. The one pity was that Jim Tunney had failed to hold his seat. He had seen the party through some rough times as chairman of the parliamentary party, which had sometimes taken its emotional toll. He was a good man and I was sorry to see him leaving the Dáil. It was another example of there being no sentimentality in politics. Even the most popular politicians go in the end.

The result of the election was bad for Fianna Fáil. We were down nine seats. Fine Gael did worse and lost ten. The PDs were up four, but it was less than they had hoped for. The real winners were Labour, who gained eighteen seats in the 'Spring Tide'.

Late on in the campaign, Albert had raised the question with me about sharing power with Labour. Now it came up again. Labour's early talks with Fine Gael were not going well. I said we would benefit from a period in opposition to rebuild the party organisation, but if there was a chance of a deal with Labour, we should take it. 'Even if you talk Springer into it,' I warned him, 'it's our own supporters that'll need convincing.' There had been a vigorous debate about going into power with the PDs in 1989. Coalition with Labour was another step. We had had to put up with 'the Cruiser' and his gang for decades, always looking down their noses at Fianna Fáil, so the question was whether we could stomach Labour. My view was that yes we could. This was a new generation, with good people like Ruairi Quinn and Brendan Howlin. They were bright and practical and I already knew they had some decent ideas about the economy.

I thought we could put a good government together that would continue to build on the economic progress we had already made. In the middle of a currency crisis, facing tough decisions especially on unemployment, these were the kind of people you wanted around the place. I went to talk to Brian Lenihan. He was strongly of the view that we should do it. Albert's reason for wanting a deal was simple. Without it he almost certainly would have had to give up the leadership of the party. Reports coming back from the constituencies said he was unpopular on the doorstep. There were questions about whether the 'Albert factor' was crucial in losing a number of tight races. That Spring's personality worked so well for Labour made the contrast even worse.

After the election, I was part of a panel discussion on the *Saturday View* programme. Barry Desmond from Labour was one of the other guests. As was the tradition with that show, we all went for a drink afterwards in Kiely's. I got chatting with Desmond and he told me that talks with Fine Gael were not going well. I got the impression from him that Labour might be prepared to deal with us. Afterwards, with Martin Mansergh, I started working through the Fianna Fáil and Labour manifestos as well as the current social partnership agreement (PESP), looking for points of overlap between the two parties. It became clear to me that there was obvious potential for a cohesive Programme for Government. I went to see Albert in his house in Ballsbridge and told him. 'Do it then,' he said, so Martin and I finished our work. When Labour's talks with Fine Gael broke down as expected, we had a comprehensive draft document ready and waiting.

Following some positive talks between Albert and Dick, the Fianna Fáil team of myself, Brian Cowen and Noel Dempsey began negotiating with Labour. Between us we made a strong team. Dempsey was great with the detail, very methodical about looking for ways to negotiate on specifics. Brian, of course, had that toughness when we needed it. He had only come into cabinet that year, so I was just getting to know him well. He was bright and a real fighter, and I liked that he was really committed to the party grass roots. He was a guy who was prepared to stay up all night talking to members at those 'chicken and chips' dinners. Not a lot of TDs are prepared to do that, especially once they get into cabinet. I liked politicians who put in time with the same people that would be out campaigning for the party on a rainy Wednesday night in the winter.

It has sometimes been said that Albert wanted us to do a deal at any cost. That's unfair. Labour had just had a good election, so they were in a very strong position. Fergus Finlay, Dick's main adviser, later put it about that he was the dominant force behind the negotiations. Typical Finlay! He knows how to spin his own story. In reality it was Fergus and Martin Mansergh who drafted the agreement together as the negotiations were going on. It helped when Albert and I went to the Edinburgh European Council Meeting in December. The decision was made in principle at that meeting on EC Structural and Cohesion Funds for the years 1993 to 1999. Back home that meant money would be available to a new government to fund the important infrastructure projects that were being agreed in negotiations. This was the famous IR£8 billion for Ireland, which would be finalised at a European meeting the following July. There were personnel changes that helped us with Labour as well. Pádraig Flynn was nominated to the European Commission just as the talks began. Labour certainly didn't like him. Having him on the negotiating team or even in cabinet would have been a problem for them.

The Labour team of Quinn, Howlin and Mervyn Taylor was tough but fair. One of the issues was over cabinet seats, since Charlie had given the PDs two ministers when they only had six TDs. In the end, Labour got six out of fifteen, with Spring to be Tánaiste. They had done well, but they had got a good slice of the vote and were the obvious 'winners' in the election. So we had to reflect that. I thought it would be a good government. Albert with his business background as Taoiseach, Spring with his sharp intellect in Foreign Affairs, Ruairi Quinn in Enterprise and Employment working closely with me in Finance. When the new government met together for the first time on 12 January, I felt positive we could give it a really good run.

Spring had a reputation as a prickly character. As time went on, he and Albert seemed increasingly uncomfortable in each other's company. Sometimes I would get stuck with the pair of them after meetings, and I would just try to laugh away, keen to keep the conversation going and to avoid the long silences. It was murder. Albert would sometimes use me as the peacemaker too. If they had a row, I was sent to see Spring. Usually it was something and nothing – Albert saying something, Dick taking offence – but because the two often didn't seem able to talk to each other, I was dispatched to help them kiss and make up.

That was always made easier by the fact that I liked Dick and had no difficulty dealing with him at all. He always knew what he wanted and I respected that. Most of the time when we had to work closely together, such as when we co-chaired the European Investment Bank meetings in Paris, he was easy-going and engaging. He was sharp in the Dáil as well, good with speeches and the technical detail. Around the country, he had built up a lot of popular support. Dick was very private though, so I never really socialised with him. Partly that was also because we were both so busy. I would have been closer to Quinn. I got along well with him and liked him. For the best part of three decades our lives overlapped. We had been in Dublin Corporation together, had shadowed each other in various ministries, worked together in government and would end up leading our respective parties. He was a good politician and a good minister. If things had turned out differently a few years down the line, we would have had no problems running a government together as Taoiseach and Tánaiste.

Some of the advisers were a different story, however. They seemed suspicious of us, although when Dick's brother Donal was around, things were easier. He was a very likeable guy. Finlay and John Rogers didn't seem to trust Fianna Fáil at all, but again I always seemed to get on all right with them. I believe Finlay later said that if it had been Dick and myself in 1993 instead of Dick and Albert, we might have lasted much longer and would likely have got re-elected.

That didn't mean there weren't a few hairy moments. I remember the tense negotiations at a ministers' meeting in Brussels about the structural funds. Dick made it clear that as Minister for Foreign Affairs he wanted me off his territory. I wasn't going to make a big issue out of it, as the details always got worked out at the Ecofin meetings anyway. There was also a bit of a set-to with Brendan Howlin, the Minister for Health, who took badly to my offer of help during a strike with the dental assistants. Brendan got very heated about that one, but the reality was that the Programme for Economic and Social Progress was in danger of coming unstuck. By and large, though, I had good relations with the Labour ministers. Inevitably there were tensions, which the media were always trying to stoke up. Advisers would be running around trying to get headlines saying, 'This issue MUST be sorted immediately.' But the ministers I dealt with were more concerned with the issues than spin, so they were always straight with Finance. It was all very practical. Everything had to go through my department, so it was busy, but the atmosphere seemed good to me, even if the two leaders were not getting on.

To be honest, the Reynolds era was a strange one for me. I was so busy in Finance, I kept myself to myself and got on with the job. I did my best, helped by my adviser Brendan Ward, to provide a good service to all of the party. Although I was a senior minister, I was not part of the Taoiseach's inner circle. I got on well with our coalition partners, but obviously was not one of their party. I had to spend a lot of time looking over my shoulder, making sure that I didn't get isolated in cabinet. That worked for the most part. I only got badly caught once, over the introduction of a tax amnesty in 1993.

I had given a huge increase in powers to the revenue inspectors in my 1992 budget. Abolishing most of the tax breaks and tax shelters to allow us to reduce rates of personal taxation meant that Revenue needed to be able to audit the system more aggressively. That got some people complaining about 'draconian powers'. There were editorials about it most weeks. The *Sunday Business Post* especially went to town on it. The idea came from somewhere that we should give defaulters one last chance to put their affairs in order. A lot of the backbenchers were agitating for the amnesty, probably because constituents were writing to them about it. Albert definitely liked the idea, which seemed to appeal to his business background. But I hated it. It certainly did not appeal to my accountancy background. The department and Revenue weren't for it either. So I put up a strong paper to cabinet saying we should not proceed. I pointed out there was 'money within the country' in disguised accounts and bogus non-resident accounts which 'could readily be transferred abroad to avail of the tax remissions'. Revenue was already very close to making a number of big breakthroughs using their new powers. An amnesty now would put those audits at 'high risk'. The so-called Investigation B was anticipated to raise IR£101 million. That dwarfed sums that might be raised through the amnesty itself. Principle and common sense, I argued, told us not to proceed. Years later when the Ansbacher report came out, I felt vindicated in that advice.

Albert was not convinced and pushed ahead anyway. When it came to making a decision at cabinet, I knew I would need Labour support. I tried talking to Ruairi, but he was non-committal when I raised it with him. I got the sense that Labour were happy for me to make the running for them, although I was reassured later when I got a tip-off the night before cabinet that all the Labour ministers would be voting against it. When it came to the meeting, Albert pressed hard for the measure. I said both the department and Revenue were opposed. Then I waited for the Labour guys to row in behind me. Nothing. They just sat on their hands looking sheepish. I don't know if Albert had done a deal with Dick. Perhaps they just didn't think it was worth the candle. That left me completely isolated. Not only did I not have the support of my own colleagues; there was no support from Labour. The only choice for me was to swallow it, or to make a lone stand. That would have meant having to walk, because if I say we're not doing it and then cabinet decides to do it anyway, that's a resignation issue. That would have achieved nothing. But I was furious and I let Quinn know it. I believe I wasn't the only one who was angry. Willie Scally, one of Dick's closest advisers, resigned over the decision, although he was talked out of it afterwards.

The irony was that I had to go out and sell the policy to the media. They could see straight through that. They knew I had opposed it, that I had said it would not raise the huge sums everyone seemed to expect. It certainly wasn't going to clean up the system, because the big players would just be using the amnesty to go offshore. I couldn't disguise my anger. I saw myself on the news that night and you could see it in my face. The whole thing was a disaster. At least later on we were able to put the money raised from the amnesty to good use on various projects, including renovating the National Museum at Collins Barracks.

Taxation issues were a source of conflict too between Albert and Dick the following year. The Institute of Taxation had put forward proposals on a new scheme for ex-pats, which Albert strongly supported. I thought it seemed a good way of encouraging ex-pats to spend money in the country, although I wanted to put in safe-guards to prevent abuse of the system. But it turned into a contentious issue between the two leaders. During a break in Kerry, I got an irate call from Albert saying that Dick was not going to support the tax measures and would not accept them coming to cabinet. He asked me to meet Dick. That meant bringing my officials into the office on Good Friday to sort out the detail, before I went back to meet Dick in the Europa Hotel in Killarney. 'The Taoiseach is not a happy camper,' I told him. 'I know,' he said. A while afterwards, I heard that Albert wrote him a long letter, most of it in block capital letters. That was not the sign of a relationship which was going to last.

The lack of trust between Albert and Dick would play a major part in the crisis that crucified us in the autumn of 1994. I don't think anyone can say with certainty that they know exactly what happened in these few weeks. The situation was a mess. Nobody seemed to be thinking clearly. No one knew what the issue at stake really was. What I do know is that we ended up throwing away a good government, because the Taoiseach and the Tánaiste couldn't get their act together. The man at the heart of the crisis was Harry

Whelehan, the Attorney General. I never knew Harry particularly well even after he joined the government in 1991. He was friendly enough, but he never seemed to have much interest or feel for politics. He had got a bad press for the way he handled the X case in 1992. As it turned out, trying to move him is what ended up bringing down the government.

On 20 September 1994, Mr Justice Liam Hamilton became Chief Justice. Albert wanted to put Whelehan in to succeed him as president of the High Court – the second most senior legal appointment in the state. Dick had his own candidate. Albert was out of the country at the time, so at the next cabinet meeting, chaired by Dick, it was announced that the Taoiseach and Tánaiste would be having a chat about it on the telephone in due course. No one thought anything of it. If you had told me then that they wouldn't have signed off on a compromise candidate and that the government would soon fall, I would have laughed you out of the room. Not sending Harry to the High Court wouldn't have been the end of the world.

The problem was that the whole thing just started to drift. Albert and Dick wouldn't deal with it decisively between themselves. Whelehan was in, then he was out, and then he was back in again. Dick got into a tangle proposing another candidate who didn't want the job. His poll rating slumped. Labour TDs went on the radio in big numbers to say that the issue should not bring the government down. A ministerial committee – 'the Four Wise Men' – was set up, involving Brian Cowen, Noel Dempsey, Ruairi Quinn and Brendan Howlin, to find a solution. Albert didn't ask me to be on that committee, which surprised me. Not that I thought the committee was a good idea. When you start dealing with these kinds of single issues by 'kitchen cabinet', you're asking for trouble. We needed quick decisions, not committees. Albert should have given it to one person with a legal brain and told them to liaise with everyone, get it sorted. Instead there was chaos.

Our only hope was that it might just blow over. A compromise was cobbled together between Dick and Albert that would get Whelehan appointed but the system for future appointments reformed. Then the story broke about the paedophile priest, Brendan Smyth. It turned out an RUC warrant for Smyth had sat in the Office of the Attorney General for months. So off we go again. Labour threaten to leave the government. Albert gets a rush of blood to the head on 11 November and appoints Whelehan president of the High Court without Spring's support. Labour walk.

For most of this I was left as a spectator. I asked Albert if there was anything I could do to help, but he said he was getting to grips with it. There were committee meetings going on half the night, trying to work out what the hell was going on. Labour kept stepping in and then out of the coalition. I remember one meeting of the Fianna Fáil ministers that went on for ten hours, with everyone getting more confused, tying ourselves in knots. Because I hadn't been brought in on the issues, there wasn't much I could contribute. This material was so complex, it was the lawyers like David Andrews and Brian Cowen who took the lead in trying to make sense of it all.

I was sitting beside Albert when he was making his statement on the Smyth case to the Dáil on 15 November. A thick folder was passed to me containing suggestions for answers prepared by the Taoiseach's office and what turned out to be notes from the new Attorney General, Eoghan Fitzsimons, on another paedophile called Duggan. Albert's supporters later got angry that I didn't pass it straight along to him. Those people have obviously never done Leaders' Questions in the Dáil. I was getting wads of stuff over my shoulder every minute from Noel Dempsey and others, giving me relevant answers to questions as they came up to pass along to Albert, who was subjected to four hours of this. If there was anything in that report that needed saying, it should have come in a summary for Albert to digest in the ten seconds before he had to answer another question. In fact, the newspapers would comment afterwards how I was one of the few who bothered to stay beside Albert throughout his entire ordeal, helping as best I could and adding regularly to the leader's pile of notes, which fell into greater disarray by the minute.

That was my contribution, backing Albert up as best I could. Aside from anything else, if new information had in fact come to light, all he would have had to do was go back to the House immediately and make another personal statement. Albert said he read the report by the Attorney General in his office straight after returning from the Dáil. If it contained vital material, there was time for him to go back to the House and explain that new information had turned up. He could even have given a press conference. That would have been the way to get the details out. Not that it was clear to me then or later what was so significant in the sheets passed to me. When there was an inquiry afterwards, Reynolds said he thought the report by Fitzsimons was 'wholly unreliable' and 'misleading', so I don't see how that would have helped him.

Part of the problem was that there was no one close to him who could tell him 'stop'. Flynn was in Brussels; Máire Geoghegan-Quinn was a supporter, but I'm not sure he was even listening to her. David Andrews had the authority but was detached. Cowen and Dempsey were still young fellas in cabinet. And then there was Harry himself. Jesus, he must have wanted that court job badly. Albert was a businessman of the 'let's shake hands on the deal' type. He had given Harry his word. He wasn't going to shaft him now. Instead, Harry's appointment had ended up shafting the lot of us. Albert Reynolds resigned as Taoiseach on 17 November.

I had been at one remove from the whole crisis, but my anger at losing a good government came spilling out during an exchange in the Dáil. Albert had been answering questions for hours and had gone for his lunch. But the opposition, who were now in control of the House, were demanding that he come back early. That was just bad manners, so I let fly at Fine Gael's Gay Mitchell, who was lecturing us. 'You're a waffler,' I told him. 'You've been waffling around this place for years.' He looked a bit taken aback. Gay is one of those guys who gets very irritated by criticism. He can say what he likes about you, but the minute you have a go back, he's giving out like a fishwife. His trick was always to come into the House, make a sharp intervention and then vanish. He had been the same on the Corporation. That always got him into the newspapers. I always thought he was a spoofer, showing up without any notes and making a speech like he was an expert on every subject. The truth was it was just hot air. And I told him so. It's probably not a good idea to lose your head in the Dáil, but sometimes you have to let rip with these guys. I just thought to myself, 'I'm not putting up with this,' so I gave it to him both barrels. We've got on well and laughed about it since.

The reason I was so annoyed was that Fianna Fáil and Labour had turned out to be a really strong team. The partnership government had delivered a programme over two years that had been beneficial for the country. Albert had done a brilliant job on the North, helping bring about IRA and Loyalist ceasefires. He had put a huge effort into the Downing Street Declaration, which was a seminal moment in the peace process. Those achievements would be his legacy and can never be underestimated. On the economy, we had low inflation, stable industrial relations, falling tax rates, higher growth rates, low interest rates and growing employment. These economic points may not have figured large in the hothouse atmosphere of the Dáil, but they were making a real difference in the everyday lives of the majority of citizens. Confidence around the country was high. The economy had expanded by 8.5 per cent over 1993 and 1994. Our debt ratio was down. The OECD was predicting another good year. Within two years, the Reynolds coalition had delivered the lion's share of the most comprehensive programme for government in thirty years. The country was on the move. Now that had been put in jeopardy, and for what? No one really knew the answer.

Things moved very quickly in the hours after Albert's resignation as Taoiseach. Almost straight away people started approaching me about succeeding him. Within about an hour I had a sense that I had the numbers. People were encouraging me to declare immediately. I consulted a few people I trusted in the parliamentary party, including among others John O'Donoghue, Dermot Ahern, Noel Dempsey, Dick Roche and Micheál Martin, who would all be part of my small campaign group. I spoke to Brian Lenihan by phone, because he was in hospital. I saw my brother Noel. I phoned Tony Kett and Chris Wall in the constituency. Then I stepped outside for a walk to think things through. I knew who my supporters would be. I had a fair idea of my own strengths and weaknesses. The question wasn't necessarily whether I could get it. The question was whether or not I wanted it. The answer to that might seem obvious, but anyone will tell you that being leader, a potential Taoiseach, is a world away from being a government minister. Your life, including your private life, is always under scrutiny. When it all hits the fan, you're responsible no matter what. You can't just be master of one portfolio, you have to be on top of everything. That's a big ask for anyone. Of course I was ambitious, I'm not going to hide that. But anyone who takes on that job without thinking it through is mad. Over the previous years, it had been in my mind that when Albert Reynolds retired, I would run for the leadership. So even though I had not expected it to arise for a while yet, I still felt prepared. I took a few moments by myself to clear my head and by the time I had finished a walk around the gardens in Merrion Square, I knew that I was ready to give it a shot. I returned to Leinster House. 'We're on,' I told the lads.

Dick Roche was to the forefront of my campaign. I knew he understood that good organisation is key to winning an election and that's what he delivered. John O'Donoghue, Dermot Ahern, Noel Dempsey and Micheál Martin gave us good coverage with TDs from around the country. Brian Lenihan was active from his hospital bed with Dublin TDs. David Andrews rounded up Albert diehards. We were briefing the media. The only other candidate to emerge as a

with the TDs that day. We had been through a tough time and just wanted to move on. I made a speech to them, saying that I didn't want any cliques, and that I wanted us to draw a line under the divisions of the past. Whether we were going into opposition or back into government, I told them, there was a big job to do revitalising the party in the country. We had to reinvigorate ourselves. People who had left the party because of factions had to be brought back. Unite and work together, that was my message. At the press conference at the Burlington afterwards, I was glad to see people from all the different sections of the party socialising together. That was the kind of buzz we needed to get us going again.

For all the excitement at the Burlington, there was one celebration I was looking forward to more than any other. Afterwards, I came back to my mother in Church Avenue. A crowd had gathered, just like in 1977. My mother met me at the door. She gave me a big hug and then brought me inside for a cup of tea. There were a few tears about Dad not being there to see me coming home as the party leader, a successor to Eamon de Valera. I know how proud he would have been. Family were coming in and out all the time, drinking pots and pots of tea. That was handy enough for me, as I was off the drink just like every November. Everyone was congratulating the girls. Miriam dropped in to say well done. She had been so much part of my success, even though it had cost us. I had a few moments alone up in my old bedroom at the top of the house. All those years ago I had been reading books about Pearse and how the Dáil works, studying for my Leaving and my accountancy exams. It had been a long old journey.

Moments like this in your life are humbling. I slipped away from Church Avenue while all the celebrations were still going on and dropped in to the six o'clock Mass at the Pro-Cathedral. I had some time to reflect, and afterwards everyone wanted to say well done. There were people from everywhere, the poorest flats in the city, those up from the country who had been shopping, all the old people who had been going to Mass every day of their lives for years and years. It took me more than half an hour to get outside onto Marlborough Street. After an interview on *Kenny Live*, I headed back to Drumcondra to Fagan's, which was jammed. I put my head in for a while, but I thought, 'I'm off the drink, I'm away across the road to take it easy.' It had been a long day.

Back in St Luke's I just said, 'Thank God' and turned in. Tomorrow was Sunday – a day for relaxing with the girls. The question of who would be the next Taoiseach was still to be settled, but that could wait for another day.

Today I was just happy to call myself Uachtarán Fhianna Fáil.

9

FAREWELL TO THE ANORAK

Becoming leader of Fianna Fáil was one of the proudest moments of my life. But it didn't take long before I was brought back down to earth.

First, I had to deal with Albert. He found it hard not being leader any more, and he had been in office for fewer than three years. Albert's frustration was clear because, as he said himself in the Dáil, he felt it was 'the little things' that had tripped him up. He had to come to terms with his disappointment in public, because he remained acting Taoiseach.

Albert came with me to Government Buildings after I had been elected and we had a private conversation just before a press conference. Clearly he wasn't happy, but he played the game. He would have preferred Máire Geoghegan-Quinn as his successor, but he congratulated me and said he was making me Tánaiste to try to make it 'business as usual' until he had gone. Relations would be very tense between all of us for the next two weeks. The Smyth and Duggan cases were still causing controversy. Albert didn't really want to deal with them, probably because they had helped bring about his downfall. That put me in a difficult position, because I needed to know everything before I started dealing with Labour to try and put the government back together. Dick Spring was very sensitive about the whole issue. The last thing I needed was to be saying something to him that turned out to be wrong. More than anything else I needed to be accurate. And to be accurate I needed information. Those early chats with Dick were friendly. He was naturally cautious about future prospects, but I got the sense that he wanted to come back in. He definitely seemed more relaxed with me than he had been with Albert. We just had to try to get the whole Whelehan business behind us.

It didn't help that Albert's relationship with Eoghan Fitzsimons, Whelehan's replacement as Attorney General, was strained. The atmosphere in meetings was terrible. Albert, understandably, was in bad humour. Fitzsimons was combing through material about the child sex abuse cases. It appeared to me that he didn't entirely trust the cabinet. And while all this was happening, Albert had to keep going over the thing that finished him as Taoiseach. It was a difficult time. The air of secrecy and paranoia around the place was terrible. There were stories about phone taps and rooms being bugged. I think my office in Finance was swept a few times by Special Branch in those weeks. I don't know where they thought any surveillance might be coming from, whether it was journalists or an inside job. Things were tense, anyway.

With that kind of atmosphere, people are always likely to overreact when something controversial crops up. That's what happened to Labour when Geraldine Kennedy published another story on 5 December about Harry Whelehan. I was on my way to Brussels early that morning for a vital Ecofin meeting. I read the story in the *Irish Times* on the way to the airport. It said that Reynolds had asked Whelehan to resign on Monday 14 November because of the Duggan case, but that he had then gone into the Dáil the next day to defend

Whelehan's 'suitability for high judicial office'. That seemed a bit strange to me, but then the whole sorry saga was strange. I can't honestly say there seemed to be anything new. Máire Geoghegan-Quinn had already said most of this in the Dáil a couple of weeks earlier. I arrived in Brussels around 8 a.m. No sooner was I there than I got a phone call from Noel Dempsey. 'Brendan Howlin's been on to me, jumping up and down. Dick's very upset.' I was amazed. 'I'll talk to Springer when I get home,' I said. Soon afterwards, my partner Celia Larkin phoned. She told me that the media were having a field day with the story. A few hours later I got another call. 'Things are getting out of control,' she said. 'You've got to get back.' Albert, who was in Budapest, had refused to show Dick the Attorney General's report on Smyth and Duggan. I sent a message to Dick's office saying he could look at anything he wanted. I would fax it over myself if need be. By this stage it was clear everything was unravelling. As soon as I was able to leave the Ecofin meeting, I headed straight for the airport. The government jet flew me back to Dublin. I was in Government Buildings by around five o'clock to find absolute pandemonium.

People on our side were spitting blood, saying the Attorney General's office had leaked it. It was clear that Kennedy hadn't just made this stuff up. Obviously there was material in the report that had not been given to cabinet at the time, but that would not be unusual. Even to this day I cannot see where the 'conspiracy' was. It wasn't in anybody's interest to be holding anything back on the Duggan case or any other case. When I spoke to Spring personally, I made that point to him. 'Look, Dick, I really don't know what's going on here,' I said, 'but you can see anything you want and talk to anyone you like.' I think I did everything I could to persuade him that we could work well together. But I knew that he was having real doubts.

I talked to Fitzsimons and told him I wanted to know everything that had gone on. He was nervous and edgy. He had only been in the office a few weeks and now found himself in the middle of a storm. After I had finished with him I knew he would be no help in convincing Dick, because he still seemed to have so many suspicions of his own. I held a lengthy meeting of the Fianna Fáil ministers at which it became clear to me once again that Fitzsimons was uneasy with us. I finally left Government Buildings well after midnight. Nothing had been resolved. There had been no word from Labour. I got back to St Luke's and went straight to bed. I had been up for around eighteen hours, so I went out like a light.

The phone upstairs in St Luke's rang around two that morning and the noise scared the life out of me. It was Spring on the line. 'I'm sorry, Bertie,' he said, 'I've decided to pull out.' I was surprised. I told him that I had been trying all day to get comprehensive information for him. He accepted that. 'It's all too much, Bertie, it's too much,' he said. I asked if there was anything else I could do. He said no. We said goodnight. The whole conversation had taken five minutes. Nobody lost their temper. By the end of it, I was no longer 'Taoiseach-in-waiting'. I had been thirty-six hours away from forming a government. Now it was 'Welcome to life in opposition'.

For a couple of moments I didn't know what to do with myself. Then I picked up the phone and called a few people. I remember trying to get hold of Joe Walsh, the Cork South West TD, who had been advising me on the negotiations with Labour. I rang down to Jury's Hotel and spoke to the desk. 'You're joking me,' the woman said, 'you're not Bertie Ahern!' I never did get to talk to Joe. I also phoned Gerry Hickey, my programme manager in Finance, and a few of the key guys in Drumcondra. 'You're better off without Spring,' was Chris Wall's verdict, or words to that effect.

I was sick about what had happened. There was nothing in this as far as I could see. No one could honestly say that the government, including Reynolds himself, was intentionally trying to hide paedophiles. We had just gone from one mess to another and here we were letting a good government fall by the wayside. Looking back on it now, I can't help thinking that Labour wanted to manufacture a row. You can always find a reason for an argument if you want one. The truth was that we were trying to put the jigsaw together, fitting all the pieces, to get answers about what had gone wrong. But these things go on all the time in government. Stuff happens, you try to deal with it. There are always a few bits of the jigsaw you never find, but when you see the overall picture you make a judgement and then learn from the experience. The frustration was that public opinion showed that people wanted us to carry on. Dick would pay a price for that at the next election.

It was quite a shock to me. I was ready to take it on. Then it was gone. And you say to yourself, 'It's gone now, is it gone forever?' I didn't break down in tears or anything, but the next few days were hard enough. One minute I had been picking out names for my cabinet, telling Charlie McCreevy he was going to be Minister for Finance. The next I'm thinking, 'How in the name of God am I going to get the party up again?' At the time I had felt I was ready to be Taoiseach. I knew the issues, thought the party was ready to move on with me, and believed I could run a good government. Now I'm not so sure. When you become leader you need time to plan. You can't just go in there without any ideas. That's why I didn't run in 1992 – I didn't feel that I had it all sorted out in my head. That had changed by 1994 and I was raring to go. I didn't know it at the time, but not getting Taoiseach straight away was a blessing in disguise. It gave me the opportunity to work out a plan. And it allowed the party to get organised. We had been through a rough period, losing two leaders since 1992. The party organisation needed a root-and-branch reform. Once I got my head round it, I realised I had been given a real opportunity. When Dublin won the All-Ireland nine months later, I knew things were starting to look up again.

I was sorry that the relationship with Labour soured. That could have been the start of something that would have realigned politics in Ireland. I don't doubt that I could have worked well with them if I had been elected Taoiseach. I remember saying to Ruairi Quinn when it was all over, 'Listen, I'm after giving you a great economy. Just do nothing and I'll pick it up again in a couple of years.' I still got on well with Ruairi over the years, and to be fair he did a good job of keeping things going as Minister for Finance. But I never let him forget that I had handed him the first current budget surplus since 1967.

A few people said afterwards that I blamed Geraldine Kennedy for what went on. I even heard that I had cut out the article from the *Irish Times* and kept it in my wallet. That's just not true. I saw her a short while afterwards. I think she was a bit nervous when she saw me coming over, but I told her that there were no hard feelings. She had just been doing her job. We had a chat about the issues, and I said that I had read the article several times over without being able to see what was in it that had got Labour so hot under the collar. To my mind it was just a massive breakdown of communication.

That's where I think Fergus Finlay might have played a role. There was always something about Finlay that gave the impression that he thought he was above Fianna Fáil. I've worked well subsequently with him on a number of causes, such as the Special Olympics. But in the period 1992–94 I always got the sense he saw himself as the moral conscience of the nation. That seems to have been crucial in advising Spring during that critical time in 1994. Finlay always looked uncomfortable dealing with us. He seemed on edge, so you never knew what he was saying to Dick. I don't think I ever felt I could trust him. That's fair enough, because he worked for Dick not me. If Finlay had been a bit more upfront with us, we might have been able to get to the bottom of what was worrying him. I'm not the right person to say how important that was in the end.

Being leader brought a lot of changes for me, not least on a personal level. I've never been what you would call a clothes horse.

For my early days in politics that was all right. I was always the fella in the anorak with the long hair, who didn't really look much like a traditional type of politician. I liked that, because it's who I really am. With me, what you saw was what you got. But being leader is something different. People wanted to know that you could represent the party and the country. You couldn't be rolling up to meet some president or prime minister and have them thinking, 'Who's this scruffy git from Ireland?' I had realised that when I became Minister for Finance. I would be attending meetings with business people or with other ministers in Brussels. There would always be bankers coming in to me or foreign investors. So without anybody really saying anything, I became conscious that I had to be wearing a decent suit and tie. The hair gradually got shorter. But still when I got back to Drumcondra, I couldn't wait to throw off the pinstripe suit and get out canvassing in my old anorak.

When I became leader, that was when I had people trying to get at me. There were all kinds of image consultants saying, 'You've got to get your suits pressed every day', or, 'We're sending someone round to do your hair.' Worst of all, I had to start wearing make-up for television. 'Get lost!' was my first reaction to that. I would be well used to a bit of powder for interviews in the studio, but I wasn't going to be walking around the place plastered in make-up just so I would look good on the *Six-One News*. Eventually it was Celia Larkin who sat me down and told me the hard truth that I would look all blotchy otherwise. I remember the first time I went into the Dáil with it on, I felt a right idiot, but I didn't get much ribbing. It's just part and parcel of modern politics. I remember sometimes I would meet Tony Blair for meetings and his face would be bright orange.

The media loved having a go at the coat. There was even a cartoon strip called 'Anorak Man'. To be honest I didn't want to get rid of it at all. Celia probably wanted to burn it. In the end, we decided to auction it for Drumcondra National School on Church Avenue. That raised a few thousand pounds for them and gave everyone a bit of a laugh. A local publican called Tom Kennedy bought it for his pub. When I've finished in politics I might see if I can buy it back. In reality, being packaged is a side of politics that I don't feel comfortable with. I'm just an ordinary guy and have never taken to being told I need to change my 'image'. There would be people telling me about what the public liked and saying things such as, 'You need more pastel shades.' What the hell did that mean? It wasn't something that came easily to me. I was happy-go-lucky on these kinds of matters. I resisted most attempts at a 'makeover', but I was fortunate to have Celia to give me sound advice. P. J. Mara and Chris Wall were also good at getting the message home. In the end I went to see Louis Copeland in Capel Street. I had grown up with him and his family in Drumcondra, knew them well, and had played football with them. He made sure I got some decent suits, but ones that were still me. 'Nothing too loud,' I told him. Louis has been responsible for making me look respectable for years now.

Suited and booted for the job, I knew there were more important things to worry about than the length of my hair or the 'colour palette' of my shirt and tie. Like getting Fianna Fáil back on its feet. One of the things I was keen to do in 1995 was to bring some of the talented younger guys through, like Dermot Ahern, Micheál Martin and Noel Dempsey. They would all play major roles in each of my three governments. They were sharp guys, with a talent for organisation, who I wanted to get a grip on the party across the country. We had been through a rough time over the previous few years. We had been in two unstable coalitions and lost nine seats in a general election. I wanted change, but the question was how to achieve it. 'Softly' was the conclusion I came to. There was no point coming in like a bull in a china shop, throwing your weight around the place. You don't have to shout 'I'm in charge' to assert your authority. Albert had arrived in 1992 and sacked most of the cabinet. That had got him off to a bad start. Factions had been looking to get their own back from day one. That wasn't my style. I wanted to unite the party. That meant keeping most of the current front bench, even if I wasn't close to some of them. Reynolds had got rid of people he didn't like. Haughey had done the same. Even Lynch had done it. I wanted to end that by picking people from across the party. I brought back Ray Burke. I went to Máire Geoghegan-Quinn, who had stood against me and asked her to join the frontbench team. Pat Farrell had supported Geoghegan-Quinn, but I kept him on as general secretary of the party. When he came to see me, I think he believed he was about to be sacked. But I told him he was doing a good job and that I wanted him to stay. He went on to work his guts out for me and the party, so that turned out to be the right decision.

I also asked Charlie McCreevy, who had run Máire Geoghegan-Quinn's campaign, to come on board. His was the appointment that probably attracted the most attention, because I gave him the Finance portfolio, the most senior appointment on the front bench after Leader. I wasn't particularly close to Charlie at that time, but I did admire him. He was a good, efficient politician. He was a straight talker, could be very tough and, despite appearances, was a hard worker. He also had a touch of genius about him, not to mention the odd flash of madness. I had first got to know him when I was whip, when to be honest he had to be watched to make sure he turned up for votes. I think in those days he was more interested in his accountancy practice than Leinster House. But I observed him for the short period he was a minister under Albert and saw how hard he worked. He made a lot of unpopular decisions in Social Welfare. That's the test for any government minister. I was impressed that he always kept his head while he was getting hit. That's important. I thought he had some of those qualities that I had liked in Ray MacSharry all those years earlier: straight guy, not prepared to be rolled over and always ready to face down challenges. That turned out to be one of the best calls I made. Over the years Charlie and I did not always agree on everything, but we worked very closely together. I was never one for shouting at people in meetings or at the negotiating table, but that

became director of elections. I brought in Padraic White, former managing director of the Industrial Development Authority of Ireland (IDA), as director of policy. They were all bright people, so they attracted other bright people who wanted to work with them. We also started thinking about making sure that we communicated the right message to the voters. Fianna Fáil had a reputation as an old-fashioned party, but that was completely at odds with what we had done to revitalise the economy. I didn't want to abandon our traditions, but I did want voters to understand that we had a vision for a modern, progressive and prosperous Ireland. Changing the logo was a small but important step in that process, because it gave us a clean, fresh image without losing our heritage as the Republican party.

I also tried to open the party up. Too often politics can seem like a conversation within the walls of Leinster House. I started having meetings and conferences around the country to involve more people. There was an all-day session for the whole National Executive at the Royal Hospital in Kilmainham, which was very important for opening up discussion. I brought the whole parliamentary party away for workshops to talk about ideas. Then I got local councillors and the elected officials from CDCs to come to Leinster House. A lot of them had never been in before, so it helped break down the 'them and us' attitude. That meant they started talking to us, telling us what was happening on the ground. We also did a large number of rallies throughout the country for ordinary members, packing out places like the National Stadium in Dublin and the Neptune Stadium in Cork. So in all these ways and many more I started to bring the party closer, drawing together different bits of the network, activating all the resources that the party had.

The first real breakthrough came at the by-elections in April 1996 in Dublin West and Donegal North East. We won both of them, electing Brian Lenihan Jnr and Cecelia Keaveney, after superb campaigns run by Pat 'the Cope' Gallagher and Jim McDaid in Donegal, and Noel Dempsey in Dublin. This was the first sign that we were getting things right. The elections were well run, and there was a sense of freshness about what we had to offer. The vacancy in Dublin West had occurred following the death of Brian Lenihan, the man I had admired most in politics. Throughout the years that followed, there wasn't a difficult decision or a crisis to face when I didn't think to myself, 'Now what would Brian's tactics have been here?'

A period in opposition was not just good for the party, getting us into shape for government; it was also good for me. I felt I had mastered the Finance brief well in the early 1990s. But leading the party is about being on top of every brief. You have to have an answer on social, economic and foreign policy. And on top of that, you have to have a strategy for the North. Although I had been interested in the North since my first visits there in the late 1960s, I had not been particularly involved in the political issues as a minister. I had watched with great admiration in 1992 when Albert Reynolds had decided to make a big push on the North. This would be the outstanding achievement of his time as Taoiseach and one that I often think he's not given enough credit for. Haughey had helped prepare the way by getting the back channels up and running, using Martin Mansergh. If anything, Martin had that bit more freedom to operate under Albert, who told him to 'find a way forward' and then left him to get on with talking to the Republicans. And because Martin is a brilliant guy and absolutely 100 per cent straight, everyone trusted him. Albert had a couple of other indirect channels of his own with the Republican leadership. Eventually he worked out the basis of an agreement with John Major in the Downing Street Declaration of 1993, which in turn led to the IRA and Loyalist ceasefires. Although eventually the ceasefires would break down, they had been important and positive developments.

Opposition gave me the chance to develop my own ideas on the North. It also allowed me space to begin making and using my own contacts. I had a number of meetings with Sinn Féin in the weeks leading up to Christmas 1994, just days after becoming leader. I wanted to assure them of my personal commitment to the process. Even though by this stage we knew there would be a new government, it was important to make the point that Fianna Fáil would help the process in any way we could. I started visiting the North more regularly. I went to Nationalist areas like Andersonstown and into the Falls Road, where Gerry Adams showed me the famous Bobby Sands mural. I visited the Conway Mill Centre in West Belfast early on and was struck by the really positive desire that there was to bring a sense of normal life to the area. I also paid early visits to Derry, Strabane, Omagh and the border areas. Wherever I went I was given a warm welcome, not something I had been told to expect. Quite a few people pointed out that they didn't see many politicians from the Republic. I remember one really old lady saying to me, 'The last time I saw someone from Fianna Fáil here was Dev in 1918.' That was funny, because the party hadn't even been founded in 1918, but it also showed how we had not really bothered with these areas. I wanted them to know that we were interested and wanted to get them a fair and peaceful settlement.

I also took the time to meet some Unionist leaders. I didn't go into the staunchly Loyalist areas at this stage, but I did become the first leader of Fianna Fáil to visit the headquarters of the Ulster Unionist Party (UUP) in Glengall Street. That gave me a real insight. I remember Ken Maginnis and Jeffrey Donaldson were there. They both had some very strong words to say about Articles 2 and 3 of our Constitution, and the need to decommission IRA weapons. But for all the strength of their feelings and their obvious suspicions of the South, they could not have tried any harder to be courteous and welcoming. It was a bizarre mixture of cups of tea and polite chit-chat mixed in with what usually gets described as a 'full and frank exchange of views'.

That would be the first of many meetings with Unionists and Loyalists, some in public and others not. The Church of Ireland was very important in facilitating some of those talks. Robin Eames, the

Archbishop of Armagh and Primate of All-Ireland, was a very impressive and thoughtful character. I think it helped that he had a strong Unionist background, so everyone accepted his sincerity when he tried to reach out to different communities. He went out of his way to help me on many occasions, including personal ones. Glenn Barr, who had been active in the Ulster Workers' Council and then the Ulster Defence Association (UDA), was also really helpful. I had got to know him when he was working with the unemployed in the North in the 1980s. I also gave him a hand with the superb project he was running with Paddy Harte to establish the Messines Peace Park in Belgium. Glenn introduced me into some of the working-class Protestant areas of Belfast. I started talking informally to people in the Loyalist groups. That was a real eye-opener. A lot of the guys I met had, like the IRA, killed people in cold blood. The murders on both sides of the conflict disgusted me, but I also recognised that if we didn't deal with these people and bring them into the process, we would get nowhere.

The need for that became even more apparent when the IRA ceasefire ended when a bomb went off in Canary Wharf on 9 February 1996. Within ten weeks, the IRA had planted five other devices in London. On 15 June, the Father's Day weekend, a massive bomb exploded in Manchester, a city I have a huge affinity with. I felt a sense of frustration during this period – at the carnage and destruction, and at the waste of a historic opportunity. In the months prior to the end of the ceasefire, a serious logjam had developed in the peace process not helped by parliamentary arithmetic in Westminster. John Major's government was becomingly increasingly dependant on the support of Ulster Unionist MPs and it was no coincidence that the British government's position shifted to require the decommissioning of weapons as a precondition for Sinn Fein's participation in all party talks. The impasse in the process was, however, never any justification for a return to violence. As I said at the time, 'the IRA hold sole responsibility for the renewed bombing,' but it was everyone's responsibility to put the process 'back together again, if possible, before further tragedy occurs.'

In my view, the failure to get all-party peace negotiations started 16 months after the initial ceasefire was indefensible. The deadlock over decommissioning meant that the process was drifting endlessly. I saw that for myself in the Forum for Peace and Reconciliation established by Albert Reynolds, which had been meeting in Dublin Castle regularly since the ceasefire in 1994. I played an active role in the Forum, but it would constantly frustrate me the way the government used to breeze in and out. I knew they had other things to do and it's not always possible to give your attention to everything, but even so. Few if any of their senior people bothered to stay at all. I would be there meeting all the delegations from the parties, the churches, and the various groups. And they would be saying to me, 'Where's the government?' The general consensus seemed to be that the Rainbow were only interested in talking to the British government. Fianna Fáil was deeply critical of John Bruton refusing to meet John Hume and Gerry Adams together as well as John Major's implicit rejection of the Mitchell Report. What followed from the IRA, commencing at Canary Wharf, was completely and utterly wrong. So I was tough on Sinn Féin after the bombings and said some hard things to them in public and at private meetings. But angry as I was, I also knew that we had to listen to them and to work with them. This was the only way to stop the renewed cancer of violence spreading throughout Northern Ireland.

There were commentators who tried to hammer me on the whole issue of the ceasefire. Some have even suggested that we quietly and cynically got a message to the IRA that they should hold off renewing the ceasefire until after the general election in 1997. That was rubbish. To start with, if the British government had handled the process right in the first place, the ceasefire never would have broken down. The Rainbow government didn't help matters either. If they had kept their eye on the ball a bit more, there would have been no need for Fianna

Fáil to be involved. But more importantly, it shows a complete lack of understanding about how the process works. You can't turn something like a ceasefire on and off like a tap. You have to work at it. That was what the government had failed to do. That left a void which someone had to fill. There was no ceasefire. The IRA were back at war. No-one was meeting Sinn Féin because the violence was back on. The Forum stopped meeting. Everything was a complete shambles. I felt that the Rainbow government had thrown away all the good work done by Reynolds. Somebody had to take the initiative. I started dealing actively with Sinn Féin and the Ulster Unionist Party, trying to create the nucleus of a way forward. I wanted to build up contacts at every level in both communities to show that if I was Taoiseach, I would take the North seriously.

One man I did meet during this period who certainly did have a clue was the British Labour leader, Tony Blair. He asked to meet me after the IRA ceasefire broke down in 1996. We had a private meeting in the Gresham Hotel and subsequently would meet in Westminster and in Leinster House. We both agreed that if elected Prime Minister and Taoiseach we would take a hands-on role about the North. A few things struck me about Tony at that first meeting. I liked him straight away. He was very sincere and practical. I had heard he could be a bit preachy, but he didn't strike me that way. In fact, he was very down to earth and wanted to listen as much as talk. It helped that he loves football. That season Man United and Newcastle were rivals in the Premiership, so there was plenty to chat about. Alastair Campbell, Tony's brilliant press secretary, was always great for finding ways to put me and Tony together in environments where it was easy to talk informally. And because Alastair is mad about football as well, those meetings often involved watching a match. Tony had a real love for and knowledge of Ireland. I'm often struck that we know much more about the English than they do about us, but that wasn't true of Tony. He had a Donegal connection through his mother, which I hadn't known until he told me. Apparently he went to Rossnowlagh Strand every summer until he was a teenager, when the Troubles started. He wanted to get back to better times. He was committed and that would make a big difference during some of the really difficult days ahead. When Tony got elected on 1 May 1997, I was delighted. John Major had definitely made an important contribution, one that doesn't get enough recognition, but I knew that Tony was someone I could really do business with.

It wasn't only the North facing the challenge of violence in 1996. The death of the journalist Veronica Guerin on 26 June was a shocking event. Veronica's murder was not just the tragic loss of a brave and talented woman; it also dealt a huge blow to Ireland as a democracy governed by the rule of law. Her murder, coming so close to that of Detective Garda Jerry McCabe, provoked revulsion, shock and outrage throughout the country. The simple reason was that people saw how criminals and drug barons posed a very real threat to the security of the state and to ordinary people's lives.

Veronica's death was a blow to me personally. I had been friendly with her for years. I had first got to know her in the early 1980s. Not many people knew that her writing career had begun as secretary to the Fianna Fáil delegation to the New Ireland Forum. She had been an active member of Ógra Fianna Fáil when I was chairman. She was active in Charlie Haughey's Dublin North Central constituency. I always liked the way she enjoyed the cut and thrust of politics. That was typical of Veronica. She never did anything by halves. There was so much energy there. She was a very bubbly person, full of life. Every time I think of her, it's up on somebody's shoulders cheering at Ógra conferences or at an election count. Like me, she was a Man United fanatic. I would often bump into her on the early Saturday morning flight over to Manchester to see a game and we would have a right good chat, more about soccer than politics.

I remember after the death of Garda McCabe walking from his funeral for about a mile down the road with Veronica. By this stage, shots had already been fired into her house and threats had been made against her young son, Cathal. Looking back to that day of Garda McCabe's funeral, I've often asked myself, should I have said something to her, told her to be careful, maybe to ease off? To be honest, I don't think it would have made any difference. To Veronica, journalism meant uncovering the truth behind the criminal under-world. In that task she was absolutely relentless. This brought great personal risk with it. In the end she paid the highest possible price. When I heard the terrible news, I was shocked right to the core.

Before her death, Veronica had been helping John O'Donoghue develop our criminal justice policy. She had spoken at a justice confer-ence John had organised for the party. What she told us made the hairs on the head stand up. Veronica named names, detailed criminal activity and violence, talked about the connections between criminality and drugs. It was frightening stuff, but made the issues brutally clear. John was putting together a very ambitious and hard-hitting legislative programme ready for when we returned to government. The centre-piece of that was the introduction of a new Criminal Assets Bureau to target the proceeds of crime, which he was developing with the barrister Eamon Leahy. In the days after Veronica's death, in the face of public outrage and fear, there were demands for something to be done straight away. It was clear that the government didn't have anything to offer except hand-wringing.

When it came to the debate in the Dáil it was left to me to announce a series of measures that I thought needed to be introduced. Eventually the government adopted legislation on the Criminal Assets Bureau that we brought forward. It only happened once in a very blue moon that an opposition private member's bill was taken in government time. It was embarrassing for the government and that was made worse for them when the Minister for Justice, Nora Owen, was late coming into the House to hear John move the second stage. The bill turned out to be among the most significant developments ever made in Ireland in the ongoing battle to combat organised crime.

That was an important moment for us as a party. It was not scoring cheap political points during a tragedy. Politics and government are about being able to make changes in people's lives, responding to challenging events. In the immediate aftermath of the deaths of Veronica Guerin and Garda Jerry McCabe, we showed people that we were ready for government, that we had been thinking about these serious issues and had ideas for dealing with them. Drug barons and criminal gangs, the Provos: these were powerful organisations and you would be right to be fearful about crossing them. But society demanded it of us. The government seemed paralysed, but in opposition we had been working on a strategy for the peace process and we had been looking at how to deal with crime. There were good proposals from Micheál Martin that would form the basis for the Knowledge Economy, one of the best ways to get people out of poverty and away from crime. By the time we got to the election in 1997, I felt we had revitalised the party with a programme for government that was planned, dynamic and progressive.

When the Dáil was dissolved on 15 May and a date set for an election on 6 June, everyone felt relieved. In the Dáil I thanked the Taoiseach for finally putting everyone out of their misery. It was probably inevitable that the media portrayed the election as a battle between the leaders. That certainly worked to my advantage, especially with John Bruton. There was a lot made about the fact that he didn't seem to like me much. He would quite often talk me down in the Dáil, so it never looked as if we had a great deal in common. During the campaign he said I was the most overrated man in the country. 'God bless him, he's been out in the sun too long,' was my reply to that one. That was just politics. In reality, there was no personal dislike. We went back a long way. I remember putting my back out playing football in the early 1980s. He was Leader of the House, and I was his opposite number, so when we had business to transact on Dáil reform, he came to my home. That was a thoughtful gesture from a busy government minister. Another time when I had helped him out with a problem he had with a constituent, he presented me with a book. So John could be rough in debate, but in person he was very friendly. He was there as the EU Ambassador to Washington when I went to address the US Congress years after. He was very gracious in what he said to me that day, and later in what he told the media. That meant a lot.

It was unlucky for John during the campaign that he could come across as a bit high and mighty. There was a bit of 'I'm Taoiseach and I'm going to lord it over you'. I remember he did a live interview on the news from the back garden of his big house in Meath. 'Jaysus,' I was thinking, 'does he even know what he looks like?' It was like seeing some nineteenth-century landlord. When he got caught out talking about 'the fucking peace process', it only seemed to confirm how out of touch he was with the fears and concerns of ordinary people. His colleagues weren't much help. I would be out to schools, churches, hospitals, and there would always be lots of people around the place. John more often than not seemed to be on his own. I don't know where his cabinet disappeared to. There was one great photo op he did with Dick Spring and Proinsias De Rossa, the leader of Democratic Left, where they were walking through Temple Bar on their own. They were supposed to be the leaders of the 'people's parties', but they didn't seem actually to want to meet any real people. We couldn't buy publicity like that.

I wasn't worried about De Rossa and Democratic Left. They were insignificant. In fact, statistically we had more members than they had voters. They had been well organised in opposition, but once they got into government, they had let down the people they were supposed to look out for. In the first Rainbow budget in 1995, they had only given a IR£1.50 a week increase on old-age pensions. I absolutely hammered De Rossa as Minister for Social Welfare. We were raking in taxes by this time. Here was a chance to help vulnerable pensioners and the poor. Instead he completely shafted them. He deserved to be politically buried for that.

Spring was different. The polls made it clear that the 'Spring tide' was definitely going out, but whatever about the Labour Party and even the way they had pulled out of government with us, I felt that he had done a good job earlier in the North. I remember one time talking to him after the ceasefire had broken down when he said how important Albert and Fianna Fáil had been to the peace process, and I wondered whether now he wished he had done things differently in 1994.

The planning that I had put in place from the minute I became leader worked like a dream in 1997. I remember P. J. Mara saying to me that if Charlie Haughey had allowed him to manage the national vote better, there would have been no messing around with coalitions and minority governments. PJ might be a great one for the stories, but the truth is he is a sharp political operator. He understands voters better than most people know their own kids. The strategy I worked out with him and Ray MacSharry, Charlie McCreevy and Chris Wall was to run a minimum number of candidates to spread the vote more effectively. Rather than giving all the no. 1 votes to the strongest candidate, we divided constituencies into areas with strict rules about transfer arrangements. That had worked in the two by-elections the year before. Now we were going to make it work nationally.

Right from the start, the election committee said to me, 'Listen, the numbers say the people like you and we want you out there pressing the flesh.' In some ways we were going right back to an old-style 1950s campaign, except with the benefit of television. Basically, I was meeting the people and asking them to vote for us. We also had a brilliant media team in Jackie Gallagher, Mandy Johnston, Sinead McSweeney and Gerry Howlin making sure that our key messages got out each day. There were some good events organised. PJ had me go over to the opening of the new Planet Hollywood restaurant on Stephen's Green. It was part owned by Sylvester Stallone, so because he was turning up, there were thousands of people outside. The atmosphere was brilliant. They brought me onto the stage. Politicians don't always go down well at these events, but I was pleased to get a good cheer. Afterwards, Mandy was raving about the pictures. This was around the same time that John Bruton and the lads were in Temple Bar on their own, so the contrast couldn't have been better. There was a party on all right, but they weren't at it. Stallone by the way was a nice guy, but shorter than I had expected. He gave me his jacket.

That was a nicely managed bit of publicity for us, but sometimes in politics it's the unexpected moments out and about with voters that catch the mood of an election. I've had a fair few of those in my time, but one of the funniest came at that election. I was on the campaign trail in Galway doing a walkabout on Shop Street. Out of the corner of my eye I could see this schoolgirl coming at me at a hundred miles an hour and I'm thinking, 'Jeeze, what's this about?' And she just jumps into my arms and gives me a big smacker. I could hear the click, click, click of the cameras and knew this one was going to get used. The journos absolutely loved it, laughing and getting the girl's name. Sure enough, it was on the news that night and all over the papers in the morning. The pictures made it look as if we were having a right old snog on the streets of Galway. The campaign was delighted. The story kept running for the next couple of days and all the time the message was that 'young people love Bertie'. I met Helen Muldoon again six or seven years later when she had been through college and I was glad to see that our brief encounter hadn't done her any harm.

Funnily enough, that event seemed to capture the sense of energy we had in the campaign. I was putting in long days, campaigning for eighteen hours at a time. We used a helicopter to fly around from constituency to constituency. There were endless interviews with local and national media, as well as countless rallies at which I would deliver my stump speech. But most of the time it was meeting people, people, people to let them get a look at me and make their minds up. That philosophy was at the heart of our campaign slogan: 'People before Politics'. It was Drumcondra '77 on a bigger scale. I remember then people had thought I was mad to concentrate my efforts going door to door on my own to meet voters. That was what got me elected. I was always confident that if I could talk to as many people as possible in person and through the TV that they would get a sense of who I am and what I'm about. The tight discipline of the campaign was pure Drumcondra as well. We had been preparing for this since 1994. We had the policies and we had the plan for the election. The election committee used to meet at 6 a.m. every day to adapt what we were doing to any changing circumstances. Organisation, discipline and hard work: that's how you win elections.

The one area we couldn't control gave us our biggest headache: our potential coalition partners, the Progressive Democrats. During the campaign, they promised to cut 25,000 jobs from the public service, which the media pointed out would mean a hundred people losing their jobs every week for an entire five-year period of government. A lot of our policies were designed to improve health and education. That seemed to be having a big impact in pulling in transfers from Labour. Now here were the PDs apparently saying they were going to sack nurses and teachers. That didn't go down well. When Mary Harney appeared to criticise single mothers, there was more bad publicity. Mary and I had already agreed to meet in the Green Isle Hotel during the campaign. I still got on very well with her. She admitted that the PDs were having a problem getting their message across in the campaign. That would end up being very costly for us both in the election.

At the end of the campaign there was a lot of focus in the media about the leaders' debate between me and John Bruton. These are weird occasions, because although you've been debating each other in the Dáil for years, let's be honest, not many people are paying much attention. Then suddenly everyone is saying this is going to make or break the campaign. Coming near the end makes that pressure even greater. You don't want to screw up. You want to get your points across. For me, as the new boy on the block, I had to show that I knew what I was on about and was Taoiseach material. We did a lot of preparation beforehand. We even got a friend of mine, Patrick Sutton, to do some role play as John Bruton. Initially that was difficult to take seriously, because his impression, with a lot of heavy sighing and waving the hands around, was hilarious. John's real mannerisms were tame in comparison. One time, when Patrick kept talking over me, I completely lost my rag with him. That was great, because when Bruton did exactly the same thing on the night, I just kept my cool.

There's always a surreal air about those TV debates. I guess everyone knows about the famous Kennedy/Nixon head-to-heads and how they 'won' the election for JFK. In reality I don't know how much difference they really make unless you are decisively beaten. RTÉ go to great trouble to make sure the two candidates are kept apart. Different arrival times, different corridors, different researchers. When you're brought into the studio, there's a quick hello and a handshake for the photographers, and then you're off for an hour of debate. As soon as it was over, they were in straight away to get us both up and off again. No chance for a chat. I'm sure me and John would have managed all right, but nobody wanted to take the chance. I was pleased with how it had gone on the night, although predictably the papers gave it to John. I certainly didn't do anything to 'lose' the election. That was the first of my three leaders' debates and by the end I felt I had got the measure of them.

Election day itself started the way it always did: the morning leaflet for voters in Dublin Central asking them to vote for Marian McGennis and myself. Then I went off to vote. It was great being with my own local friends in Drumcondra, thanking them for all the hard work they had done. Being leader means you have to rely even more on your constituency activists, because you're having to travel round the country. There's really not much more you can do by that stage other than have a chat and let the people make their decision. I remember I got my first early night for months that evening and then slept in probably for the first time in years the next morning. By habit I never go to the count early, so I just stayed at home quietly, doing nothing much. Bowl of soup, a sandwich. Quick visit to Church Avenue for a cup of tea. 'Are you winning, Bertie?' Mam asked me. 'I really don't know,' I told her truthfully, 'but thank God it's over.'

The early assessments were that the election was going to be nip and tuck. Only by around nine o'clock did it look as if I would be able to get the numbers to form a government. When I heard that John Bruton had said he wouldn't be going on RTÉ that night, I knew we must be almost there. We were up nine seats and so were Fine Gael. The big losers were Labour, who were down sixteen, and the PDs, who were down six.

That put us in pole position, but there was still a job to do. I felt strongly that Fianna Fáil/PD was the way to go. If the PDs had done better, the two parties would have had a majority, but because they had done badly, I knew we had to bring some independents on board. For a moment I considered going to Ruairi Quinn to see if Labour were interested in a coalition, but I dismissed the idea almost straight away. Too much water had passed under the bridge. In opposition, I had worked well with Mary Harney, knew her better than most, and liked her too. Our different strengths complemented each other's. During my first conversation with her after the election I made it clear immediately that I wanted to form a government. The most important point that I made, though, was that I wanted to put together a programme that would last a full term. Commentators were already saying that Fianna Fáil was incapable of sustaining a coalition. I wanted my government to run for the full five years. John Bruton was predicting that we would not last a wet weekend. In fact, we turned out to be the longest-serving peacetime government in the history of the state.

Getting the independents on board was the usual business of trying to herd cats. I talked to a lot of them myself. Gerry Hickey, my programme manager, was travelling round the country meeting them. Donie Cassidy worked on Jackie Healy-Rae. Gerry did the same with Harry Blaney and Tom Gildea. I negotiated with Mildred Fox. They all had genuine projects they wanted to advance. Blaney had had this idea since boyhood for a Mulroy Bay bridge, which would make a huge difference to people's lives in the area when it opened as the 'Harry Blaney Bridge' in 2009. Jackie wanted the roads widened around Kenmare. Mildred had a number of schools projects. These and others were all good ideas and I had no complaints about TDs using their moment to get things done for their constituents. 'I'm not Santa,' I remember saying, 'but if you understand that this can't all be done in a year, we'll get these projects going.' To be fair they accepted that, and once they committed to the government, they stuck with us.

The one person who overplayed his hand was Tony Gregory. He came to me looking for a meeting. There was talk he might be Ceann Comhairle, but what he really wanted was a seat in cabinet. 'That's just not going to happen, Tony,' I told him. He started asking about being a 'super junior', coming to cabinet meetings. That was never going to be possible, but I suppose he was putting the bar high in case we came back to him. As it happened, we didn't.

On 26 June 1997, the 28th Dáil elected me Taoiseach by 85 votes to 78. At forty-five, I was the youngest person to hold the office.

John Bruton gave me a generous welcome. In our private meeting that day, he had been gracious and helpful, only asking that I would maintain our commitment to the Ireland–Newfoundland project, which had been a particular interest of his. I was happy to do so. For myself, I felt deeply humbled by the honour the Dáil had just conferred. 'Having spent twenty years here and having had an interest in politics from a very young age, it is hard to put into words the honour of this position,' I told the House. 'The only way I can repay it is to work every hour of every day to show I merit it. I will do that on behalf of my party, the Dáil and the people of the country.'

Up in the gallery, looking on proudly with the girls, was my mother. There had been enough hard times in her life. She had seen the Black and Tans in her family home and lived through the civil war. She and my father had brought up a family when Ireland had been one of the poorest states in Europe. At the time she had instilled in us that if you worked hard, there was nothing you could not achieve. Now, at eighty-six years of age, she was there to watch her youngest son become Taoiseach.

At the end of my speech I glanced up to look at her. There were no tears or big demonstrations from her. She had a faint smile on her lips, but I knew she was thrilled, probably thinking of my dad as well.

'Go raibh míle maith agaibh,' I said.

10

UP ALL THE TREES

Maybe the first day as Taoiseach is the best. All that positive energy, no decisions taken to upset anybody.

After accepting the nomination for office, I left Leinster House through the Kildare Street entrance, where a big crowd of supporters had gathered to cheer me on my way to Áras an Uachtaráin. There were a lot of people from the constituency there, friends who had supported me throughout my political career. At the Áras, President Robinson was friendly when presenting me with the seal of office. 'I think this might be the last time I'll do this,' said the President, who had recently announced that she wouldn't be seeking a second term. 'I definitely hope so,' I told her, 'otherwise I'll be Taoiseach for the shortest time in history!'

Back in Leinster House, the new cabinet gathered in the Sycamore Room. There was a lot of excitement in the air. Fianna Fáil had been out of office since 1994, and the PDs since 1992, so there was a real sense of being glad to be back and wanting to start the job. There was no doubt that opposition had done us good. We had already developed a dynamic policy agenda. Now we wanted to get on with it. I kept a balance of interests from across the spectrum in the party, holding on to people like Brian Cowen and David Andrews, who had been strong supporters of Albert Reynolds, bringing back Dermot Ahern, John O'Donoghue and Mary O'Rourke, who had been sacked by Reynolds, and introducing new faces, such as Micheál Martin and Síle de Valera. I wanted a united cabinet that would reflect all strands of the party. That would involve a bit of work on my part, but it would be worth it in order to go the full term. 'A house divided against itself will not stand,' as my mother used to say. Mary Harney as Tánaiste and Bobby Molloy as a 'super junior' minister attending at cabinet were happy to be on board. Despite some bumps along the way, the PDs would remain in coalition throughout my entire time as Taoiseach.

I had to make two difficult decisions in naming the cabinet. The first involved Séamus Brennan. I had a high regard for Séamus. We had often found ourselves on different sides during heaves in the party, but we never had any personal difficulties. Completely the opposite. He was absolutely straight, but Séamus had political cunning and a really tough side as well. He would say what he thought even if you didn't want to hear it. I admired that. It was exactly what I wanted in a Chief Whip, someone who was respected by the backbenchers for his even-handedness, who would not be afraid to tell me what was happening, and who had been around long enough to know every trick in the book. I had been whip myself and I knew it was going to be a vital position in my government. Between the coalition and the independents, it would take a lot of care to keep the government going for the full term. Séamus knew I wanted to go the full five years. He had exactly the right skills and experience to mastermind that. To be honest he was disappointed, because he wanted his own ministry and a proper seat at the cabinet, but it only took a few seconds before he happily accepted the role of Chief Whip. I told him I would give him a free hand to reform the Dáil and deliver votes for the government. 'Do that for a term and I promise you'll get your own brief next time,' I told him. I kept my word in 2002, when I made him Minister for Transport.

Not putting Séamus into the cabinet was tricky enough, but it was not the most difficult decision I had to make. That surrounded the appointment of Ray Burke as Minister for Foreign Affairs. It turned out to be one of the biggest misjudgements of my political career. At the time, there was no doubting Ray's abilities. He was a very experienced minister and I knew he would be robust but skilful in dealing with the North. As Minister for Justice, he had had dealings with the Northern parties and officials, so he had already covered a lot of the ground. I knew we would be getting into the issue of renewing the ceasefire and finding a way forward in the peace talks as soon as we got into office. Burke had already come with me to meetings with Tony Blair, Mo Mowlam, David Trimble, Sinn Féin and the Loyalists, so he had the experience and knowledge, and knew the key people. The North was not a place for the thin-skinned. You had to be a tough and hardened politician for these kinds of talks. As Mo Mowlam later said in her memoirs, Burke 'was a straight talker who I felt we could do business with' and had 'what I thought were the right instincts: pragmatic, looking for a deal'. So there was no argument about Burke's ability. The question was about his past.

For years there had been persistent rumours and allegations about Ray Burke and planning irregularities. Dermot Ahern, a colleague I've always trusted completely, mentioned to me that he was hearing all kinds of stories about dodgy goings-on. That put us in a very difficult position. Here was Burke, an experienced politician and well able for the important job I had lined up for him, surrounded by all these rumours. I had to dig deeper. When Garda Commissioner Pat Byrne came to see me to discuss security for the government and for myself, I asked him directly if there was anything questionable in their examination of planning irregularities in North Dublin with regard to Burke. He was categorical that there was not. To ensure we had the fullest information, I also sent Dermot Ahern to find out about particular allegations surrounding a builder in England. Dermot went to London to speak to the builder's son, Joseph Murphy Jnr, who vehemently denied that anything irregular had occurred. Having read and re-read Dermot's note of this meeting, with the builder categorically answering 'no' to each of the questions that Dermot put to him, I still can't see anything that at the time should have stopped me from appointing Burke.

I had faithfully and rigorously followed a process, but perhaps I should have been more sceptical. Hours before Burke was appointed, at the church service in Dublin Castle for the new Dáil session, I asked him outright. 'Ray, I need your word there's nothing in any of this.' Without blinking behind those huge glasses of his, he looked me in the eye and said, 'It's absolute rubbish, Bertie. There's nothing there.' In the end I had to take him at his word. I had looked into the background. I had asked the Gardaí. I had sent a senior politician on a recce. I had confronted the man himself. I even tried to divide out the foreign policy portfolio, giving some of it to David Andrews, to emphasise that I wanted Burke for his negotiating skills in the North, but that turned out to be a constitutional non-starter. In fact, although there was plenty of comment in the Dáil about that arrangement, Burke's fitness for office was not an issue. John Bruton noted that Burke was 'qualified to hold any office'. Dick Spring called him an 'able politician'. Hindsight is always twenty-twenty, but in reality you have to make these calls as you see them. It comes with leadership. But even if I did it for the right reasons, I got this one wrong. That mistake would sap a lot of the government's energy for its first six months.

That was all ahead of us. But at the time I had to get used to being Taoiseach. When I arrived at Government Buildings from the Áras, the civil servants, as they always do for this occasion, came out to welcome me. The Secretary General to the government, Frank Murray, was there to greet me alongside Paddy Teahon, the Secretary General at the Department of the Taoiseach. Frank was a very accomplished and polished individual. I was sorry that he retired soon after I arrived, to be replaced by the very able Dermot McCarthy. I already knew Paddy Teahon, because, fifteen years earlier as whip and a minister of state in the Department of the Taoiseach, I had liaised with him over Dáil questions on the Central Statistics Office. He was an outstanding public servant, who understood how to use power during a period of great change.

The main physical feature of the Department of the Taoiseach is a long central corridor, maybe a hundred yards, with big inset windows. I soon realised that this corridor was a kind of bull run, especially before and after Leaders' Questions. To get from my office to the House, I would have to walk, or sometimes run, the length of that corridor to get to the perspex bridge that leads to the Dáil. You would have to be stupid to get in my way as I did the journey out, but on my return I would see all the advisers waiting along the corridor hoping for 'a quick word, Taoiseach'. Sometimes I felt like putting my head down and ignoring them just to get a bit of peace, but I knew they were only doing their job, so there was business to be done along the way. I don't think I broke my stride, so they had to be ready to say what they wanted in the briefest time possible: efficient for me, efficient for them.

Near to the Taoiseach's rooms, there was the office of Gerry Hickey, the programme manager who was my political eyes and ears in the department. Working with him were Jackie Gallagher, Paddy Duffy, Joe Lennon and Martin Mansergh. Olive Melvin was the gatekeeper to my diary. No one got to me without her say-so. Immediately outside my door sat Brendan Ward, the private secretary to the Taoiseach. The Taoiseach's office itself is a nice spacious room, with elegant wood panelling. John Bruton had hung a portrait of John Redmond over the fireplace. I replaced that with one of de Valera. Interestingly, John also had a picture of Lemass. I kept that one. Above my own head, I put a picture of Pádraig Pearse, whose image had always been near my desk, even as I did my homework in Church Avenue. Later I added a wonderful picture of Thomas Francis Meagher, who had been a hero of mine since JFK presented the colours of the 'Fighting 69th' to the Oireachtas in 1963. In 2008,

I would return the compliment by presenting Meagher's sword to the Congressional Friends of Ireland. In front of my desk there were a couple of chairs and a sofa. Someone had done that old trick with the furniture of making sure that anyone coming in for a meeting always sat lower than the Taoiseach. Behind my main office there was a gloomy sitting room, which I never really used. There was also a door to a meeting room, which was handy for putting two sides together for negotiations, if only because they never knew when I might just call in to see how things were going. The office was the place where I conducted most of my public business. I never really warmed to it though, maybe because the view was hopeless. There were big bay windows, but they started about halfway up the wall. Sitting at my desk I couldn't see a thing. Sometimes I would stand up to look out the window, with its view of all the comings and goings in the courtyard below. But to be honest, I was always glad to take my papers back to Drumcondra. The office was the office. St Luke's was where I felt at home.

Right from day one I said that the North was 'the priority I would put above all others'. I wanted peace on the island. I also thought that would bring prosperity with it. If we could get a multi-party agreement, I knew that would help drive the economy, which in turn would bring in the resources to reform health and education. It was a very simple message, which I had been plugging all through the election campaign. Now I felt we had the mandate to do it. I said straight away that I would be taking personal responsibility for the North, working with Ray Burke and Liz O'Donnell at Foreign Affairs. Liz was in the government as a member of the PDs. She did add glamour to our negotiating team, but you wouldn't want to underestimate her ability. As Liz O'Donnell or Mo Mowlam would have told you, the Unionists weren't always used to dealing with women politicians, especially such formidable ones. And because her father had been a good GAA man, who played for Eoghan Ruadh club in earlier times, she knew how to banter with the best of us.

That summer saw a great deal of progress on the North. Multiparty talks had resumed in June, which resulted in the publication of a 'Document on Decommissioning'. Around the same time, Tony Blair published the text of an aide-memoire sent to Sinn Féin after a couple of meetings held in May. This called for the ceasefire to be restored within five weeks. Then after a six-week 'testing period' Sinn Féin could enter talks. It also envisaged the talks finishing by May 1998. On 1 July, I travelled to Belfast for my first official meeting with the Secretary of State, Mo Mowlam. A few days later I had my first meeting as Taoiseach with Tony. 'Can you bring Sinn Féin on board?' he asked me. 'I can,' I told him.

In the days leading up to Saturday 19 July I had met up with Gerry Adams. I had often seen him in St Luke's as opposition leader, including the night before I was elected Taoiseach, when I wanted to reassure him of my continuing commitment to the peace process. But these were our first official face-to-face meetings. That Saturday, the IRA issued a brief statement announcing the 'unequivocal restoration' of the ceasefire. There was criticism that the statement did not refer to a 'permanent' ceasefire, but Tony and I felt this was enough to get all-party talks going in September. Unfortunately, Ian Paisley's Democratic Unionist Party (DUP) and the UK Unionist Party (UKUP) both withdrew around this time and did not return.

By this stage I knew Adams. But in a way I felt I never really got to know him at all. This despite the fact that over the next eleven years hardly a week went by without us meeting to talk, often in Drumcondra on weekends. I had first met him in the 1992 general election when he was campaigning for Christy Burke in Dublin Central, and, of course, I met him from 1994 onwards when I became leader of Fianna Fáil. Adams is a very serious guy. He would never come in with a bundle of jokes. There wasn't much small talk. Sometimes he could be cross and difficult. He always had it worked out in advance how far he was prepared to go and how he could get there. He definitely wasn't someone who halfway through a conversation would say, 'You know, you're right. Let's change tack.' But he was a good listener. I always felt he was exploring what was being said. Sometimes he would come back to me and I could see that there had been an impact. I learnt as the years went by that he was also fair in passing on what had been said. I would be in a meeting listening to Republican representatives and I would be thinking, 'God, I'm listening back to myself here.' That was because Gerry had passed it on almost word for word. This made it easier to deal with him. Quite often he would say, 'What's the argument I should make if I was making your case?' That was good tactics and helped build a certain level of trust, but Adams was hard work. It was never like that with Tony, where there would be jokes and chat about football in between the serious stuff, and the odd 'That's a good point, let's do that'. With Gerry it was always business. He was always right, even when he was wrong. Occasionally you might see the human side. I remember a dinner at Chequers when Gerry presented me with a birthday card signed by himself, Martin McGuinness and Tony Blair. Sometimes as well there would be acknowledgement of the amount of effort I was putting in to find common ground with him. So I fought with him, fell out with him in public and in private, but in the end he proved to be one of the good guys in the process, because he delivered. We understood one another.

Martin McGuinness was a different type of person. While Adams could be narky, McGuinness was more personable. He would ask about my family and talk about sport or fishing. He was more friendly and approachable. He was also more emotional in talks. Gerry would usually be fairly bland about things, so you could never be sure if he was happy or annoyed. If Martin was angry, you knew it. The one occasion they both hit the roof was when, after a number of very serious incidents in January/Feburary 2004, I came out and said that I had always assumed Gerry was a member of the IRA. At our next meeting on 23 March, the two of them came storming in. They ranted about the government trying to undermine Sinn Féin by criminalising the party. In these situations, I always leave people to blow off steam, refusing to get drawn into a shouting match. But on this occasion, Brian Cowen, now Minister for Foreign Affairs, was in the room with me, along with Michael McDowell, Minister for Justice. Brian was getting angrier and angrier as the meeting went on. Eventually he stood up and banged his fist on the table. 'You will not speak to the Taoiseach of our country in that way!' he roared. McGuinness jumped up and the two of them stood eyeball to eyeball, neither saying anything. After I'd calmed things down, Adams went into grievance mode. Michael hadn't said much up until this point, but he rounded on Sinn Féin, backing up my position that there was ongoing criminality. 'You know it and I know it,' he told them. 'Don't try to cod me!' So harsh words were often exchanged and discussions could be robust.

One of the most demanding aspects of negotiating with Adams and McGuinness was having to put the violence with which they were associated to one side. Many said these guys had blood on their hands. But I felt we had to look to the future and I saw them as men who were trying to lead a movement forward. I knew that they would often leave negotiations to go and talk with people on the Army Council. My own officials would be involved in some of that too. Paddy Teahon and Dermot Gallagher would be meeting members of Sinn Féin who we knew were IRA. When it came to substantive issues, like putting weapons beyond use, we knew that only the Army Council could deliver. Sometimes we found that distasteful. It frustrated and annoyed us, but we understood it was part of the process. Pragmatism was the price of getting the job done.

I knew one or two people myself who had gone into the IRA around the time of Bloody Sunday, though none of them would have gone up through the ranks. It was part of my background. But there were people around the country known to some Fianna Fáil members who would try to feed us information. One or two of them may have been acting on some kind of authority, because what they said turned out to be accurate. But most of this was nonsense. It's amazing the number of people who liked to flirt with the idea of the IRA even though in reality they knew absolutely nothing about it. So I would always look over the flow of information with a sceptical eye. About 5 per cent of it might be accurate. That was another good reason why it was important to keep the lines of communication open with Adams and McGuinness. That didn't mean I wouldn't criticise them when I needed to. They were furious with my comment about Gerry and the IRA, and when I accused the Provos of carrying out the Northern Bank robbery. But in general by talking to Adams and McGuinness we established a way of keeping a tight hold on the negotiations.

Dealing with the Brits turned out to be more straightforward, although I knew that the possibility for misunderstanding was always there, given our shared history. Robin Cook, the British Foreign Secretary, always liked to tell the story of our first meeting in the Foreign Office. It got better with every telling, as Robin was a clever man with a good sense of humour. I walked into the room that day in 1997 and there in front of me was a huge portrait of Oliver Cromwell. I suppose Cromwell's an iconic figure in England, although for very different reasons than in Ireland. Robin had that little smirk on his face as he sidled up to me, and asked, 'So what do you think of him, then?' 'He's a murdering bastard,' I shot back, 'that's what I think of him.' That wiped the smile off Robin's face. The officials froze. You could see them, thinking, 'Jesus, what are we going to do now?' No one was saying anything. I let that hang there for while before I said, 'Use another room next time, but let's get on with it now.' Then we got down to business. The Cromwellian conquest is a horrific period in our history, which has long impinged on our national consciousness. But our job as politicians was to overcome the problems born out of the divisions of history, not to be constrained by them.

Even with Tony there would be moments of real tension when

harsh words were exchanged. Conversations in my first couple of weeks in office took place in the context of the upcoming Orange Order Parade in Drumcree on 6 July. The parade was permitted to proceed, with RUC protection, sparking days of widespread disturbances. That would be the third consecutive year of serious trouble. I remember Tony phoning very early on the Sunday morning that the parade was due to take place to tell me about the decision to let it proceed. He said that the security people on the ground had been observing it all night and that their advice was to let it go. 'That's a mistake, Tony,' I told him bluntly. 'There will be bloodshed.' I felt the decision was very unhelpful. We were trying to get the ceasefire back on. There had been violence around the parade before. It wasn't worth it. My real worry was that this would throw us off course and that inevitably it would have a knock-on effect within the Nationalist community. I told him that I was going to have to say something along those lines in public, which I did later that day. The point is that we could talk frankly like that without taking it personally. We were always direct and, over the years, we would say things to each other that were tough. But there was always a sense that from our own different national interests we wanted to get this sorted. I was always amazed how, not just with me, Tony had the ability to absorb any amount of stick. There were a few times over the war in Iraq when I think maybe it got him down. But most of the time, even during the darkest days in the North, he was always positive and optimistic. However hard he got hit, Tony always bounced back, usually smiling.

It was also important to know that we could talk privately. Tony and I addressed that in our own way. Right at the start my officials were saying that each time it could take a week to get a phone call in to Whitehall. Paddy Teahon told me that was because the officials on both sides needed to tape the conversations, and that MI5 would be listening. 'To hell with that!' I told him. Apart from anything else, once you're told something like that you can't get it out of your head.

But I had a personal rapport with Tony. I didn't want that interfered with by knowing half the intelligence services around the world were listening to our calls. I had a chat with Tony and we agreed that we would talk on our own phones. At least that arrangement meant we could call whenever we wanted, even if the spooks were listening. I would say we spoke several times a week for the whole time he was prime minister. Sometimes it might just be for a minute from the car, but it kept us in regular touch and in control of the process.

The resumed ceasefire was announced on 19 July and in operation from the following day. I gave a press conference in the park opposite St Luke's. There was a great feeling that day, with everyone saying, 'Thank God the ceasefire is back on.' Most of the questions I got that weekend were about the ceasefire, but I was also asked if I had any reaction to press reports about Ray Burke. Rumours about Burke had been swirling around for a long time, so these latest didn't seem like anything new. As I said on *This Week* a few days afterwards, 'We were up every tree in North Dublin,' checking them out. Now he was such a prominent minister, the media really turned up the temperature. Throughout the summer, there were new stories about planning and corruption. Burke went down to Killarney for his holidays and no sooner was he there than he turned round to go back to Dublin to give a press conference, where he said he had received 'in good faith a sum of IR£30,000 as a totally unsolicited political contribution'. Burke subsequently made a statement in the Dáil and said he wanted to draw 'a line in the sand'. But in my view this wasn't going to go away. Only something like a tribunal would give a degree of clarity on the matter. It would be better to get the planning issue looked at over the next six months and then that would be the end of it one way or another.

I felt sorry for Burke but I was also angry with him. Here was a man of great ability and experience who was already making an impact on the North. He was taking a pounding in the media and from the opposition, unfairly in my view, if, as he said, there was nothing illegal about any payments. But he had brought a lot of this on himself. If he had come to me in June and laid it out, then we would have known the circumstances on which we were making the appointment. But he told me there was absolutely nothing of concern. Then it comes out, drip, drip, drip, and you can never turn it off. We had set out on the first day of the government believing there were no problems at all. If he had said to me or to Dermot Ahern, 'Look I got this money . . .' then we could have said either, 'Yes, you're in,' or, 'Sorry, no you're not in,' knowing exactly what we would have to stand over. But here we were only five minutes down the line with a situation where we have to establish a tribunal to look at the issues and Burke resigns. Burke was very bitter about all this and made it clear that he thought I had sold him out. All along I felt that I had behaved honourably.

Burke resigned as a minister and a TD on 7 October, the day of his brother's funeral. The next day I appointed David Andrews as Minister for Foreign Affairs. Although Burke had now fallen out with me, I still felt disappointed that such an effective minister had been hounded out of office. 'Due process has gone out the window,' I told the Dáil. 'Is that the way we are supposed to run our democracy? How will we attract good people into political life if years of service can be forgotten in a moment, as reputations are torn apart without just cause being shown?' There is no doubt that I missed his experience and commitment on the North. I worked well with David Andrews, who could be very shrewd, but I had to watch things more carefully than before. Burke had always been more hands-on.

Burke found it hard to forgive me for his downfall, even though he had made his own bed. There were a few words exchanged in a pub in Swords during the resulting by-election campaign. He seemed annoyed when we went down the tribunal route. He believed that when he went into the Dáil to explain himself, that should have been the end of it. Unfortunately, as time went on, it became clear that those weren't all the facts. At that point we did not know what had gone on, but what eventually came out was enough to get him sentenced to six months in prison for tax evasion. Did I feel that he had let me down personally? Regrettably I did. He knew that some people were telling me not to appoint him a minister, that I went out on a limb for him because I respected his experience and effectiveness. We were a new government with a big job to do on the North. Not telling me all the facts was not just a question of letting me down, he had let us all down. Even in the autumn, if he hadn't resigned his seat, my view was that he might have come back. Senior people in the government were agreed that a tribunal was the best way to deal with it. Mary Harney thought so. So did Charlie McCreevy. We all thought it was the best way forward. I was in a coalition government. Even if I had wanted to, I don't think I could have delivered my own colleagues if I had said, 'To hell with it, there's not going to be an inquiry of any sort.' It didn't make sense. I certainly don't think I let Ray down or that I shafted him. To this day, I've always highlighted the role he played in the peace process, even drawing attention to it in my final Fianna Fáil Arbour Hill commemoration speech in 2008.

Burke was not the only senior figure in the party that I fell out with in my first year as Taoiseach. Albert Reynolds suffered another setback, and looking around again for scapegoats, he settled on me. He had gone as leader of the party at the end of 1994 and took it very hard. Back then he was starting to make progress on the North, so I think he was disappointed to see his chance snatched away from him. In the six months or so leading up to the general election in 1997, certain representations were made to me by Albert's supporters that he might consider running for the presidency if Mary Robinson decided not to go for a second term. I wasn't sure if he was up for it, but one day I saw him in the Dáil and I raised it in conversation. 'I hear that's something you might be interested in,' I said. He seemed pleased and we agreed to discuss it. We met for lunch. I told him that my focus was completely on the general election, but that obviously I saw him as a candidate if he was interested. I was conscious that other people might come into the field, but at that time there was nobody else, so I wanted to see what he was thinking. My priority was that we had to have a serious candidate.

Because of the way in which he had fired so many members of the government on his first day as Taoiseach, Albert was not popular with everybody in the parliamentary party. Over the summer other names were floated. John Hume was mentioned as the all-party candidate. Ray MacSharry was being encouraged to run. David Andrews had his supporters, and for many he already looked like a president. The first to declare his hand as a serious rival to Albert was Michael O'Kennedy. He was an interesting candidate, who back in the 1980s had been spoken of as a future leader of the party. Some people might not have been aware that we were friendly, but I had great admiration for him and his loyalty to the party. Albert was still the front-runner, but there was definitely a lot of debate going on.

As soon as Mary McAleese entered the race, though, everyone understood that we were in a new ball game. Ministers started saying to me that she looked like the real deal. She had impressed at the New Ireland Forum in the 1980s. She had been an academic in Trinity College Dublin and in Queen's University Belfast. She was an excellent communicator and worked at RTÉ on the *Today Tonight* programme. Her personal story in the North was a compelling one. And as a woman with a young family, she was a very powerful role model. Once she declared, a lot of people were saying inside and outside the party that it was time to put the controversies of the past behind us and to move forward. That was how the balance started to swing. I recall the day before the election talking to Charlie McCreevy, who had been a big supporter of Albert, and to Tony Kett in St Luke's. 'It's slipping away from Albert,' Tony told me. 'What do you want us to do?' I told them to tell people the truth: that I was voting for Albert, because I had promised it to him, but that this was my personal vote. It was up to the parliamentary party to make its choice. I did not see it as part of my role to influence the vote.

Going into the party room at Leinster House that morning for the selection meeting, I still wasn't sure who was going to win. It all seemed tight. The three candidates made short speeches. Mary's was the best. Albert looked uncomfortable, as if he felt it was demeaning to have to ask for votes. Less than three years ago he had been in the same room as the leader of the party and Taoiseach. When it came to voting, I supported Albert and showed him my ballot paper. Apparently Brian Crowley turned to Albert afterwards and said, 'You're fucked now, Albert.' I don't know why he said that. And I still can't understand the comment, except to say that it shows the level of paranoia growing up around Albert. That doesn't mean there weren't people in the party out to get him. I believe Gerry Collins, who Albert had sacked from cabinet, travelled back from the European Parliament to vote, and sat on the front row for the meeting of the parliamentary party. Certainly there were those looking to see Albert defeated. But I wasn't one of them. In the end Mary McAleese won convincingly. Albert kept his composure, but he was very upset about the result. He had thought he was going to win until close towards the end. To miss out at the last minute really hurt. But the truth was that Mary McAleese was a serious, formidable candidate. She came with a late charge and quickly got people saying what a great candidate she was. She also appealed outside the party. The PDs liked her for herself and because she was not Albert. From every point of view, Mary McAleese was an excellent choice.

I was sitting beside Albert at the count and commiserated with him afterwards. Some of his supporters seemed to blame me for his defeat. They should have been asking why they hadn't run a better campaign for him. Their only criticism of me could be that I didn't go out there and win it on their behalf. There was no arm-twisting or ringing around. And of course I had to be careful not to offend

Michael O'Kennedy, with whom I had worked for years and who was also a trustee of the party. I'm afraid the conspiracy theorists who say we had this all worked out, keeping Mary McAleese back until the last minute, were just kidding themselves. I understood that it was hard on Albert, as he had already been through one big disappointment. But that's life in politics. And we all know that. Unfortunately in the years to come, Albert would never miss the opportunity to try and give me a kick when the chance arrived, and did so on several occasions. Most of them I ignored, but I was surprised and disappointed when he decided to have a crack at me during the 2007 general election, which could have damaged Fianna Fáil's chances of winning.

The presidential campaign itself went well. Winning 45 per cent of first preference votes, Mary McAleese easily beat her main rival Mary Banotti, with Dana, Adi Roche and Derek Nally trailing in behind. It was a tough campaign, but we had the best candidate and a strong team involving Noel Dempsey, Brian Lenihan Jnr, Noel Whelan, Martin Mackin, Tom Reddy and Brian Murphy. Her victory felt like a fresh start. Here was the party under my leadership with a great candidate for president who from her first day in office commanded the respect of the entire country. She has never been a Fianna Fáil president. She has always simply been the President. She has that kind of all-embracing dignity. Even in the campaign when people tried smearing her or throwing lines back at her about the Troubles, she kept her composure and grace under pressure. Her quiet diplomacy during the peace process would be vital. And she has extended the hand of friendship to all communities in the North, bringing people down to the Áras.

At our regular meetings, we always kept in touch about the peace process. We would discuss issues and how she might use her constitutional role in a way that would promote goodwill, cooperation and understanding. She was modern, efficient and very dynamic, in particular putting real effort and thought into her speeches, which would often challenge the easy line on controversial subjects. In particular, the speech she made at University College Cork on the ninetieth anniversary of 1916 is one of the best I've ever read. Martin, her husband, also established a role for himself, building close contacts with the Loyalist groups and organising small dinners and functions to bring them into the process. He worked on that very quietly and has never really been given the credit for it he deserves.

My monthly meetings with the President were always very enjoyable. After the business on the agenda, we would have a more informal conversation across a range of issues. Over a cup of tea, we talked about where she might be travelling and how she could extend our relationships abroad. For example, in the years leading up to enlargement, she helped build links with the new countries coming into the EU. I never found her anything other than helpful and proper. Sometimes it was a relief to get away from all the hustle of life in Government Buildings to sit down for a good talk with someone who was interested but wasn't really after you for anything. One issue that we did not succeed in bringing to fruition was a visit by Queen Elizabeth. In my view there is no doubt that eventually this will happen. I always made it clear that first we had to have the institutions of the Good Friday Agreement in place, as well as the devolution of policing in the North. Once this happened, it would allow us to issue a formal invitation and the fine details worked out. I was sure that Queen Elizabeth would want to lay a wreath at the War Memorial Gardens in Islandbridge. But we also wanted to make sure that she would lay a wreath at the Garden of Remembrance in Parnell Square. As it turned out, the visit didn't take place on my watch, although I sounded out my cabinet colleagues on the idea. What my dad would have thought about it, I hate to think.

Such influences of family and background have always been more important to me as a politician than most people have realised. In some ways my political life has always been a dialogue with my upbringing. Certainly that was the case on the economy. When I was growing up in Drumcondra in the 1950s and 60s, there were three big employers in the area. Lemon's Sweets, the button factory and the plastic mac factory between them employed over a thousand people. Even if not especially well paid, these jobs were vital during a time of high unemployment in the state. By the early 1980s, when I had just started out in national politics, all three had gone, ending with Lemon's. There was a lot of unemployment in the area, which in the north-east inner city was as high as 85 per cent. While poverty was bad enough, the lack of hope was even worse. That's why creating jobs was so important to me as a minister and after that as Taoiseach. Social partnership was a complex mechanism that generated all kinds of economic activity while allowing the government to get on with running the country. Effectively that was my remit for twenty-one years: helping to set it up in 1987 and then bringing it to 2008 under six agreements. Partnership was geared towards getting the country to the next phase of development. But above all it gave people jobs and self-respect. We went from a million people in jobs to more than two million. We introduced the minimum wage – something the Rainbow coalition had rejected. Reforming the tax system was just as crucial. Those on low salaries, even at the level of the new minimum wage, were still paying too much tax. That was something we tackled, bringing down tax rates across the board and taking thousands of people out of the tax net altogether.

By keeping discipline for two decades through national agreements, we worked together and made our economy one of the best performers in the EU and the industrialised world. During my years as Taoiseach, Ireland had the lowest level of unemployment in the EU; the second lowest national debt; the second highest minimum wage; the biggest spend in the EU on infrastructure; the fastest growth of all OECD countries in spending per capita on health; and the most generous tax and welfare system in the world for single-income families on the average industrial wages. Over that period Ireland finally caught up and surpassed average EU living standards. I will never regret those years of great success. Record economic growth helped drive social progress. It helped lift hundreds of thousands of people out of poverty, to increase pensions and child benefit, to modernise schools, health facilities, roads and communications infrastructure around our country and to create over 500,000 jobs.

But we were not profligate. We recorded budget surpluses in ten out of our eleven budgets during my time as Taoiseach. My approach was to balance sustained increases in spending against the need to reduce our national debt. The year before social partnership was established, 30 per cent of the entire tax take in the state was used to service the national debt. We managed to slash that to just over 4 per cent by my last full year as Taoiseach.

I never understood why some commentators said we were Thatcherite. It never made any sense to me. Seán Lemass used to say that Fianna Fáil was the real Labour Party. And I believe that. Throughout my political career I had thought that we were the only party capable of ensuring that the decent hard-working people of our country gained their reward from a more prosperous society. I have always believed that a healthy economy can do more for the marginalised than a depressed one. A rising tide lifts all boats.

Today we're faced with a huge economic challenge, but in so many ways we are better placed to tackle it than we were in the mid-1980s. That's down to the hard work of the Irish people and to our ability to act together.

We need this spirit as much today as we ever did.

11

THE BEST OF WEEKS,
THE WORST OF WEEKS

Every Taoiseach since Jack Lynch has come into office wanting to end the Troubles in the North. I was no different.

Peace talks in Belfast had been going on without much success throughout the autumn of 1997. We had identified a three-strand process, looking at internal Northern Ireland issues, North–South issues and British–Irish issues. Basically, nothing was agreed until everything was agreed. It was also understood that those talks would proceed on the basis of 'sufficient consensus': if there was a clear majority in both the Unionist and Nationalist communities, that was enough to move forward. The early stages of talks were frustrating. The parties just stuck to their usual positions. The UUP wouldn't even talk to Sinn Féin. But I kept plugging away with Tony Blair. International summits were always useful. Because we were talking about other issues, it gave Tony and me the chance to discuss Northern questions more informally on the margins of these meetings. In late November at a special Employment summit in Luxembourg, we had the chance to go over some of the key sticking points, such as prisoner release and how to get the UUP and Sinn Féin talking to each other. On difficult issues like these it was vital that we could communicate directly. Even if we couldn't solve the issues, it was important we always knew where we stood with one another. Progress was never going to come in a rush. We would get it inch by inch. 'The devil is in the detail' soon became a phrase we were sick of hearing. But it was true.

You also had to watch every single word. The week after I met Tony in Luxembourg, the new Minister for Foreign Affairs, David Andrews, put his foot in it. In a radio interview on 29 November, he said that North/South institutions would be 'not unlike a government'. David Trimble went ballistic and phoned me to say that Andrews should go. A few days later, Andrews met Trimble to apologise for his misuse of words, but it was a bad moment. Andrews himself came to see me to offer to resign. 'I think it might be for the best,' he told me. 'Not at all,' I replied. 'You know what these guys are like. It'll be any old excuse.' But it was difficult. I had brought David in to steady the ship after all the trauma of Ray Burke. While Burke would have been reading every last brief, David was never as interested in the detail. He was more relaxed. He also had a bad back problem around that time and he didn't like sitting at his desk or at the negotiating table for too long, so he would often be up and walking around. Most Unionist politicians didn't like him. Burke was tough, but they respected his intensity. Andrews they found a bit offhand, and they certainly didn't like his Republican background. He irritated them with his manner. But in fairness to David, he stuck with it. The incident brought the two of us closer together. I backed him up with the Unionists and he knew that he had my confidence.

That was just one task in a whole autumn and winter of difficulties. Parties were either pulling out of the talks or threatening to do so. Then we had to deal with a Republican splinter group, the Real IRA. That was a worrying development, because although it was known that there were differences emerging within the Provos, this formalised them. It was a challenge to the whole project. Intelligence briefings were telling us that the new group could draw off significant numbers. These included senior figures like Michael McKevitt, who had been Quartermaster General of the IRA. They were going round the country holding meetings, drumming up opposition to the peace process and raising money for arms. It was all very unwelcome. When I met Tony for the Luxembourg European Council in December, we were both very concerned. 'We've got to push this thing forward,' I said, 'because otherwise we're going to lose the Republicans.' We both agreed that in the new year we would try to produce a fresh document.

Part of the problem with the peace process was never knowing when something was going to happen. Christmas that year had been reasonably quiet. Then on 27 December I got a phone call in St Luke's on my way out the door to the Leopardstown Races. Billy Wright, the founder of the dissident Loyalist group the LVF, had been murdered in the Maze Prison by the INLA. Wright was infamous in the Catholic community and, even though he was controversial within Loyalism, I knew his death would create serious tensions. In the end, it was Mo Mowlam who sorted it out. In January 1998 she went into the Maze itself and persuaded Loyalist prisoners not to carry out their threat to wreck the negotiations. That was a brave thing to do. If she had failed, her credibility would have been completely undermined. When Tony told me what she was planning to do I was speechless. Fair play to her though: she was an incredibly courageous woman and this was just one example of it. In the thick of the final peace negotiations, Tony as prime minister naturally came to the fore. But he was always quick to point out that the work Mo did over a long period got us to a position where a deal was possible. That was a massive legacy to leave behind when she finally lost her battle with cancer in 2005.

All this time, painstaking work was going on behind the scenes to move things forward. I was lucky to have a fantastic team of officials working with me. They were led by Paddy Teahon (Secretary General, Department of the Taoiseach), Dermot Gallagher (Second Secretary General, Department of Foreign Affairs) and Tim Dalton (Secretary General, Department of Justice, Equality and Law Reform). My special adviser, Martin Mansergh, also played a vital liaison role. There was a dedicated talks team in Foreign Affairs, coordinated by Tim O'Connor. We had people in Belfast led by David Donoghue and in the embassy in London under the ambassador, Ted Barrington. On the British side, the key official was Jonathan Powell, Tony's Chief of Staff, along with John Holmes, the Principal Private Secretary at No. 10, and Quentin Thomas, Bill Jeffrey and Jonathan Stephens in the Northern Ireland Office. Alastair Campbell was as central as ever.

By January 1998, we had a one-page document intended as an outline of an acceptable agreement. After the two governments presented the document, I was never off the phone with Tony and the party leaders trying to finalise the draft. Gerry Adams, in particular, was worried that the language on the North/South Ministerial Council didn't put enough emphasis on executive functions. By and large, though, the document was seen as a significant move towards getting an agreement. On 16 January I formally wrote to Tony suggesting that we make the document the basis for a preliminary draft agreement. It might only have been the heads of an agreement, but at least it showed the range of ground that we were going to cover. I remember sitting down with Dermot Gallagher in particular, poring over the detail of this, figuring out where we could get movement on all the various issues.

Around the same time Martin Mansergh and the Attorney General, David Byrne, began working on new language for Articles 2 and 3 of the constitution. They were vital as well in making sure that the parliamentary party remained fully involved and understood the line the government was taking. Accompanied by David and Martin, I held a series of four meetings with members of the parliamentary party early that year, bringing them through the proposed new language on Articles 2 and 3 and explaining what we were trying to achieve in the negotiations. To give up Articles 2 and 3 was huge for everyone and we all needed to be clear about why this constitutional change was on the negotiating table. David and Martin were superb in those meetings, which were vital in making sure that we went into the formal talks with the support of our own parliamentary party.

David would also be vital in finding a solution to how exactly we might put the proposal to amend Articles 2 and 3 before the people. We were confident that many in the South would be prepared to abandon the claim of sovereignty over Northern Ireland, but only in exchange for securing the full terms of any deal we might reach in the negotiations. David devised a step-by-step constitutional process, which involved requesting the people, in referendum, to amend Articles 2 and 3 in specified terms but only if the North voted 'yes' to any British Irish agreement. In effect, the people would approve the proposed Articles 2 and 3, but the amendments would only come into effect when the government declared that the terms of an agreement had become operational. This was a radical approach and the first time such a procedure would be adopted to amend the Constitution. It was typical of the imaginative way that David approached his position as Attorney General.

This was just one example of the work being done on all sides to keep the peace process moving forward. Much of this was about building trust, getting the parties to deal with one another. The British and Irish sides worked well together even when there were differences. For me, though, there was one massive issue of trust that had to be faced. I wasn't one for insisting that there had to be an inquiry into every violent act carried out by the British security forces. You couldn't forget the past, but you also had to move on. Sometimes that was hard, even unfair. And I knew that there had been victims. But what I wanted from Tony was recognition that this kind of behaviour had happened.

On 23 January 1998 I went to Derry to lay a wreath in the Bogside for those who had been killed on Bloody Sunday and to meet some of the relatives. I called once again for a full inquiry into the events of 30 January 1972. An apology would have been nice, but what I really wanted was the facts to be made known. By this stage there was a lot of media speculation that Tony was planning to make an announcement about Bloody Sunday in the House of Commons the following week. It looked as if he was going to say no to any inquiry. The next few days were among the most intense and difficult of our relationship.

As for so many of my generation, Bloody Sunday had left a huge mark. I had been there on the day the British Embassy was burnt down. The events in Derry had driven a lot of people, including friends of mine, to give up on politics and to join the IRA. The awful events of Bloody Sunday had been a blow against the civil rights movement that had done so much good and brave work since the mid-sixties. So when the Widgery report came out in April 1972, throwing whitewash over the actions of the British Army, and somehow trying to blame the victims for what happened to them – well, let's just say that was a turning point in the Troubles. If the British weren't going to come clean about this one, then it told us they didn't have the level of seriousness we needed to move the peace process along. So this was a hugely significant moment.

If the call for an inquiry was rejected, that would have soured the relationship between Britain and Ireland, and between me and Tony – probably for good. That led to a series of very sharp exchanges with Tony. He was coming under fierce pressure from his officials not to concede. I remember talking to him in the car a couple of days before he was due to make his statement to the House of Commons. I made the driver pull over by the side of the road so I could concentrate fully. He told me there would be uproar if he did. I told him we may as well just give up then, because what those paratroopers had done was horrendous. 'What will happen if

I can't do it?' he asked. 'Then you may as well phone back in ten years,' I replied.

In fairness, I think Tony really wanted to have the inquiry. And I was certainly aware that speaking bluntly to him, more bluntly than I had ever spoken to him before, was not going to be unhelpful. He could go to his own people and say, 'Bertie's hopping mad on this one . . .' More importantly, it meant that he understood me. Usually everything in the North was compromise and shades of grey. But this was a black-and-white issue for us. The Irish government had presented a detailed analysis of the events of Bloody Sunday to the British government. It showed conclusively that a case remained to be answered.

So I was pleased when Tony phoned me the night before the anniversary to say there was going to be a new inquiry. I thanked him for what he was doing. We both knew it was a significant moment. It had been a hard call for him to make when he was under so much pressure to say no. Officials in London were telling us there were lots of people on the British side who didn't want this dragged up again. Better just to bury it. In the end, though, I couldn't see how anyone could disagree with what he said in the Commons: 'It is in the interests of everyone that the truth is established and told.' 'That's all we want, Tony,' I told him afterwards, 'the truth.' The new inquiry gave fresh impetus to the talks and it helped our credibility in the North. Everyone knew I was saying this had to happen. If it hadn't, that would have left me looking weak.

This turned out to be important, because the next couple of months were bad. The Loyalist Ulster Democratic Party (UDP) were ejected from the talks following the murder of three Catholics by the Ulster Freedom Fighters. Then attention turned to Sinn Féin after two murders were attributed to the IRA. I told Tony on the phone that we would support the expulsion of Sinn Féin if it was clear the IRA had been involved. We had also just kicked the UDP out, so we had to be even-handed. If there were problems with the Shinners, they would be treated the same as everyone else. You would have got officials worrying about issues like this, but as soon as Tony and I talked, it was sorted out. More and more that would become the way things were worked. Cutting through the bureaucracy, and dealing with difficulties directly. Sinn Féin were kicked out, but were expected to rejoin talks on 9 March if the governments were convinced the ceasefire was being fully and continuously observed.

When Loyalists murdered two friends, one Catholic and one Protestant, sitting in a bar in Poyntzpass, Co. Armagh, we all could see how events might spiral without progress in the talks. As soon as there is no political activity or dialogue, everything is thrown into a vacuum. And as soon as there is a vacuum, you're likely to get more killing. There had been a cycle of mayhem in the North for so long. Everyone had the jitters, just waiting for the next incident to happen. Discussions about letting Sinn Féin back into the negotiations were very tense. Eventually they were allowed to rejoin on 23 March. Two days later, Senator George Mitchell, who was chairing the talks, publicly announced a deadline of 9 April for the agreement. 'It could be discussed for another two years or for another twenty years,' he said. 'It isn't that there hasn't been enough time, it is that there has not been a decision required. I believe the time for that is now.'

That kind of tough action was typical of Mitchell. It had been a real commitment taking on the task. When he first put a set of principles in place, he was treated with contempt by some of the parties at the talks. There was a great long debate about whether they would even allow him to chair the meetings at all. This was a guy who had been Majority Leader in the US Senate. But he just took it on the chin, let them abuse him until they had blown themselves out, and then got on with the job. I was impressed with that. He wasn't just some high-powered American coming in to swan around. He was a serious player who was going to get stuck in. But he also made it clear that he wasn't going to hang about wasting his time on all this. His wife, Heather, had given birth the previous October, so he had an additional reason to want to be at home. He had allowed the talks go on since the late summer, but now he was saying that it was decision time. I thought that was the right approach. Put a time frame on it. The North seemed to be taking up every hour of my day. So why not try to bring this to fruition, and see what happens?

Mitchell's involvement was an indication of how committed the Clinton administration was to the peace process. When I visited Washington for St Patrick's Day a few weeks before the final negotiations were due to begin in Belfast, I had a long session with the President. It was clear that he had immersed himself in the situation, and I was able to talk him through our concerns and priorities. Later on, that would become important at the most intensive moments of the talks in Belfast, when the President stayed up all night to encourage the various parties to take the last remaining steps to peace. I also had a breakfast meeting with the Secretary of State, Madeleine Albright, and individual meetings with Senator Edward Kennedy, Senator Chris Dodd and Senator Patrick Leahy, who were all influential supporters of the peace process.

On the evening of Wednesday 1 April, I travelled from Dublin to Downing Street to meet Tony Blair. Afterwards I had to admit that there remained 'large disagreements which could not be cloaked'. Officials from both governments had been in intensive talks throughout the week about Strand 2 of the process – the North/South issues. Those were very difficult discussions, as we were nowhere near a draft that could be given to the parties. Our talks overlapped with the Asia–Europe summit that Tony was hosting. Things became almost comical. There were endless sessions and dinners. We would be ducking out to talk and all his officials would be hovering around, trying to get him back into the room and do his social duties. 'Yeah, be there in a minute,' he would say, which would keep them away for a while, but soon they would be back again fussing around him. I don't know what all the other leaders thought of this. One who seemed to think it amusing was the Chinese premier, Zhu Rongji. Unusually for a summit of this kind, I sat next to him for all the working sessions, the lunches and the dinners. He had been to Ireland earlier in his career, so he chatted enthusiastically about that. But as the hours went by, he noticed that I was getting notes passed along from Tony. I was scribbling replies, and then sending them back down the table. He would have been well within his rights to be annoyed, but in fact he seemed to find it funny. He asked what we were discussing. I explained to him about Northern Ireland and the talks that were due to take place the following week. He sat listening intently as I explained about the peace process and a little bit of our eight hundred years of history. He was fascinated by this, and told me something about Hong Kong, which had been returned to China only the previous July.

By the Friday evening, it was clear that we weren't going to get any agreement on a draft text. Tony phoned Mitchell to ask for a delay. Officials would keep going at it over the weekend. Tony and I would be in constant touch by phone. I would be holding meetings with some of the parties in Dublin. Everything was a race against time. When I got back to the airport, I was already running late. I was due to attend a constituency Mass in the Church of Christ the King, Cabra. I had planned to call into my mother on the way, but we were too far behind schedule. As the car shot past Church Avenue coming in from the airport, I made a mental note to call into her the next evening. I had meetings scheduled all day, but would drop in afterwards. That next morning, I was in St Luke's at seven-thirty to start my meetings. Martin McGuinness was coming in to me, only then I got a message that there had been a mix-up and he wouldn't be there until later. I was annoyed, because I had even asked my secretaries, Sandra Cullagh and Olive Melvin, to come in specially to make breakfast for us. We ate the breakfast and then I went to Government Buildings for a meeting with the SDLP.

It was around midday, while I was in that meeting, that I got the message that my mother been taken ill with a heart attack. She had been rushed to the Mater, but never regained consciousness. I felt a stab of guilt. I still feel it to this day. Over that weekend, I was right around the corner. I passed the end of our road on the way in from the airport. I had sat down and eaten breakfast in the morning after the mix-up over the meeting with McGuinness. The house is only a five-minute walk from St Luke's, a minute by car. I could have been in to see her. I was busy, the schedule was always so tight, but you say to yourself, 'You should have made the time.' Maybe I should have gone home rather than attend the constituency Mass. Then on Sunday, if I had gone in early at any stage, I would have got to see her. That's how it should have been. I went to the Mater that afternoon, and stayed through most of the night. I was glad to have the chance to hold her hand for one last time. My mother died around six o'clock on Monday morning.

I don't really know how I got through that week. I suppose you don't think about it, you just get on with it. In the hours after Mam's death, I decided to keep going and did not cancel scheduled meetings with opposition leaders on the impending negotiations. They were kind in sympathising with me, but I made it clear that it was easier for me if we got on with business. Then I was flying backwards and forwards between Dublin and Belfast, sometimes several times in the one day. My mother was buried in the Republican plot in Glasnevin with my father. We were at the graveside just at the end of the service, when one of my officials appeared. I could see he was embarrassed, but he had to tell me we needed to go, because we were flying to Belfast half an hour later. On the way I went up to where the family were going to have a meal in the Skylon Hotel and all I could do was walk the queue and thank everyone for being there. Then I had to leave. I know my mother would have understood, but I remember saying to myself, 'Jesus, is there no other way of doing this?' You can only do your best, but sometimes you know that however hard you try, your best isn't quite good enough. Even once the talks were over, the following weekend, I didn't really get a moment. I was up at my mother's house. My brothers and sisters had given me the letter that

Mam had written to us, which was unopened. They had left it to me to read out, not because I was the Taoiseach – they never cared much about that when it came to the family – but because I was the youngest. It was very emotional reading that, but immediately afterwards, a phone call came in from Kofi Annan about the peace process. Even in that moment of grief, with the family together, politics was never far away.

This period of great personal sadness had coincided with an extremely tense and dramatic time in the peace process. On the Tuesday evening of the week my mother died, Tony Blair had phoned asking me to come to Hillsborough for a breakfast meeting the following day. He had just arrived in the North himself and believed that the talks were in danger of collapsing. That was when he made his comment in a press conference about the 'hand of history' on his shoulder. It was typical Tony, who always had a liking for one-liners. When he phoned me that evening, he was really apologetic, because he knew that I had been at my mother's removal. But he said that he believed I had to get there as soon as possible. I had needed a walk to clear my head, so I was on the phone for around two hours to Tony and then George Mitchell, as I was walking up and down Griffith Avenue. Mitchell couldn't understand how we had been talking for so long and I was still on the same avenue. It's miles long and I had walked both sides.

Meeting Tony meant leaving in the early hours of the following morning. It was a frank discussion. He told me Adams had said 'I'm out' if prisoner releases were linked to decommissioning. He also outlined Unionist opposition to the Strand 2 draft. 'Trimble's not bluffing,' Tony told me. 'He's about to walk.' Tony wanted the North/South part of the agreement watered down, but I stressed that substantial North/South cooperation was fundamental for us. 'What we're doing with Articles 2 and 3 is historic,' I told him. 'I'm not having the North/South institutions turning into chat shows.' The text could be revisited, but the substance had to be maintained. Any revisions would have to be made in the context of the overall draft. 'To be honest, Tony,' I said, 'if we get an agreement people are going to wonder what all the fuss was about the North/South stuff. It's not like we're not already doing it in the EU.'

When I arrived at Castle Buildings, something happened that touched me deeply. As I was walking in, all the TV camera operators and the photographers put their cameras down as a mark of respect to me on the death of my mother. Then Eamonn Mallie, a senior reporter in Belfast, said a few words about how sorry they were for my loss and how everybody understood the personal sacrifice I was making in attending the talks. I was moved by this. It is in the nature of our different professions that politicians and the media sometimes have a confrontational relationship. But we are all just trying to do our jobs to the best of our abilities. This was a shared moment of solidarity at a very difficult time in my life. Although inevitably we would soon pick up our swords again to resume battle, I never forgot this demonstration of kindness and empathy.

Inside the talks, the atmosphere at Castle Buildings was absolutely awful by this stage. Everyone had long faces, walking around looking like they knew we were going to fail. People were quoting the opinion poll from the *Belfast Telegraph* saying that only 5 per cent thought the talks would be successful. I kept saying that I knew the odds were against us, but that there was no stone I would leave unturned to try and succeed. I met Sinn Féin, and immediately afterwards went back to Dublin for my mother's funeral. By the time I got back to Castle Buildings, around 6 p.m., all hell had broken loose. Jonathan Powell had given Mitchell new language about linking 'participation in democratic bodies' to decommissioning and making significant concessions to the Unionist position around security, policing and justice issues. We went ballistic. It wasn't just the substance that rankled. It was going to the chairman behind our back. I told Tony frankly that if that's the way we were doing business, then the pessimists were right, and we weren't going to get anywhere. Powell is actually a sound guy and he stepped up right away to say that he had made a mistake and apologised. That seemed to break the atmosphere.

When Tony and I met Trimble and the UUP later that night, we had a very positive discussion about Strand 2, including the areas identified for cooperation and the various implementation bodies and institutions. Exhausted by the end of the night, I flew home to Dublin. On a point of principle, I never slept in the North, always returning to my own jurisdiction. I only changed that after the Good Friday Agreement. It was a big deal for me.

At breakfast at Hillsborough the next morning, Tony was annoyed that the Irish and UUP delegations had not made further progress to agree language on Strand 2. I had to tell him frankly that the attitude of the UUP had left a lot to be desired. Liz O'Donnell and John Taylor had been having a right ding-dong across the table. Liz is forthright, and Taylor really didn't know how to handle her. The main point was that they did not want Westminster legislation on implementation bodies. We saw that as crucial, because otherwise what was to stop the Unionists blocking it in the Northern Assembly?

Once we returned to Castle Buildings that Thursday morning, it was non-stop until 5 p.m. the following day. To be honest, we could hardly have found anywhere worse to do it. Castle Buildings is a dreadful place. The food was terrible. Corridors were narrow and badly laid out, with low ceilings. It was claustrophobic. There never seemed to be any fresh air or decent light. Every party had their own rooms, which were all over the place. So there was a lot of toing and froing, going from one meeting to the next. Stale air, bad food, no light: to be honest it was not a place to lift my spirits when I was still mourning my mother. To make matters worse, there seemed to be no escape even for five minutes. We weren't allowed out into the grounds for security reasons. I've always been one for a walk when I need time to think, so it was a nightmare being trapped inside this dump of a building. On one occasion, after being up all night negotiating, I got fed up with being inside and just barged through a security door to get out into the gardens with Dermot Hobbs, my security guy, and Joe Lennon, my press secretary. It was a beautiful crisp morning, with fresh snow on the ground, and we spent a few minutes watching the rooks making their nests. For a moment I was back in All Hallows. Then a couple of burly security guys came running over, wanting to know what the hell was going on. They would have given anyone else a right bollocking, but there are certain advantages to being a prime minister. When I told them I needed a bit more air, they reluctantly agreed, but insisted on remaining there with us.

I might have been trapped in Castle Buildings for the most part, but so was everyone else, and that suited my negotiating style. It was just like the old days with the trade unions. Tony's negotiating style was a bit different to mine. He tended to stick to his own rooms. I preferred being mobile, using casual conversations as well as formal negotiations. You might be heading off to see Trimble and suddenly Adams would be coming down the corridor. So if an opportunity presented itself for a quiet word, I took it. Those conversations were important, because they just happened, no agenda or anything. I had learnt from my younger days that negotiations under pressure give you the chance to get to know how people tick, and you can use that to get over any trust issues. That had a knock-on into the real meetings too. I remember one time with a Loyalist group, when there were Republicans in the room too, and one of them turned to me and said, 'We've worked out that you're the only one in the room who hasn't killed anyone.' What the hell do you say to that, except get down to business. It was chilling, but that's what you have to do if you want a deal.

The real trick was to keep everything moving. There were discussions with the UUP going on here, and with the Shinners there, I had to make sure that Mitchell was kept informed, had to see what Tony was doing on prisoners, let him know where I was on Articles 2 and 3: all these balls had to be kept in the air, and obviously if you dropped one, the whole lot would fall to the floor. I had believed all along that everything was connected, and we just had to get the different bits to join up. Sure enough, that Thursday we started to make headway with the language on North/South, which saw Trimble move towards acceptance of Westminster legislation. There was one moment when we pushed Tony a bit too far with our draft language and he slammed the paper down on the table in a rage, shouting, 'What the bloody hell are you all playing at?' I knew we were chancing our arm a bit, but even so we managed to get the Unionists to accept some of the new language. Eventually, around midnight, a deal was finally done between the two governments on the full text of Strand 2.

That had an impact on Strand 1 – internal Northern Ireland issues. The UUP and the SDLP had been going through the motions on that for most of the day, but when they heard we were making progress on Strand 2, it seemed to give them a kick up the backside. They did a deal around 1 a.m. John Hume and Séamus Mallon came to see me absolutely delighted. I had never seen John so buoyant. He is a very serious guy and had been through a lot to bring peace in the North. Now he told me he thought that a deal could be reached. As a backdrop to all this, Ian Paisley had led a group of protesters up to the gates of Castle Buildings around midnight and had been given a load of abuse from a group of Progressive Unionist Party (PUP) supporters. It really did seem like the tide was turning.

These high spirits lasted about five minutes. We had been hearing talk during the day that Sinn Féin were thinking about walking. I wasn't too concerned, because they were always saying that. Tony and I had arranged to meet them in the early hours, but then they presented us with a massive document that included more than fifty questions they wanted answered. Mo Mowlam went absolutely crazy. I've never seen anything quite like it. She was shouting and swearing at Adams. She was sometimes accused of being too close to Sinn Féin, but no one who saw her that night would have said so. She could be quite brash, which wasn't always to Tony's taste.

When everything had calmed down, I started going through the points with Sinn Féin one by one. These were examined and replied to in detail through the night. Adams kept getting regular calls from President Clinton encouraging him to keep trying. By dawn we had removed most of the obstacles and, after my encounter with the rooks in the gardens, were set for a meeting of the two governments and Sinn Féin to thrash out the remaining sticking points. We decided to keep this meeting small, which meant that Mo Mowlam and David Andrews would not attend. David was relaxed about it, but I could see that Mo was hopping mad.

When we went into that meeting with Sinn Féin, everyone knew what was at stake. Prisoner release was the big issue. The whole deal could turn on this one. In a way it was Tony's call, because we only had a small number of prisoners in our jurisdiction, and that would prove difficult enough, especially when dealing with the killers of Jerry McCabe. But it was huge for Tony and only he knew how far he could go. And as it happened, he went much further than I thought he would or could. In the end it came down to a question of trust between Tony and Sinn Féin. The atmosphere in the room between the four of us had been professional and workmanlike. Sometimes in these meetings there can be a great deal of grandstanding. But this time it was strangely calm and focused. It was like everyone in the room suddenly realised that Tony's 'hand of history' was really there. We came out of that meeting believing that an agreement would be reached. Sinn Féin were saying they would have to go back to a special Ard Fheis, but they weren't threatening to walk out or saying the deal was unacceptable. Afterwards, Adams generously thanked me for the effort I had put in.

Later that morning, I had a set-to with David Trimble in a meeting with Tony Blair. David wanted to give me a lesson in Irish history, delivered with his usual charm, but that did not bother me. For years in these kinds of circumstances, I had developed the trick of looking for a picture on the wall, and then thinking about the inspiration for it and how the artist might have gone about painting it. Around the world, I had often found some beautiful art to consider. Paddy Teahon, on the other hand, looked as if he would like to hit Trimble. To be honest, I think it was David trying his luck, hoping we would be so desperate for a deal that we might water down proposals on the North/South bodies. When he realised we weren't going to do that, he backed off. It was typical of David. He was a big one for respect and was very sensitive to 'proper' behaviour, especially towards himself. I don't think I ever saw him with the top button of his shirt undone or heard him curse. So I never really understood why he always felt he had to get so excited to make his point. I suppose that was part of his make-up. He rubbed some people up the wrong way, and I had my fair share of difficult meetings with him, but eventually we would get on all right. I always particularly admired David for having the strength of character to negotiate with Sinn Féin, when his close friend, the Rev. Robert Bradford, had been gunned down in broad daylight by the IRA in 1981.

By the morning of Friday 10 April, we thought we were close to a final text of the overall agreement. Mitchell's team were asked to put the document together and to prepare copies. We had wanted to bring it to a plenary session that morning, but because of the sheer bulk of documentation which had to be prepared and copied, it took time for Mitchell to circulate the text. Tony and I were worrying that the final session was going to be far from a formality. We had already got word about divisions within the UUP. While the Unionists were in a meeting, I briefly left Castle Buildings to go to a Good Friday service. The parishioners, ignoring the security detail, were very welcoming when I chatted to them afterwards, wishing me luck in the negotiations and asking if we were going to get a deal. I remember there was one woman there with her young fella who looked like he couldn't wait to get home to play with his football. It struck me at the time that with a bit of luck we might be able to give him a future where 'the Troubles' were just a history lesson.

The lesson you learn with the North is never to take your eye off things for a minute. By the time I got back to Castle Buildings, the UUP, as we had feared, had had a bust-up about the final text. Mitchell postponed the plenary session. Over the next hours, an intensive process of bilateral contacts took place between Tony Blair and David Trimble. It was Tony's job to deliver the Unionists, but I offered all the support I could, including meeting Trimble to try and reassure him. Late that afternoon, Tony sent Trimble a personal letter offering assurances about decommissioning. Trimble called the chairman to say that he was ready to sign. That seemed to clinch it.

George Mitchell opened the plenary session just after 5 p.m. It was a strange occasion. The TV cameras had been let in, so the informality that had grown up even at times of high drama had suddenly gone. Now we were all on show. Usually at the end of these things, there's great humour and a bit of messing. Looking back on the pictures now, we all look very serious, like we felt the historical importance of the occasion. But partly it was because we were all exhausted. The effort that had gone into those last few days and weeks was massive. The strain was beginning to show. And there was tension as well. I had it in the back of my mind that someone might want to open up another point. So when the chairman asked everyone to state their position, I was holding my breath. I knew Sinn Féin were not going to say that they supported the agreement, or that they could speak for the IRA, but they came up with a form of words that showed they were not opposed to it. That allowed Mitchell to say that the meeting was adjourned '*sine die*'.

I looked at Tony. He looked at me. We had arranged it beforehand. While the others were still sitting around or shaking hands, we jumped out of our seats and went through the door to where the microphones were waiting. What was vital was to get the message out that this was an agreement. It was not a stage on the way to agreement. This was it. The deal was done. Now we moved to implementation. As I was walking down with Tony, there were no profound words about what we had done. I told him I was looking forward to going home to my family. He wanted to get to Spain, where Cherie

With Ted Kennedy –
a great Irish-American

With Nicolas Sarkozy before the
match between Ireland and France at
the 2007 Rugby World Cup

With Pope Benedict XVI

With Hillary Clinton,
an important influence
in the Peace Process

Simply the best. With Sir Alex Ferguson

Put me in, coach!

GAA All-Star Awards with
members of the Dublin Panel

With Celia Larkin

Inspecting the guard of brave Irish men and women serving with the UN forces

Visit to St Columba's School, New Delhi, India.
With John O'Donoghue, Mary Hanafin and Micheál Martin

G8 Conference, 2004.
The man in the yellow trousers.

Social partnership at work.
Between Bill Clinton and Newt Gingrich

With George Bush at the EU/US
Summit at Dromoland Castle, 2004

Tony Blair, 'a true friend to Ireland'

The Day of Welcomes, Farmleigh,
1 May 2004

'I have to shake
hands with this man!'
With Ian Paisley, April 2007

Early days in the
Peace Process.
With John Hume
and Gerry Adams

Georgina's wedding, 2003. David Keoghan, Miriam, Nicky Byrne, Georgina, Cecelia, BA

New additions to the family. Jay and Rocco, 2007

'Ireland is at peace.' Addressing a Joint Meeting of the US Congress, April 2008

'Ireland's hour has come.' Westminster, May 2007

Speaking for Europe. UN AIDS Conference

Three in a row. Accepting the Seal of Office from President McAleese in 2007

My last Cabinet Meeting, May 2008

'Handing on a tradition to the future': St Catherine's Infant School, Cabra, 2009

and the kids were waiting for him. But the negotiations established a deep bond between us. That would be vital in what turned out to be the years of intensive talks that lay ahead, trying to unblock the many obstacles to implementation.

A room had been set aside so that we could sign the agreement immediately, again to make sure that no one would try to reopen the negotiations. I hadn't seen the cover to what we were about to sign, which the British had entitled 'The Belfast Agreement'. 'It's not the Belfast Agreement,' I said to Tony, 'it's the Good Friday Agreement.' Tony is very religious, so that appealed to him. Eventually it got the official title, 'The Belfast Agreement signed on Good Friday'. But to this day, it is known around the world as the Good Friday Agreement. Sometimes I was asked why I had worn a black tie to sign the agreement. Of course, it was a mark of respect for my mother.

Flying back to Dublin that night was strange for me. Someone produced a bottle of champagne and there was a mood of great celebration on the plane. I shared that, because I knew we had achieved something amazing over those few days. I was pleased that I had held it together all week, but I was still also in mourning. The intensity of the negotiations; shuttling backwards and forwards between Dublin and Belfast; attending my mother's funeral between meetings. It had all been a strain. When we arrived back at the airport, there was a crowd of TDs and supporters waiting to meet us. That was very moving. I had never believed in all that rent-a-crowd nonsense, but on this occasion it was clearly spontaneous and I was glad to see everyone there. John Bowman from RTÉ had turned up as well and I agreed to record an interview with him for the sake of the archives. Perhaps it was only on my return that I realised how much the Good Friday Agreement meant to people. Everyone had been watching the negotiations on television throughout the night. Seeing all those faces of colleagues, friends and family was very moving. Later, President McAleese phoned with congratulations, as did Ted Kennedy. There are not many moments like these in life when you feel that you've done your best and everyone is grateful for the effort you have made.

There was one moment, though, that I had been dreading. The car took me from the airport, back to St Luke's. Passing Church Avenue was very difficult. The whole week had been a blur. Now I was back and my mother was not at home waiting to hear all about it. She would have been quizzing me and wanting to know what it all meant. One of our last discussions in the week before she died had been about Articles 2 and 3, when she had asked about what I was getting in exchange for rewriting the Constitution.

Going by the top of the road made me realise that so much had changed in the last few days. It had been the best of weeks. It had been the worst of weeks. We were on the road to peace in the North. And Drumcondra, the place that means more to me than anywhere else, had suddenly become emptier.

12

PS, I LOVE YOU

Two steps forward, one step back. That always seemed to be the story with the Northern peace process. Sometimes it felt more like one step forward, two back.

On 22 May, the people of Ireland, North and South, voted to endorse the Good Friday Agreement. The vote was 71 per cent in favour in the North and 94 per cent in favour in the South. 'The decision of the people of Ireland, Nationalist and Unionist, to endorse the Good Friday Agreement represents an historic watershed,' I said afterwards, 'between a past riven by political division and a new future based on mutual respect, concord and agreement.' However, it soon became clear that there were still some who remained committed to violence and hatred.

At 3.10 p.m. on Saturday 15 August, the latest in a series of bomb attacks took place in the centre of Omagh, killing twenty-nine people, including a woman pregnant with twins. Another man injured in the blast died of his wounds two weeks later. The Real IRA claimed responsibility for the bomb on the following Tuesday, although they denied intending to kill anyone. We had been getting reports from the security services that the Republican dissidents were well organised.

That was one of the reasons we were worried about them. Now they had committed one of the worst acts of terrorism in the bloody history of the Troubles. The 500lb car bomb had been left outside S D Kells, a shop where children went for their school uniforms. The reaction across the whole island was one of disgust and revulsion.

Exactly a week afterwards, Tony Blair and I attended a memorial service in Omagh. We agreed that the horrendous tragedy had to be used to push the peace process forward. We also agreed that we both had to come down on these dissident groups like a ton of bricks. Following ratification of the Good Friday Agreement, Martin Mansergh and Father Alex Reid had been in talks to try and persuade Republican dissidents to cease further violence. The INLA a week before Omagh had indicated their intention of calling a ceasefire later in the month. The political case for opposition to the agreement, claiming the backing of international law, was put forward at a meeting in July by the 32-County Sovereignty Movement, which was aligned with the Real IRA. This was responded to and refuted, but efforts to stop the bombing campaign had clearly had no effect. Now I laid out the other option for them in new provisions to strengthen the Offences Against the State Acts. I explicitly left open the possibility of internment. Omagh had been a terrible reminder of what these people could do. None of us were prepared to go back to that. By 7 September, the Real IRA and the INLA had both announced ceasefires.

Even before Omagh, the situation had been strained. There had been all the usual tension around Drumcree during the marching season. The Orangemen had been banned from entering the Garvaghy Road by the new Parades Commission. Inevitably, violence and protests followed in Loyalist areas throughout the North. Then, on Sunday 12 July, three young Catholic boys from the Quinn family in Ballymoney, Co. Antrim, were killed when their house was petrol-bombed. That was an horrific event. Of course it was condemned, but then these terrible things always were. People were sick of words.

They wanted things to change. The vote in favour of the Good Friday Agreement had been a command to all political leaders to begin the work of peace. Omagh, the killing of the Quinn lads: these were proof that not everyone wanted to listen to what the people North and South were saying.

One person who wanted to add his voice to that of the people was President Bill Clinton. He arrived for a three-day visit in September and paid his respects at Omagh. That was really important, because it gave the seal of approval of the United States to the whole process. It said that the men of violence were not going to derail us. This had been a terrible tragedy, but the President was there to encourage the population in the North to stick with the initiative. One thing that was obvious to everyone during the visit was how up to speed Clinton was on the whole Northern question. Certainly you could see how he empathised with people. He held the hands of survivors or the families of victims, and you could see he was personally affected by it. There was real emotion there. But when he talked in private about the problems we faced, he wasn't fuzzy about encouraging us to do our best. He was incredibly hard-headed and practical. He had kept in close touch with George Mitchell during the negotiations surrounding the agreement, and stayed up all night throughout the talks on Holy Thursday and Good Friday. Throughout that process he had rung Tony or me regularly to see how it was all going. If we needed to talk to him, it was surprisingly easy to get through to him in the White House. Obviously I would only call him if it was something of substance, but when I needed him on the line, he was there.

And he had a great grasp of the situation. He got to know individuals, he was even fluent in all the abbreviations of the various parties, which is never easy at the best of times. He never seemed to get his UUPs mixed up with his DUPs, or worse, with the UVF. So he knew who was where and had a very good feel for the personalities involved. And this wasn't participation from afar. He came to the island of Ireland an unprecedented three times during his presidency, and also made an emotional return a few months after he left office. That was the measure of his commitment to the peace process.

For me, part of the fascination of Bill was the way he would grasp the issues. Obviously he was well briefed, but it was more than that. He had an instinct for what was involved in decommissioning, he knew the issues of putting arms beyond use, and could decode the language of the paramilitaries. And that wasn't just on the North. I was at a dinner with him once while he talked about the problems of India and Pakistan, with their various sects and groups. That's not an issue that a Taoiseach has to deal with in any great depth, but I came away from that occasion feeling I understood the problems of the region and it triggered my own thoughts about parallels with the North. It was like Bill had drawn a picture in my mind. Obviously there's a trick to it, that ability to clarify without making it simplistic.

With Bill there was real insight and that inspires confidence. I remember in the early hours of the Good Friday negotiations, he was on the phone to me, to Tony, to Trimble, to Adams several times. Around 1 or 2 a.m., you're thinking, 'Well, OK, it's only nine o'clock or something in Washington.' Then he's back on to you around 4 a.m., and you're thinking, 'Fair play for staying up.' When he's coming back to you at 6 a.m. and then 10 or 11 a.m., saying, 'I think I'm just going to stay up with it now,' you realise that this is the most powerful office-holder in the world giving you his full attention. That keeps everyone on their mettle.

Hillary Clinton has always been very committed to Ireland too. Her style is very different to Bill's, maybe more direct. But anyone who saw her with the victims of violence like I did will know there's also a sensitive side to Hillary. She would be there with victim support groups, or with people who had lost their sight or their limbs, and she would sit listening to them like a mother. I've seen people in those situations more often than I care to think about, going back to my own days in the Mater. You can't fake it. If you're just doing it for show, everyone will see that. With Hillary it was genuine, a real solidarity. She was obviously getting the briefings too, because she was excellent on the detail, especially on the women's projects which sometimes got overlooked. In some ways her grasp of detail was even better than Bill's. There's no doubt they made a formidable team, and Ireland benefited from that.

Clinton's visit gave the peace process a boost, and when David Trimble and John Hume were jointly awarded the Nobel Peace Prize, there was a renewed feeling of momentum. John obviously had been working at the peace process for years, so that was a reward for a lifetime trying to find a way forward. But I was glad Trimble got recognition too. He's a good guy in my view. Yes, he could be bad-tempered, and I had my fair share of difficult times with him. But he really did try to bridge the divide. He had shown that after Omagh, when he went to all the houses where the bodies were laid out to pay his respects. It wasn't that long ago that he would have been seen as one of the roadblocks to agreement. Now he was trying a complete about-turn. The Nobel Prize recognised that. A week after the announcement, all parties finally agreed on the make-up of the ten government departments of the Northern Ireland Executive, the six new implementation bodies, and the six areas for North/South cooperation. Treaties establishing the North/South and British–Irish institutions would eventually be signed in Dublin Castle in March. That was the same month that Rosemary Nelson, a high-profile Catholic lawyer, was murdered by a splinter loyalist group, the Red Hand Defenders. I had met Rosemary many times and admired the courageous way she took on controversial cases.

One of the inevitable consequences of the Good Friday Agreement was that it raised the profile of Ireland abroad. We started lobbying hard to win a seat on the UN Security Council. We hadn't been there for a generation, and diplomatically I felt that we could punch above our weight in this forum. It would give a new level of expertise to our own officials, and would also let the world know that we were capable and competent in dealing with major issues like, as it turned out, 9/11 and the war in Afghanistan. Sometimes it takes a small country to make the permanent powers listen, because we are not seen as a threat. That often gives us the opportunity to say, 'Listen, let's have a bit of common sense here . . .' David Andrews did a terrific job in lobbying, making particular use of the credibility we had built up in Africa through Irish missionaries. Richard Ryan, our UN Ambassador, was also superb. We used different tactics with different parts of the world, and Tony Blair was helpful to us with the Eastern European countries. We were up against some fairly tough competition in Norway and Italy. I remember at the UN Millennium Goals summit in New York one month before the vote, watching King Harald V of Norway and Italy's Giuliano Amato canvassing the floor for votes. I had to use my best constituency techniques to match them. It was worth the effort. The day we were elected in October 2000 was one of my proudest as Taoiseach.

The Good Friday Agreement not only gave Ireland more influence in the world, it also made the island more attractive in the global marketplace, not least in the new markets opening up in Asia. One of the first things I had done on becoming Taoiseach was to ask the departments of Foreign Affairs, and Enterprise Trade and Employment, and Enterprise Ireland to devise an Asia strategy for Ireland. We had already had some success in attracting Chinese investment to Ireland, but we weren't actually doing much business in China. We had exported IR£34 million of goods, but our imports were almost ten times that figure. The potential to improve the balance of trade in our favour was clearly enormous. I had struck up a good relationship with the Chinese prime minister, Zhu Rongji, in London when he had been amused by me passing notes to Tony under the table. That helped facilitate a week-long visit to China in September 1998 to include Beijing, Shanghai and Hong Kong. It was the first official visit by a Taoiseach to China, so I was well aware what an opportunity it was. I had meetings with President Jiang Zemin and with Zhu Rongji, and was invited to address the prestigious Foreign Affairs College.

In Hong Kong I met the Chief Executive of the Hong Kong government, Tung Cheehwa, as well as opposition members of the Legislative Council. This was the start of building good contacts with China, generating new markets and business opportunities. They certainly knew how to look after their visiting dignitaries. I remember giving a press conference where all the questions were about my 'great role' as a peacemaker. I was up on a huge platform, looking down on all these smiling faces. The Irish journalists didn't know what to do with themselves. 'Why can't you lot be more like that?' I joked with them afterwards.

It was after another of my trips to China that I probably had my most unexpected overseas meeting. Our plane had stopped at Novosibirsk in Siberia for refuelling. I was fast asleep until an official shook me awake. 'I'm sorry, Taoiseach,' he said, 'but I think they're expecting us.' When I looked out of the window, I could see a red carpet, a brass band and a row of dignitaries. I made myself present-able and walked down the steps of the plane onto the tarmac. The welcome could hardly have been more enthusiastic. Once inside the terminal building, a large banquet was laid out. The local television station was there to record an interview. There were warm words and extravagant toasts with vodka to mutual friendship. Only as we were leaving did I notice the photographs on the wall. It was a who's who of international leaders. This obviously wasn't the first time the good people of Novosibirsk had got a head of government out of bed.

One of the things I was often told as Taoiseach was, 'Sure, it must be great to do all that travelling.' People see you jetting around the world at the taxpayers' expense and think, 'Lucky so-and-so.' To be honest, though, you never really get to see the country you're visiting. There are always meetings and engagements laid out in fifteen-minute segments. If there's a gap in there, you can be sure one of your offi-cials will fill it. 'Excuse me, Taoiseach, while we've got five minutes, can I raise . . . ?' At times that could get frustrating, because however exciting a place might be, I often felt that I was just going from one identical meeting room to another. Sometimes, though, you could get a bit too much local culture on overseas trips, not least when it came to food. I remember a dinner on one of my trips to Japan sitting on a cushion and being served sushi and live fish. My adviser Paddy Duffy was seated nearby, and each time the host's back was turned, I would shovel some of those live fish onto his plate. 'You know me, Paddy,' I told him with grin, 'I like plain food.' In the end, Paddy had to eat two dinners and I left the restaurant starving. I sometimes thought life would have been easier if I had been able to take some of my mother's brown bread with me on my travels.

At home, one of the most difficult times in these early years of the government was the Sheedy affair. Philip Sheedy had been sentenced to four years in prison for causing the death of a young mother through dangerous driving. He was released from prison in November 1998 having served one year of the four-year sentence. When it came out that I had made representations to the Minister for Justice, John O'Donoghue, it whipped up a massive storm. Any TD will tell you that we do this kind of thing every week of the year. The father had sent me a letter making a plea for his son to be allowed day release to work on an FÁS scheme. My office had followed it up with the Department of Justice, asking, 'What's the story?' Then the press started saying that because the father knew my friend Joe Burke, this must have been some kind of a favour for the 'Drumcondra Mafia'. They even tried to drag my partner, Celia Larkin, into it, because she was friendly with the wife of the Supreme Court judge, Hugh O'Flaherty, who had relisted the case. It was crazy stuff. I get letters about everyone and everything all the time. Parents would be writing to me about this, that and the other. If the office thought we could help, they would refer them on. The answer in this case had come back 'no', so that was the end of it. That is not pulling strings. Every time I went out the door I got representations. The week the papers splashed the Sheedy story, I had got fifteen representations alone during a trip to the Punchestown races.

The political fallout was bad. I had told Mary Harney on 14 April that I had made representations and she was fine with that as long as I put it on record in the Dáil. I said I would, but I missed an early opportunity to do that, and when the story broke Mary was furious. She was in Donegal by this stage, saying that she would not be coming to cabinet and generally letting it be known that she was 'considering her position'. I used Charlie McCreevy as a peacemaker and then phoned Mary to say sorry. In the end, I went into the Dáil on 5 May to apologise for not bringing my own involvement to the attention of the House earlier. That helped to calm things down, but it was a lesson. As usual I was up to my neck in the North. We were still working on decommissioning and trying to find a basis for devolution. My political antennae should have picked up on the Sheedy affair earlier. I had dropped the ball, and in a coalition government, that's not something you can afford to do. You didn't have to look very far back to Albert Reynolds and Harry Whelehan to understand that. Unfortunately, it didn't mean we wouldn't end up repeating it.

In 2000, one of the judges involved would be back in the public eye when Charlie McCreevy nominated him for a European job. Hugh O'Flaherty had resigned from the Supreme Court after the Sheedy affair. Charlie mentioned it to me at the end of a parliamentary party meeting, and I said, 'Ah sure, that's grand.' O'Flaherty was a bright guy, maybe a bit other-worldly, but someone who had been tipped to be the next Chief Justice. He had got caught up in something, lost his whole court career, and here's an opportunity in Europe where we would be able to use his abilities. The problem was that the public didn't want him to have a job anywhere. We didn't put enough thought into it. Totally different job, nothing to do with the other controversy. A million other things going on at the time. And then – bang – we were into it again. Once the decision was taken, Charlie dug his heels in about making the appointment.

That brought more trouble with the PDs. The difficulty for Mary Harney was that she had been informed of the appointment in advance

Then there were the setbacks, like the Sheedy affair or when we lost the referendum on the Nice Treaty. I just had to accept that things could go well and they could go badly, sometimes at exactly the same time. That's the skill to being Taoiseach: dealing with a lot of complicated issues all at once. Eventually you just accept that's the way it is. My view was that I wanted to try to achieve as much as I could during my time. It involves a massive amount of stamina to keep yourself going. Obviously you make mistakes, sometimes because just for a second your mind is on one of the other twenty things you've got to decide in the next thirty minutes. But you just have to move past it, learn the lesson. Every now and again I would have to remind myself, 'Jesus, we're on a mission here, you're going to get good days and bad days, so here we go.' I tried never to over-analyse the bad days. Whether it gets you down or not, you just have to keep going because there's another meeting in twenty minutes. I rarely changed my diary, even when things were going wrong. I would try not to delay the Dáil or alter the programme. Sometimes that was hard on me personally, but I always tried to keep order. Then a good day would come along, you would get a kick out of it, and off you go again. If the worst came to the worst, there was always the football. In fact, I never put in Sky Sports at home until after I finished being Taoiseach, because I didn't want that to be an option every day of the week. As soon as I left, it was my first treat to myself.

There's no doubt you have to give your life to the job. I would be in St Luke's every morning for around seven to get some quiet reading done and go over my papers. I didn't like to get into Government Buildings before nine o'clock, because it's better to let the officials settle, get their material in order. Once the Taoiseach arrives, they're expected to be on top of their game, so you have to give them a chance to prepare. I usually stayed there until around nine at night and then would head back to St Luke's to tidy up any bits and pieces. Each day there would be black cases to bring back with material to read, letters to sign, decisions to be made. Even if I went which would be planned out to the minute. Then the security was a nightmare. In films you always see all these guys in their black suits, dark glasses, talking into their sleeves, so when you see the real thing, you almost think they're actors. But Clinton always seemed relaxed, and that was especially true when he came in December 2000. He was near the end of his term, with approval ratings through the roof. I took Bill for a pint in Fagan's. That was a phone call I enjoyed making. Eamon O'Malley, the owner, is a great guy, but when I called him to say I was bringing the Clintons over – well, let's just say he was surprised! He had to let Special Branch crawl over every inch of the place the night before. I invited a few people along, but word soon leaked out that the President was coming, so there was a massive crowd waiting for him. Bill knows how to work the room. He genuinely loves meeting people. That was a massive night for me. Back in 1963, I had stood on the Drumcondra Road to watch President Kennedy drive into the city from the airport. Now here I was as Taoiseach bringing the President to my own community for a drink in the local. It was a proud occasion and good for the area. And it was good for the President as well. Look at the photographs from that night which went round the world, and you can see from his smiling face a genuine pleasure in doing something that was ordinary and straightforward. Of course, there was the whole cavalcade, with the security and the media. But these were ordinary Drumcondra people who had got inside that bubble where a US president has to live. He knew that, and so did they.

I was delighted with the visit, because I had also seen Bill in less happy times. I had been standing right beside him in September 1998 as he had to take question after question from the American media about the Lewinsky scandal. Senator Joe Lieberman had condemned the President's conduct as 'immoral' and 'disgraceful'. My photo call gave Bill his first opportunity to reply, when he said for the first time that he was 'very sorry' about his relationship with Monica Lewinsky. Talk about grace under fire. Bill kept his cool all the way, standing there with his hands behind his back, showing no sign of unease or defensiveness. When the cameras had gone, he had a few things to say about Lieberman. The senator was old guard and I was surprised he had chosen to break the tradition of not embarrassing the commander-in-chief while abroad. That had given the media licence to do the same. Behind the scenes, you could see how drained Bill had become by the whole thing. He had lost a lot of weight and he looked tired. Partly that was the heavy schedule, but it must also have been the strain of having his private life dragged through the papers. No doubt this must have been difficult for Hillary as well. To have to endure such a public humiliation must have been awful, but you never would have guessed it. There was not one hint in public or in private that she was remotely concerned. That was classy.

Any relationship in the public eye comes under scrutiny. I knew something about that myself. My separation from Miriam had been a public issue and my relationship with Celia Larkin became one too. I first got to know Celia in 1976 when she joined Fianna Fáil in Dublin Finglas. She was a long-time political ally of mine in the constituency and she was our representative on the National Youth Committee. Celia would subsequently run for the party in local elections. She had come to work for me in Government Buildings in 1982 and stayed working with me until 2000. She was really bright and excellent at her job. She had a good political brain. She was also very professional, and could see how to make my office run faster, better and more strategically.

In the period after my marriage broke up, the office really did become my home and Celia and I were spending even more time together. We both worked incredibly long hours and were hugely committed to politics and to public service. We got on well and there was a definite attraction between us. Just being in her company put me in good form. She was witty and highly intelligent, stylish and very good-looking, and a relationship between us blossomed.

Of course it was a relationship that attracted a lot of attention. Ireland in the late 1980s and the early 1990s was a much more conservative society than we live in today. A divorce referendum had been comprehensively defeated in 1986. The Church, which frowned on second relationships, still held considerable sway and we did get some abuse. But most people were generous and had a 'live and let live' attitude. Celia sometimes worried that our relationship might damage me politically, but I never gave that much thought. The most important thing for both of us was being together, because that made us happy.

Thousands of people had experienced the trauma of marriage break-up and had set out on a new relationship. I felt that Celia and I were entitled to a second chance at happiness. In this we may have been no different to so many other couples, but there was an inevitable spotlight on us because of my job. Few people in Irish public life at this stage admitted to living apart from their spouse. Fewer still were openly in a second relationship. Celia and I did not set out to challenge the system, but I was determined no longer to live a lie. She was the woman I loved and we were committed to each other. I was going to be open and upfront about that. I wanted her at my side. By the time I went public about the break-up of my marriage and then later about Celia, Ireland was gradually becoming a more tolerant society. People were that bit more relaxed about second relationships. Sadly, there were still some who tried to make something of it and I'm sorry to say that a lot of the nasty stuff was generated from within Fianna Fáil.

Celia is a courageous woman and she had to be to put up with the inevitable criticisms that came our way. We were breaking new ground and it was often difficult to have our personal life held up as a subject of public discourse. I greatly admired the way Celia refused to let this get her down. She always held her head high and battled on. I know at times she must have been hurting, but she never complained. It certainly was not easy for either of us being one of the first and the most prominent 'second relationship' couples in Irish public life. We were held up to intense scrutiny, but I do believe some good came out of it. We made it easier for anyone coming after us. Now thankfully a politician's marital status is usually seen as his or her own business. The novelty of a separated public figure or someone in a second relationship is gone.

I have always maintained that the Irish people are generous and compassionate. In looking back, I think it is important to acknowledge that most people were prepared to judge me on my policies, not on who I was or was not living with. Some others may have had doubts, but they quickly realised that the country was not going to collapse because I was in a relationship with a woman who was not my wife. Obviously a few held to the line that we were wrong and they condemned us. That is their view and they are entitled to it. But I strongly contend that nobody had the right to abuse me or Celia because of the choices we made. It was personal and it was our decision to make.

Celia was by my side for the first five and a half years of my time as Taoiseach. She helped me enormously through the stresses and strains of political life. Celia was a great sounding board for ideas and a very shrewd strategist. Away from the goldfish bowl of Leinster House, it was a great help to be able to discuss with her whatever issues might be bothering me. She had no agenda except what was best for me. People have tried to bad-mouth Celia, but it's beyond me to understand why. She is a very kind and loyal person. She is great fun to be around and she never let me become so immersed in my work that I forgot my friends. I was working huge hours, but she always made sure that I was happy in my personal life. Celia understood the game and she understood me, which meant knowing exactly when to talk politics and when to drop it. That was a great support. She pulled her weight too. Celia had a special quality of putting people at ease, and whenever visiting presidents or prime ministers were in town, she would look after them brilliantly. She took a lot of care in studying the briefs for these visits as well as for the ones we made overseas. And she always looked great. Although some chose to criticise her, I always believed that she was an outstanding ambassador for our country. I remember during the Clinton visit in 1998 watching her at a reception talking to all these important people. She was a natural and I was very proud of her.

That's not to say it was all plain sailing. In 2001 there was a big row when we hosted an event together for the newly elevated Cardinal Connell. During the reception we had to listen to him give a pointed speech on the importance of marriage, but at least he turned up. We had hosted a stack of receptions previously, which the Hierarchy had attended. This one created a huge problem though, with some of them writing to say they would not attend. A few were promising me eternal fire and brimstone. Two of the mostly harshly worded letters came from Cardinal Daly and Archbishop Brady. Those letters could not have contrasted more strongly with the warm and compassionate letter I had received earlier from Archbishop Robin Eames when the *Church of Ireland Gazette* had seen fit to pass comment on my relationship with Celia. I persisted with the event for Cardinal Connell, but it was not a night either Celia or I would particularly want to go through again. But at the end of the day she was my partner and I wasn't going to hide her away. That was why on the night that I became leader, at my first press conference, I had said it straight up. I wasn't going to skulk around. As far as my public life was concerned, I was legally separated from my wife. I now had a partner. My own conscience was my own business.

The girls, Georgina and Cecelia, were always my top priority. I was determined they would know that just because I was no longer with their mam, it did not mean that I loved them any less. I would always meet them on my own, went on holidays with them on my own. That was exactly the way it should have been. Miriam was absolutely brilliant. It was a very difficult situation for her. Most people who go through a break-up deal with it in their own way. She had to keep reliving it year after year. Every time someone made a public comment about it, there it would be all over the papers again. Most of the journalists were all right, but you would always get a few who would be up at Miriam's house trying to get a quote out of her. It must have made it more difficult for her to move on. But she never once said a word against me, when she might have had good cause. In fact, she said almost nothing. Although it hadn't worked out for us, there's a loyalty in Miriam that breaks my heart, because probably I don't deserve it. Ours was a funny old way to live, but really it was just the same as for thousands of other people in the country. It's called life.

When Georgina got married in August 2003 to Nicky Byrne, I had the chance to thank Miriam in front of our family and friends for the wonderful job she had done raising our two very special girls. It was a great day, with beautiful weather and a wonderful setting in Château d'Esclimont, not that far from Paris. It wasn't an easy thing to say, but I acknowledged that I wasn't always there for the girls in the way that I should have been. Most of their upbringing had fallen on Miriam, so that was a tribute that had to be paid. I think from the start we had both decided that whatever else happened the kids were going to suffer as little as possible. Although Miriam took the lion's share in raising them, she was always good about making sure I got time at the weekends and then that I could take them away in August. If I was going somewhere exciting like New York that coincided with the school holidays, then she let me take them along. So Miriam had most responsibility in the home, but I still felt as if I really knew my kids and had a proper connection with them. Of course it must still have been hard for them, but I hope they didn't suffer too much from the separation. The fact they turned out so well tells me we must have dealt with it OK.

The wedding got a lot of attention, but from the family's point of view it was two people getting married who had been sweethearts since they were fifteen years old. I remember Georgina asking me if she could bring this lad with her for Sunday lunch. Two things struck me straight away that I liked. He was a very polite young man, and he was mad keen on football. Turned out he was very good at it as well, and I've spent years trying to put the ball past him. He played for the Ireland youth team, got the opportunity to go to Leeds United as an apprentice and subsequently turned professional. Being abroad was very hard on him and Georgina, but they stuck at it. Unfortunately Nicky never quite got the height to be a top-class goalkeeper. That was tough for him, because he had such great natural ability. So he came back, played in the League of Ireland and then got his big break with the band.

What I know about pop music you can write on a postcard – I'm more of a Leonard Cohen and Neil Diamond man myself – but what I recognised with Westlife is that the music business has some similarities to politics: there are lots of people with talent but not all of them are prepared to work every hour that God sends to make it. These boys were so dedicated. They were great entertainers, but they still had to drive around places in the van, doing gigs in different places every night, talking to every local radio station wherever they happened to be. They were disciplined. I'm sure they had some good nights out, but they never seemed to go on long benders in the way some bands do. Even when it took off for them, I remember thinking, 'It'll be great if you can get two or three years out of this . . .' Then I was thinking, 'They're five years at it now, fair play . . .' In June 2008, they celebrated ten years with a massive concert in Croke Park. 'I thought they would get a couple of years,' I told Georgina, 'but now they've outlasted me as Taoiseach!' These days I've got more time to play with two fantastic grandkids, Jay and Rocco. If they end up making Georgina as proud of them as I am of her then she'll be very lucky indeed.

My job has put the girls in the public eye since they were youngsters, but now both Georgina and Cecelia are recognised as much as me. That comes with a downside too. Georgina's wedding was quite an occasion for the media. We found ourselves in this small village in France with a whole lot of press, very agitated because they couldn't get all the pictures they wanted. Georgina didn't let it spoil the day, and when *Hello!* came out with all the photographs, it was huge in Ireland and in England.

Cecelia has a great life now as well. She has a terrific partner in David Keoghan. Cecelia definitely has grit and self-belief. I remember when she was doing her master's degree in film production, she pulled out saying that she had started a book and wanted to go full-time at it. I thought, 'Jesus, that's a risk . . .' but she was absolutely determined. Maybe I said something about using her journalism degree and writing part-time, but she said, 'No, this is what I want to do with my life.' Luckily, she didn't listen to me and went off to follow her dream. Miriam read the draft of *PS, I Love You* first and told me it was brilliant, so I just put my feet up and read it in a day. By the end of it I knew she was a brilliant storyteller and that she had a hit on her hands. It came out in 2004 and was no. 1 in Ireland and in England, as well as a best-seller in Europe and the United States. Warner Brothers snapped up the rights, bringing out the film in 2007 with Hilary Swank. There had been snide comments early on that she was only getting published because of her dad, but her success soon knocked that on the head. Ten million readers can't be wrong.

So there you have it, two girls who've made the most of their lives. It still gives me a kick when people come up and say, 'Tell us about your daughters!'

As any dad will tell you, pride in your kids trumps everything.

13

KEBABS AND WELCOMES

Coalitions are unstable. That was the conventional wisdom in Irish politics. It was something I was determined to change. Throughout my first couple of years as Taoiseach, the question was always how long can this government last. Then it became how long before I took advantage of our popularity and went to the polls. Only right at the end did people realise that when I said we would run the full term all the way to 2002, I really meant it.

Throughout most of 2001 and 2002, the pressure to call an early election got more and more intense. That wasn't something I was interested in. I was getting a lot of questions from within the party, with anxious TDs coming up to me with ridiculous sayings, like 'Seize the day!' I would always just laugh and say, 'Why not go to the end?' but they would give me a knowing look as if I was pulling their leg. Charlie McCreevy was one of the few people I discussed it with sometime in early 2001. I told him I had made up my mind that I wanted to see through the full term, and asked what he thought. 'If that's what you've decided you want to do, then do it,' he told me. So that was that. An election in the summer of 2002. I loved summer campaigns, with the bright evenings and people already out and about. There's always more chance of having a chat on the doorstep when the weather's better. Who wants to answer the door to a politician on a dark, freezing cold night? For all the hot air coming into your house, you're letting even more out!

We got a sharp reminder of how the weather could affect a ballot during the abortion referendum in March 2002, which was lost on a low turnout on a wet day. I had been very sorry to lose that, because it was obviously an issue that needed clarity, but all along I had said I would only take one shot at it, so for me that was now done. Hopefully whoever tackles it next won't have Dana ranting away during the campaign, which had an influence on the level of the debate. So all things considered, I always had May in mind for the general election. Canvassers don't want to be out every night if they've got kids at home doing the Leaving Cert. Once we had gone past May 2001, I knew for definite we would wait another year. Little did I know that by the time we got there, the world would have changed beyond recognition.

I was in my office in Government Buildings on the afternoon of 11 September. I was going to be fifty the next day, so I had an extensive programme of media interviews and a big party lined up. I had just finished a meeting with Gerry Adams and Martin McGuinness and was about to have another with the new US ambassador, Dick Egan, and Richard Haass, the director of policy planning for the Department of State and US envoy to the Northern Ireland peace process. We had often put this kind of thing together so that various parties could say hello informally without actually having a meeting. The five of us were literally standing on the cross of my door, when my private secretary, David Feeney, came racing over. David is normally unflappable and is extremely professional, but on this occasion he was white in the face. 'Taoiseach, something terrible has happened,' he told me. 'A plane is after flying into the Twin Towers in New York.'

We were shocked, thinking how terrible that an accident like that could happen. No one mentioned terrorism. Adams and McGuinness went to the outer office to take a look at the TV pictures before leaving. I carried on my meeting with the Americans.

Twenty minutes later, David came back in to say another plane has gone into the Twin Towers. The two Americans literally jumped. 'Is this not the same one you told us about before?' I asked in disbelief. 'No, Taoiseach, all hell's breaking loose,' he told us. 'They think it's a terrorist attack.' Haass immediately went to my phone to call the State Department. He couldn't get through, but said he had a 'hotline' number for the Pentagon. When he couldn't get through on that number, I could see he was really worried. We found out afterwards that the Pentagon was under attack as well. In the meantime I spoke to Foreign Affairs, while I was listening to RTÉ. I remember Conor O'Clery describing what he was seeing, just keeping really calm as he watched the terrible sight of people falling from the sky. Soon afterwards, the Minister for Foreign Affairs, Brian Cowen, was on to me. He was just about to go into a meeting with Yasser Arafat. I told him that I had Haass in the office, so I asked Richard for an immediate assessment of US policy regarding Arafat. 'He must condemn the attack unequivocally,' Haass told me. I passed that on to Brian. When Arafat came out shortly afterwards and did indeed condemn the terrorists, I felt that we had been able to make a useful contribution.

Although some criticised me for it, I declared a National Day of Mourning in Ireland to express the depth of our grief at the suffering of the victims of 9/11, and our solidarity with the American people in the face of these unbelievable attacks. I know that was deeply appreciated and it came up in discussion every time I visited the US during my years as Taoiseach. The previous St Patrick's Day at the White House, President George W. Bush had said that the Irish were integral to America's pride in being a nation of immigrants. On 9/11 many people of Irish heritage vindicated that tribute. One of the first recorded victims of the attacks was Father Mychal Judge, Catholic chaplain of the New York Fire Department and the son of Irish immigrants, with whom I had met only a short time before when he had visited Ireland on a peace mission.

Dealing with the attacks on the Twin Towers must have been daunting for a new president and it was a challenge that would define his presidency. It was a question I was asked all the time as Taoiseach. 'Is George Bush really as bad as he looks on television?' The answer to that is no. On my trips to Washington as Taoiseach every St Patrick's Day and also during my period as president of the European Council, I had more access to the White House than most heads of government. I was always impressed with Bush in one-to-one meetings and was surprised that he got so tangled up on television. In meetings he always appeared totally on top of everything, rarely referring to notes. He had a different style to Bill Clinton. With Clinton, you would work your way towards a decision. He would want to know the internal political situation, what the UN and the EU were saying, how the media were reporting the story. That always gave me a feel for the decision-making process in the White House. With Bush, he would start with the bottom line – 'I don't like that guy and I'm going to get him!' – and then move to the analysis as a commentary on the decision that was already in place.

This certainly made him straightforward to deal with. I know Mary Harney thought that too when she met him in 2004 during our European presidency. She had said to me beforehand, 'Is he awful?' and then laughed when I told her he was sharp. But afterwards she came out raving about him. He was authoritative on the issues and well able to speak on them. Then he would look less impressive during television interviews on the same topics. It was as if he were two different people. I remember him telling me in great detail about the new technology they had for unmanned aircraft that could take out a target from 20,000 feet. I remember thinking, 'this guy loves armaments,' but also being impressed with the level of detail he had. Maybe he had a fault in that he saw arguments in a very black-and-white way, but he always seemed to know his facts.

I saw that on the North as well. He may not have been as interested as Clinton, but he was prepared to listen. He was getting a lot of advice after 9/11 that Sinn Féin were terrorists just like al-Qaeda. I managed to persuade him that Adams and McGuinness were genuinely looking for a peaceful solution and that the IRA could be convinced to give up violence. Bush listened to that. This was despite the arrest of three suspected IRA members in Colombia. That support from the President was important, because the peace process had stalled. There had been talks in Weston Park a few weeks before 9/11, which had put forward proposals from the two governments on how to implement the Good Friday Agreement. Now, just six weeks after the attacks on the Twin Towers, the Independent International Commission on Decommissioning (IICD) announced the first 'significant act of decommissioning' by the IRA. This would be followed by a second act in April 2002, and a 'statement of apology' by the IRA in July. There were not many positives to come out of the tragedy of 9/11, but progress in the peace process was one of them.

Immediately after 9/11 my security people were keen to bolster my personal detail. They wanted me to start changing the patterns of engagements, so as not to make everything so regular. To be honest, I wasn't going to worry too much about it. Obviously you have to let people do their job, but there's no point losing any sleep over it. We had a few incidents along the way, especially at St Luke's, but these usually turned out to be people who were a bit troubled. There were also a few minor protests around the time of the Iraq war. The security sometimes got in the way on trips abroad. There would be huge security at international conferences, when you didn't always know whether the 'ring of steel' was designed to keep protesters out or us in. Even on bilateral visits I would end up with heavy security, because it was assumed I needed it as 'the Northern Ireland guy'. I remember going for a drink in an Irish bar called Fado on one occasion in Washington. I went in with a large team of agents, which was not exactly relaxing. So I had a quick pint and got out as soon as I could. A quiet drink just wasn't possible in the climate after 9/11. Everyone was on edge. On my last official visit to Washington, the night before I addressed Congress, we had a fire alarm go off in the hotel. There was total panic. They got me out straight away, but I heard later that the advisers and officials were left to fend for themselves, a perfect situation for Gerry Hickey's dry humour. Coming down the stairs with my adviser and former government press secretary, Mandy Johnston, she asked him if everything was going to be OK. 'Of course it will be, Mandy,' he said, 'as long as the fire is above us and not below us . . .' Mandy's a tough character, but this time she freaked. Later, she had a laugh at Charlie Bird's expense. He came running to the front of the hotel, saying, 'Where's the Taoiseach, is the Taoiseach all right?' Mandy told him I was just round the corner and that he could have a word. Off he dashed. Needless to say I had already been whisked away by this stage. Fortunately Charlie saw the funny side once he realised Mandy had been winding him up.

The 9/11 attacks had an impact on the world economy too. An open economy like Ireland's will always be vulnerable to worldwide shocks. We had already been trying to react to the sharp global downturn in Information and Communication Technology (ICT). In situations like this the key is to act quickly and decisively to try to provide some impetus. We needed a stimulus to get us through that period, which included tax cuts to encourage people to keep spending in their local shops and communities. We also wanted to encourage our entrepreneurs and business people to keep faith in the enterprise economy. The alternative was to let the country stagnate. Quick action would prove highly successful. By 2004 Ireland would be growing three times faster than the eurozone average and we would have the second lowest national debt in Europe. Unemployment would stand at 4.4 per cent, compared with the 10.3 per cent in 1997. After 9/11 we could have panicked by raising taxes, which would have stalled an already spluttering economy. Instead, we gave it a boost.

As we started the countdown towards the general election, I was confident that we had a good case to put to the people of Ireland. On 25 April I went to Áras an Uachtaráin to ask the President to dissolve the Dáil and call an election for 17 May 2002. It had been a golden period for the country and the government were very proud of what we had achieved. That would become the central message of the campaign. A year earlier I had spoken to a grass-roots meeting in Donegal and introduced a new phrase for the first time that seemed to sum up where we were. 'There's a lot done,' I said, 'and a lot more to do.' That was something I had thought out with my speech-writer, Brian Murphy. Later, encouraged by my adviser, Peter MacDonagh, we adopted it as the central message of the campaign and it was plastered over billboards throughout the country. A lot done. More to do.

There's no doubt that in the 2002 campaign we wiped the floor with our political opponents. I travelled up and down the country, touring the constituencies. Wherever we went, there was genuine goodwill and enthusiasm. You could tell almost from the beginning that we were going to win. The party vote was looking very strong. The key was to attract more transfers, getting people who wouldn't normally give us a high preference to change their habits. Michael Noonan, in his first election as leader of Fine Gael, did us a big favour by fighting such a poor campaign. Fine Gael were still in disarray following the heave that had got rid of John Bruton. Noonan had been quite effective as opposition spokesperson on Finance, but he didn't seem able to unite his party or make any real connection with the voters. Everyone kept telling me how clever he was, but if you can't get through to ordinary working people, you're not going to get anywhere. His party put forward some ideas, like promising taxi drivers compensation for deregulation and offering to pay shareholders who had lost money on Eircom, which just looked mad. That cost them in the end. They lost twenty-three seats, including big-name casualities like Alan Dukes, Nora Owen, Jim Mitchell and Austin Currie.

For us, the unspoken question during the campaign was whether we would get an overall majority. There was such a feelgood factor out there, we thought we might just be able to do it. In some ways, I wish the polls had been closer, because that might have encouraged more people to come out and vote. We were a united party. We ran a very well-structured campaign that year. The only danger was people showing too much bravado. A winning campaign is an ego trip and some people let that go to their heads. I know P. J. Mara and Mandy Johnston were both annoyed about that. There were guys running around telling anyone who would listen about their own strategic brilliance and how single-handedly they were crucifying the opposition. These characters were planning to go into business and consultancy afterwards, so they wanted the world and its mother to know how great they were. The PDs were the main beneficiaries of that. Michael McDowell spotted what was happening and ran a clever campaign telling people to vote for the PDs to help keep Fianna Fáil 'honest'. The media loved that, seeing him go up a ladder there in Ranelagh, putting up his poster. He was normally such a formal Law Library type, so it was funny seeing him hanging off a lamp post, and of course the pictures went all over the place. That must have had an effect. Heavy rain on election day didn't help either. The PDs gained four seats and so did we, but Fianna Fáil were left just short of the magic eighty-four needed to form a government with an overall majority.

I was sorry not to get that overall majority, but all in all I was delighted with the result, winning two in a row. Just about the only downer on events was Roy Keane's exit from the World Cup training camp in Saipan. I had spoken to Roy at the airport before the Irish team left. He was sitting on the floor away from the other lads. He could not have been more polite to me, but it was already clear that he was not happy. After he got sent home, I offered to put the government jet on standby to fly him back if the various parties could work something out, but unfortunately nothing came of it. The World Cup was not the same without him.

After the election, I phoned Mary Harney and told her I wanted to continue with the PDs in government. I knew Fianna Fáil could get enough independent support to form a government on our own, but above all I wanted stability. The PDs had fulfilled their end of the bargain by going the full term from 1997 to 2002, so I felt we owed them something. 'Let's get on with it,' I told Mary. She agreed, telling me that she wanted it to be business as usual.

I was glad to have the government continuing along the same lines, because I wanted to take us through another full five-year term. That was my intention right from the outset. There had been a lot of gossip in the papers that Joe Walsh and Michael Smith were to be sacked. Both had been around for a long time. I had already agreed with Walsh that he would stay on to finish the agricultural reform he had been negotiating in Europe. He was pleased with that. I was tempted to replace Smith at Defence immediately with Willie O'Dea, but in the end I decided to keep him in place. That was a major disappointment for O'Dea, but Smith's card was marked. He would be moving on at the next reshuffle.

There were a few others leaving the cabinet in 2002. Síle de Valera had not been in the best of health, so I thought she was better off as a junior minister. Jim McDaid had been given a good run. Frank Fahey had got us caught up in a bit of difficulty about the 'Lost at Sea' scheme and so now seemed a good time to get him out of the spotlight. Michael Woods returned to the backbenches. Even when I knew it was the right action to take, I never enjoyed these occasions. For all the bravado that politicians have, no one likes being told their cabinet career is over. We always like to think we're the very last person who should be dropped. Some react with dignity. Others plead to keep their jobs and get very agitated around the Dáil. Fair enough, I suppose. You should be devastated when you're dropped from cabinet.

The start of my second term, just like that of my first in 1997, got off to a shaky enough start. There was a lot of aggravation about the economy. We had tried to stimulate the economy after 9/11, but when we got the figures for the first six months of 2002, we could see that the rate of growth had slowed down dramatically. That meant we would have to cut our cloth in the next budget. This would see cuts of around €250 million from a budget of billions. The media and the opposition went mad, saying we were only telling everyone now that the election was over. I knew this was rubbish and that decisive action in tightening up now would let the economy roar ahead again the following year. In the event, that is exactly what happened. We had acted quickly enough to get on top of things, but we made a mistake in not dealing with the media angle that we had misled people in the run-up to the general election. McCreevy took terrible flak. To be fair he enjoyed these battles, showing that he could deal with a difficult situation, not just the good times. But it definitely had an impact on our popularity.

So too did the financial affairs of Ray Burke, just as they had in 1997. These now came back to haunt us with the publication of the interim report of the Flood Tribunal, which said Burke had received corrupt payments from a number of builders and had made decisions as a minister that were not in the public interest. And just like in 1997, it was a national vote that gave us that bit of impetus we needed. This time it was the second referendum on the Nice Treaty. We spent a lot of time getting the campaign right, working well with the new leader of Fine Gael, Enda Kenny, who is an enthusiastic European. That gave us an opportunity to detach the arguments from everyday politics. Perhaps the economic pinch helped too, because it made everyone realise how important the EU was to our economic and financial future. We won comprehensively. That enabled us to recover our position in Brussels, which had been damaged by the earlier rejection. We also got back onside with the 'enlargement' countries due to enter the EU during our presidency.

One of the shocks for me after the general election was that my own popularity took a hit for the first time since I had become Taoiseach. I saw something somewhere saying the government was as popular as the SARS virus, which seemed harsh. After both election campaigns in 1997 and 2002, there had been analysis after analysis saying that it was the 'Bertie factor' that had won it for Fianna Fáil. I took that with a massive pinch of salt, but it was true that our pollsters had numbers showing that I was popular with the public and that to a certain extent we ran a 'presidential'-style campaign in both those elections. That took advantage of my popularity with voters, but also exposed the weakness of my opponents, none of whom were particularly comfortable with ordinary people. For a couple of years from 2002 onwards, opinion polls started to dip. The media seized on this. Some of the coverage became much more hostile, maybe because they were upset we won the election. The economic dip started things off, but it carried on long after that, because although the economy recovered very strongly in 2003, the unfavourable coverage continued. You expect to get stick as a politician. Show me a thin-skinned politician and I'll show you someone who shouldn't be in politics. But this seemed a different kind of agenda.

One thing you can be sure about is that bad media coverage and a few dodgy polls will always get backbench TDs nervous. Most of us in Leinster House are highly strung. When polls go south, we all worry about keeping our seats. Maybe if some of us put a bit more effort into our constituencies, we might worry less, but that's another story. During this period from the summer of 2002 until that of 2004, there were definitely a few colleagues on the backbenches who were out to cause trouble. We were trying to deal with the economic situation, making sure that we kept the show on the road, so the last thing I needed was people not pulling their weight. They were only a small group to be fair, mainly comprising those who were disgruntled about not getting ministerial office. But in the modern 24/7 media environment, anyone prepared to share pearls of wisdom or

compared to what was going on in the North. As usual, it was the same old story. Up and down, up and down. Back and forth, back and forth. For all the progress we had made, the simple fact remained that by the time we reached the fifth anniversary of the Good Friday Agreement in April 2003, implementation looked as far away as ever.

Part of the worry for me was that Tony would start to lose interest in the North. By now he was in the middle of a storm over the Iraq war. The Secretary of State at this stage was Paul Murphy. He was a very calm character, good at building consensus, and prepared to put in the hours on the North without getting too distracted by wider British politics. That brought new focus on the British side. We had been through two Secretaries of State after Mo Mowlam, neither of whom had really worked out. We never really hit it off with Peter Mandelson. Talks with him were always heavy weather. Partly it was his manner, which was a bit stand off-ish. I think he liked being up at Hillsborough Castle, where he could play the 'viceroy'. That always came across. I heard back from officials that he was one of those who would be sitting at his desk when you came in and then would leave you standing there while he carried on with his paperwork just to emphasise that he was a minister of the Crown. We were always doubtful about him. Nobody thought he compared to Mo. She had done her fair bit of talking to the media, but we always found with Mandelson that he was briefing the media before he had even spoken to us. No one likes to get information second-hand. There was no doubting his intelligence, or even his charm when he decided to turn it on. But he had unfettered access to Tony Blair, which made it difficult to go over his head.

Poor old Paddy Teahon found that out the hard way. He was talking to Blair on the phone, making it clear that the Secretary of State had not been a helpful presence in recent discussions. Paddy reported that Blair had seemed to be egging him on. Later I found out why. Tony phoned me and said, 'Paddy was in full flight the other day. By the way, you should probably tell him that Peter was listening.'

Ouch! It was a lesson to all of us about the kind of access that Mandelson enjoyed. When he went in January 2001, we were glad to see the back of him.

If Mandelson was a bit too smooth for our liking, his successor, Dr John Reid, was probably too upfront for anyone's good. I liked him on a personal level. He always seemed absolutely trustworthy and was good for a chat about the fortunes of Glasgow Celtic. He would become Tony's enforcer during the Iraq war and so was close to him like Mandelson. In fact, I often thought if you could have put the strengths of the two men together, you would have had the ideal politician. John was probably a bit too abrupt for the North. He was very blunt in discussions, never really alert to all those sensitivities that make Northern politics what they are. I did wonder whether it was a tactic on Tony's side. You've had silky-smooth, let's see how you get on with a tough guy. John's attitude was basically, 'Enough of this bloody nonsense, get on with it or there'll be consequences.' That kind of approach was never going to work. Worse, it was only going to undermine the position of the moderates in the process, who were coming under pressure. I think Tony recognised the error of that tactic himself with the next appointment. Murphy was no soft touch, but he had a much better feel for the place.

One person I did have a massive regard for during this period after the Good Friday Agreement was Chris Patten. He had come in to chair the Independent Commission on Policing for Northern Ireland, which produced the Patten Report and led to the formation of the Police Service of Northern Ireland. He's definitely one of the unsung heroes of the peace process. It's hard to believe that the Tories didn't find some way around this time to get him back into Parliament and give him the leadership. He's a serious political heavyweight. I dealt with him again as an EU Commissioner, when once more he was superb. Chris had a good feel for the North in the same way that Tony did. He didn't just parachute in and write his report. He listened carefully to people like Maurice Hayes, who also did

Trojan work on this report. Patten went to public meetings, took in what was being said, and tried to reflect it. That's why even if we didn't agree with everything he recommended, we had no argument with the overall report, because it was a real attempt to find a way forward. He got his fair share of stick while he was doing it, because, even though he was Catholic, many on the Nationalist side would have seen him as just a typical British Tory, here to deliver another whitewash. When I joked with him about that once, he just smiled and said, 'You should have seen Hong Kong.'

There's something to be said for that attitude. When you've already got the political scars, a few more won't really hurt. That cost us in October 2003 with John de Chastelain, the chairman of the IICD. There had been intensive talks between the UUP and Sinn Féin on a possible sequence involving the calling of elections, a statement by Gerry Adams which would be endorsed by the IRA, and a further act of decommissioning. Trimble had agreed that if there was transparency on decommissioning, he would be able to sell it. We agreed 21 October as the day when it all had to happen. Everything started well. Early in the morning, Tony announced that elections to the Assembly would be held on 26 November. Adams welcomed the move and said the implementation of the agreement would allow 'the full and final closure of the conflict'. The IRA issued a statement endorsing the speech. So far so good. Everything was set for de Chastelain to play his part.

The problem was that the IRA had taken de Chastelain to a secret location to witness the act of decommissioning and he was completely out of contact. Tony wanted to go to Belfast for the announcement. I told him that was crazy, because we didn't know what the guy was actually going to say. In the end, Tony begged me to attend, which I did against my better judgement. I knew that was a mistake the minute I set eyes on de Chastelain. He was tired and still in the clothes he had worn overnight. Fatigue seemed to affect his performance on the day. He said an act of decommissioning had taken place, but due to the nature of the IICD's confidentiality agreement with the IRA, he refused to give a detailed description. The media gave him a right going-over, pressing him strongly for further information, but he would not or could not provide it. I was furious, because I had warned Tony it wasn't going to work. Trimble immediately said the statement wasn't enough. Adams was livid that Sinn Féin had had their concession thrown back in their faces. There was a fair bit of friction between everyone involved. It's easy to blame de Chastelain. Perhaps he needed a bit more political nous on this occasion, but it was also my belief that if the IRA hadn't unexpectedly held him overnight, de Chastelain would have been in a better position to do the necessary and report a really significant stage.

That was a game-changing moment. At the elections on 26 November, Ian Paisley's DUP replaced David Trimble's UUP as the biggest Unionist party. Sinn Féin overtook the SDLP to become the largest Nationalist party. Politics in the North had become a whole different story. In an odd way that was a relief, although it required a completely new strategy. I looked at the DUP manifesto, which was calling for a review of the Good Friday Agreement, and turned that round on them by saying, 'Yeah, you're right. There's a clause in the Agreement that allows for a review, so let's do it.' I think a lot of people would have expected a rejectionist approach from us over the DUP, but I was determined to use the method that had always worked well for me in the past: moving beyond the rhetoric to deal with concrete issues one by one. That was the message I got across unequivocally in an interview with Adam Boulton of Sky News the weekend after the elections. There would be the usual ups and downs along the way, but this approach would eventually end in the St Andrew's Agreement in October 2006.

The shift in the process from the UUP/SDLP to DUP/Sinn Féin also meant the end of the leading roles taken by David Trimble, John Hume and Séamus Mallon. I felt sorry for each of them, because they had all put a huge effort into the peace process. David Trimble had seen his character dragged through the mud by his opponents, but he had always remained committed to finding a way forward. Quite often with David that had meant acting against his own instincts, so we were all aware of the difficult journey he had made. He was capable of genuine compassion, not least in the aftermath of the Omagh bombings, when he undertook the role of First Minister for all communities with dignity and statesmanship. John Hume had devoted his life to peace, carrying on even through the darkest days of the Troubles, when common sense would have told him to give up. For John it was always about legitimacy. It was his suggestion that we put the Good Friday Agreement to a vote of the whole island, because he said it would supersede the mandate Sinn Féin claimed from the election of 1918. Séamus too showed great courage throughout the process, not least when he agreed that the SDLP would sit on the policing boards recommended in the Patten Report. We owe a huge debt of gratitude to the three of them for their dedication and perseverance.

The North, as always, was still taking up a vast amount of my time as Taoiseach, but the new shift in negotiations also coincided with another massive challenge: taking up the presidency of the European Council for six months from 1 January 2004. Ireland could be proud of its reputation in this rotating office. Liam Cosgrave had been the first Taoiseach to hold the post in 1975, and like his successors had done a good job. We had a reputation for being easy to deal with, but also for efficiency and getting the job done. I was determined to keep up the tradition. That said, I knew from the beginning it was going to be a huge challenge. We were taking over from the Italians, who had done a pretty shoddy job. The intergovernmental meeting in Brussels in December was one of the worst I had ever attended, and ended in very low spirits. Silvio Berlusconi was in the chair. He's a colourful character to say the least. In private, he can be great. He's very gregarious, and chats away. There was a shared passion for football, so we were never short of something to talk about. Both of us had our own teams, although I have to admit that AC Milan were on a bigger scale than All Hampton. If Silvio was good fun, diplomacy was not his strong point. We had to try to agree a new EU constitution. It became clear after about five minutes that the Italians hadn't done the groundwork or achieved the necessary compromises to get a deal. To be fair, Silvio himself recognised that he wasn't even near to pulling it off, so he just carried on chatting and telling stories. The result of that was all eyes immediately turned to us looking for answers. 'This will be a piece of cake for you after Castle Buildings!' Blair joked as we were leaving.

There was no doubting that we were in the hot seat. I was worried, not because Berlusconi had got a logjam with the EU constitution, but that there didn't seem to be any obvious way to break it. That wasn't all bad, mind, because in a funny way it relieved a bit of the pressure. Journalists and EU officials were saying this was going to be a long process. Jan Peter Balkenende, the prime minister of the Netherlands, who was to succeed me in July, was already running around saying the issue was likely to be sorted during his presidency. I was happy to keep expectations low, but I thought we could do better than setting the thing up for the Dutch. In a way Tony was right. I had spent my whole political career putting together agreements. I had been around long enough to know most of the leaders fairly well and understood the issues. Although on the last day of the intergovernmental conference it looked as if no one would ever agree anything, I was confident I could build a new consensus. It just needed patience.

In a way Ireland was lucky it was such an interesting time. Sometimes the rotating presidency comes along when there's not much going on. We had a number of important issues to deal with. Working out what to do with the constitution was obviously a key concern. Then we also had to complete the process of enlargement. Ten new countries — Cyprus, the Czech Republic, Estonia, Hungary, Latvia, Lithuania, Malta, Poland, Slovakia and Slovenia — were being admitted to the EU on 1 May 2004. The Treaty of Accession had been signed the year before, but there was still a lot of nuts and bolts to work out before May Day. And there had been almost no thought put into the formal proceedings of entry. A lot of the Eurocrats were telling us not to make a fuss about this, saying that the new countries would just be 'in' when we got to the date. I soon made it clear that wasn't going to do. This was the largest expansion of territory and population in the history of the EU. It was bringing in a lot of countries that had been stuck in the Soviet empire all the way through the Cold War. It wasn't like filling in a form for your car insurance. It was a big deal for them, for democracy and for the European ideal. This kind of cooperation between sovereign nations was something that worked, bringing with it peace and prosperity. If that wasn't worth celebrating, what the hell was? There was a much older friendship that needed looking after as well. Transatlantic relations had hit a real low around the time of the Iraq war, so an EU–American summit meeting was planned for later in the year to try to heal the breach.

So those were the challenges: the constitution, enlargement and America. Of course, along the way there would be many international meetings and regular trips to the European Parliament. All this had to be done while carrying on the job of Taoiseach. Wherever possible I tried to divide the week: attending in the Dáil and meetings of the government, Monday to Wednesday; travelling to meetings on behalf of the EU, Thursday to Saturday. Sundays were spent reading all day to catch up and prepare. Visiting dignitaries were scheduled, where possible, for Mondays. Constituency work had to be squeezed in too, along with party work in preparation for the upcoming European and local elections. Cabinet meetings for the entire six months took place very early on Tuesday mornings in Farmleigh. I was out of the house at six thirty most mornings and never in bed before midnight. Seven days a week, from 1 January until 30 June. It was a punishing schedule with zero time for socialising. Once again, the only treat to myself was dinner with the girls on Sunday evenings.

I was extremely lucky in my own officials, particularly Michael

Collins and Eoin O'Leary in the Department of the Taoiseach, Bobby McDonagh in Foreign Affairs, my special adviser, Una Claffey, and Joe Lennon, who did a top-class job on the press. Anne Anderson was superb as the Irish Permanent Representative in Brussels. The only row we really had with the EU officials was over the terrible train bombings in Madrid that killed 191 people and injured more than a thousand. Brussels wanted me to rush out a statement, but I knew enough about these things from the North to know that you had to be sure of your facts before you opened your mouth, especially as Spain was in the middle of a general election. I needed no reminding of what those poor people were going through. I got news of the bombing when I was in the Sycamore Room in Government Buildings with the families of the victims of Omagh. They knew all about resilience in the face of terror. Brussels had nothing to teach us about how to react to terrorist violence.

The appalling tragedy in Madrid was the low point of Ireland's EU presidency. In the face of such an outrage, the Day of Welcomes on 1 May, when we admitted the ten new countries, was an important moment of affirmation. Unfortunately, the threat of a possible terror attack and also potential action by anti-globalisation protesters meant a huge security operation, the largest in the history of the state. In the event, it all passed off peacefully. There was such a brilliant atmosphere around the city. It was glorious weather, probably the only decent day we got that summer. Everyone was in good spirits. I wandered through Stephen's Green and Merrion Square before the official engagements got started and you could feel the buzz. Then it was up to Farmleigh and Áras an Uachtaráin where President McAleese graciously welcomed all the leaders of the EU countries. I was thrilled that they all came, because I know that the event had only gone into their diaries after we had taken up the presidency. I think once they were all there, everyone understood why I had wanted to do it. There was a terrific camaraderie, with a real sense of history and Europe turning a new page.

That was important politically too. The intergovernmental conference in Rome had been very bad for our sense of unity and togetherness. The Day of Welcomes reaffirmed our shared ideals. As we stood there in sunshine, listening to the RTÉ National Symphony Orchestra and Choir performing Beethoven's 'Ode to Joy', it reminded us all of what we were trying to achieve. I could see how moved everyone was by that. Politicians can be cynical about these things, but this was a real emotional moment with the music and a small child from each country presenting their national flag. Afterwards, we had a terrific party, where everybody seemed more relaxed and happy than I had seen them at these European meetings for a long time. At one point in the evening I wandered into the marquee to see the fantastic sight of Gerhard Schröder, the German Chancellor, dancing away to traditional Irish music. Gerhard's a forceful individual, and to be fair he was giving it some serious effort. He is a big fan of the Dubliners, having seen them in O'Donoghue's as a student in the 1960s, and later, during one of Gerhard's official visits to Dublin, Ronnie Drew kindly agreed to perform again in the same pub. On the Day of Welcomes, watching Gerhard in action, I thought to myself, 'If I can get the German Chancellor doing Riverdance, then I can get all the leaders to sign the constitution.'

By the time we all assembled in Brussels in the middle of June for the intergovernmental conference, it was as if the Day of Welcomes had never happened. We had done a good deal of preparatory work and circulated two major documents, but there was still a lot of difficult negotiation that needed to be done before we could reach an agreement. The first day went well, but the working dinner that night, when we discussed who would be the new president of the EU Commission, was terrible. France and Germany were supporting the Belgian premier, Guy Verhofstadt. Britain, Italy and Poland didn't want him. Everyone was narky. Chirac and Schröder were sniping at Blair and Berlusconi, with the personal bad feeling over the war in Iraq still evident. Everyone had to be given the chance to have their say about the EU president, so the atmosphere got worse and worse as it went on. Verhofstadt was in the room listening to all this, so he was seriously grumpy by the end. All the while I was trying to keep the show on the road. In the end I suggested that we park the issue. I promised to take a straw poll on the top job. I met the leaders one by one, with Ambassador Anne Anderson keeping a tally. It was like confession, with most telling me in private what they had not been prepared to say in public. A few asked me if I would be interested in the job, but I brushed that aside. By the end of the night, having spoken to everyone, it was clear that the Belgian prime minister didn't have a hope in hell of getting it. I informed the leaders. We had got nowhere.

By the next morning I knew that I had just one day to get a deal with the constitution. I told everyone that we had to focus on that and forget who might get which job. There was enough to be tackled with the constitution. I had done this so many times before. If you can get people away from making great long speeches about points of principle and get them to concentrate on specifics, that's how you make progress. It was just like Castle Buildings, when Sinn Féin had come in with a huge list of objections. Fine: let's work through them one by one. The unions had problems with social partnership. Talk them through one at time. It's always about the specifics. When you've ticked them all off, you've got yourselves an agreement.

We started off in the morning with twenty-seven countries, nine with no problems, nine with a few problems, and nine very unhappy. We started working through every objection. By teatime, we had eighteen with no problems, nine still not on board. And so it went on. Each detailed objection dealt with word by word. There were a few officials and advisers on hand to work out the exact language and make sure everyone was happy. Once we had signed off on each point, that was the end of discussion on it.

We were at it for fifteen hours, gradually whittling down the objections, particularly on issues surrounding qualified majority voting in the European Council, the number of European Commissioners and the size of representation in the European Parliament. Over the course of the night I had several one-to-one meetings, and others with small groups of leaders who needed to work together on specific issues.

In the end only Poland was holding out. Before we went into the final full session, I had a long conversation with the Polish prime minister, Marek Belka. He was only in the job a few weeks and was having terrible political troubles at home, so I knew he was under pressure to defend his position. I told him that I had gone as far I could to deal with his concerns, but that I had reached the end of the line. 'You have to make your mind up now,' I told him. I didn't try to put the squeeze on him, but I did go through it with him in great detail. In the end he agreed to proceed as long as he was allowed to have his say in the plenary meeting.

At the conclusion of the last session I informed the members that I had answered all the points, got clarification on everything and that we had a final document, which had been circulated. 'Unless there are any objections,' I said, 'I'm going to declare an agreement.' There was silence in the room. I let it hang there for the briefest moment, then called it. Immediately there was a standing ovation. Champagne appeared from somewhere. Everyone rushed at me, slapping me on the back and saying congratulations, well done. It was an amazing moment, having all the other EU heads saying what a great job we've done. Representing Ireland abroad is a proud time for any Taoiseach, and when you get it right and do the task well, it is deeply satisfying to know that you've not let yourself or the country down.

After the big press conference, I gathered all the Irish crew together, about forty of us, to say thank you and well done. They seemed proud and happy too. It had been a great team effort. 'The Paddies have done it!' everyone kept saying. There's a great photograph of me with Brian Cowen and Dick Roche. They had both played a hugely important role. You can see the delight on all our faces. 'That's one of your best photographs,' I joked with Brian afterwards. 'You're after smiling!'

Just before I had gone out for the press conference, the officials gave me the presidency room for ten minutes to compose myself. Sitting there I had the chance to take in what we had achieved. I took a couple of calls from friends. Then I phoned the girls. They had both been watching it all on Sky News. 'Sounds like you'll be moving to Brussels, Dad!' they said. In fact, I couldn't wait to get back to Drumcondra the following day.

When I did get back, I gave an interview to Charlie Bird for RTÉ. Instead of doing it in the studio, I decided to go to All Hallows. It just seemed a nice thing to do at the time, but looking back on it now I realise there was something going on in my head. Here was the boy from Drumcondra, coming back from an international summit meeting as the president of the European Council. I had played here as a small boy and worked on the farm with my father. It was the place where I had first got to know people from other countries and a place that I had come back to over the years to walk and read and think. It just felt right at what was one of the most important moments of my political career to bring everything back to where it all started.

The following day I attended a Mass in the college chapel celebrated by a friend of mine, Monsignor John Delaney, who was marking the ruby anniversary of his ordination. I just wandered in. All the visitors there from around the world were amazed, because they had been watching me on TV most of the week. The locals knew better though. To them it was just Bertie back home.

It was that same weekend when I started getting the calls. Leaders from all around Europe were phoning to say, 'Well done, you should run for President of the Commission yourself.' To start with I thought this was just people being polite, but when call after call kept coming in, I understood enough about how these kinds of things work to know it was a coordinated approach. About two-thirds of the EU leaders were on to me expressing encouragement before I had even lifted the phone to start a few conversations myself. Tony Blair was very supportive, as were Gerhard Schröder and Jacques Chirac. Even Jean-Claude Juncker of Luxembourg, who many thought wanted the top job for himself, telephoned to say that he would declare immediately for me if I said I wanted it. The question was, did I?

There's no doubt I gave it serious thought. I was confident I had the numbers. I didn't seem to have many enemies and had shown that I was capable of doing the job. The big three powers, Britain, Germany and France, all wanted me to run. So I was thinking hard about it in the week after the Brussels meeting. Obviously I took soundings from a few key people. I had a long chat with Tony Kett about it. I spoke to McCreevy and to Gerry Hickey. Naturally I talked to the girls. There was no one view that emerged. Some people were saying, go on, take it – you've done your bit winning two elections and the party will be fine. Others were asking whether I would be happy living in Brussels and sitting on an aeroplane travelling round the world non-stop. It might sound glamorous, but I can tell you it wears you down. People who knew me best reminded me that even when I was in Government Buildings I couldn't wait to get back to Drumcondra, let alone sitting in Brussels. So there was no consensus. Half the people I was talking were saying go for it. The other half were saying go for the third term like Dev. So it was 'yes, no, yes, no' the whole week.

In the end, I decided no. Partly it was because I thought there was still a job to be done at home. There was the question of living in Brussels, which didn't appeal much. And then there was the thought that while president of the commission was a good job, it was also a thankless one. Perhaps if the constitution came into effect in 2006 and they were looking for a permanent EU president of the council, maybe then I might let my name go forward. But that question hadn't come up yet. The job as it stood was not one for me. I had recently won a general election at home and I was confident that I could win another. At the end of the week I let it be known that it was 'thanks but no thanks'.

That left me with having to organise the person who would take on the job. I was in the last week of our presidency by this stage and I was determined to deal with this one outstanding issue to achieve a clean sweep for Ireland. After an intensive round of discussions, I gathered everyone together in Brussels to agree on the name of José Manuel Barroso, the Portuguese prime minister. It had been a tough job convincing some of the countries to accept him, because he had been a supporter of the Iraq war and was a free marketeer. But I liked Barroso. I thought he had something of Ray MacSharry about him. He had begun to knock the Portuguese economy into shape by reducing the country's budget deficit under the EU Stability and Growth Pact, all the while keeping his coalition together in the face of public hostility to painful cuts. That took courage and skill, both of which Europe needed. To help matters along, he was a nice guy, fluent in many languages. I was pleased to help him get the job.

Another of my key priorities during the Irish presidency had been to improve transatlantic relations. The EU–US summit at Dromoland Castle that June had been something I particularly wanted to go well. There is always huge security but it was something else for this meeting. Millions and millions of people around the world, including Ireland, had been out on the streets protesting about the war in Iraq. That had made George Bush one of the most unpopular presidents ever. The US security forces worked closely with ours during the summit, but there were a few tetchy moments when they made it absolutely clear that the President's safety was their only concern and they weren't going to worry about diplomatic niceties. Perhaps it is understandable that they are super-sensitive with their history of presidential assassinations. As if to prove the point, a photographer got a picture of Bush in his vest standing at his bedroom window in Dromoland. He looked fit for a guy of his age, but it did make you realise that if someone was pointing a camera at his bedroom, God knows what else they could have done. Still, having to put up with that kind of security all the time, I don't know how US presidents tolerate it.

As it turned out, Bush was in great form. He knew that we were trying to rebuild bridges between the EU and the US, so he appreciated that. We had plenty of informal time together and I got to know him much better than I had at our earlier meetings. I think it helped that Laura was with him. She is such a warm person and very relaxed. Her daughters had read *PS, I Love You* and she was telling me how much they had enjoyed it. That was a nice moment for a dad, thinking of the book on the shelves in the White House. There was one funny moment when I took a walk with the President through the grounds for the cameras. That was great, because it was only supposed to be a couple of minutes, but we kept going. As we headed into the woods, I was thinking, 'Jesus, what will the security be thinking of this?' But no, as we went in, there they all were, hiding behind trees. Nothing got past these guys.

There was serious business to discuss. I asked Bush outright about rendition flights passing through Shannon. He told me categorically 'No', that there was no use of Ireland for rendition. Later, Condoleezza Rice told me the same. If one of your most important allies gives you that assurance, you have to accept it unless you intend creating an international incident. He didn't hedge, or say that he didn't have the right information to hand or that he would look into it. This was a straight no. So he gave us that and we had to take him at his word.

When the EU presidency came to an end on 30 June, I felt happy that we had done a good job. It had been a challenging and rewarding time for us all. We had spent twelve months preparing for the presidency and six months running it. During that time, I had travelled the EU three times, chaired conferences around the world, including the EU–Japanese, EU–Canadian, EU–Russian and EU–Latin American/Caribbean summits, and attended the G8 meeting. At the latter, I wore my infamous canary-yellow trousers, which ended up helping me get an award as the World's Best Dressed Leader, even if no one liked them much at home. At the beginning of the presidency, I had said that our overall objective was to secure outcomes that would have a positive impact on the lives of ordinary Europeans. I strongly believed that with the successful enlargement of the Union, the agreement on the European Constitution, and the improvement in transatlantic relations we had done that. I wanted us to get back to first principles, the most basic of which was that Europe must work for its people. Too often, the debate on European issues can drift into jargon and theory. No one outside Brussels was interested in that. I passionately believe that the European Union is not a matter of theory. It has made and will make a real difference to the lives of its citizens. Without the EU, Europe could not have recovered from the devastation of world war. Without it, Europe could not have created a vibrant single market and a strong and stable single currency. And, of course, without it we would not have been in a position to embrace and support those Europeans who had suffered a half-century of totalitarian oppression.

That was why I was so proud of what we did during our presidency. Ireland had helped Europe focus on what unites us, not on what divides us.

14

BOWLING ALONE

In politics, whenever you get ahead of yourself, you can be sure that the voters will give you a good slap. Throughout the spring of 2004 I was the toast of Europe, praised everywhere for the way in which I was handling the presidency. Sure enough, near the end of my term as president, the electorate decided to hand out a drubbing.

On 11 June, local and European elections had taken place throughout Ireland. They were a disaster for Fianna Fáil. We lost eighty-one council seats and were down two MEPs. On one level I took this on the chin. All the senior people in the party had been involved in the EU presidency day and night, preparing for the upcoming intergovernmental conference, so there had been little chance of getting our heavyweights out campaigning. I loved canvassing as much as anyone, but even I was restricted. I might get off the plane on a Friday night and go door-to-door for a couple of hours, but that was pretty much it. The hit we took in the election looked even bigger because there was a large turnout. This was because we had put an important but controversial citizenship measure up for referendum, but that made it easy to say that this was a 'massive protest vote' against the government. We might not have been at our most popular, but it didn't help that we had given so much of our time and effort to the presidency rather than the campaign at home. We had seen it coming and had to accept the hard reality of lost seats.

But it was a wake-up call. We had been getting it in the neck from the media since the cutbacks in 2002. Public opinion was not happy with us either. You couldn't deny that a lot of that anger had gone into the polling booths, with people saying, 'We need to keep these guys on their toes.' I remember McCreevy saying to me a good while beforehand that we were going to get a terrible kicking no matter what we did. That was right, but there was no doubt that complacency had set in. People were starting to get a bit too comfort-able in power, taking it for granted. If you get too easy in the back of your government car, the voters are going to throw you out on the street. I was especially disappointed because we lost a lot of good councillors and stopped the momentum we had achieved back in the 1999 locals.

We had also looked like amateurs. That really annoyed me. What made it worse was that the candidate who had got himself into the greatest difficulty was someone I knew well. I have known Royston Brady since he was a kid. His brother Cyprian was one of my closest aides in Dublin Central. Royston had run his own ward in the constituency and done it well. He had energy and enthusiasm matched by an honest desire to make life better in one of the poorest areas of the city centre. He had done a good job as Lord Mayor. He was high profile and popular, so we decided to run him in the Euro elections in 2004. We hoped that he would attract younger voters, especially on the Northside. He ran alongside Eoin Ryan, a popular TD from the Southside. Eoin had a good campaign and was elected. Royston on the other hand got bogged down in all kinds of con-troversies, including one after he had said that his father's taxi had been stolen and used as a getaway car by Loyalists who had bombed

Dublin in 1974. Apparently that was true, but some of the victims' families accused him of using the bombings as a cheap way to get votes. Then he refused to turn up for interviews with the media, so he looked as if he was running away. It was real amateur stuff. I was out of the country while this was going on, but I was getting frantic phone calls from some of the guys who were helping run the campaign, telling me that Royston had completely lost it. Afterwards, when he didn't get the seat, he started to get into the blame game. I never rose to that, because I didn't want the office of Taoiseach dragged into a slagging match, but he seriously fell out with a lot of my crew.

There's an old saying that it's good to be lucky in your friends, but it is even better to be lucky in your enemies. This was the case for us in 2004. However badly we had done in the elections, we were fortunate that the opposition really didn't know how to take advantage. Fine Gael and Labour entered into their 'Mullingar Accord' that summer, which promised an alternative programme at the next general election. That was a house built on sand right from the start. It was always easy for us to exploit the differences between the two parties, and within each party, as they argued over the next few years about what new government would be like. They spent so much time debating what they would do when they were in government that they completely forgot they had to try and kick us out first.

Part of the problem was that a lot of people didn't think the 'Taoiseach-in-waiting' was up to the job. That would dog them all the way to the next election. Enda Kenny is a straightforward and decent person, and I admire what he did with revitalising the grass-roots organisation of Fine Gael in his early years as leader, because that was something I did with Fianna Fáil in 1994. But I think the problem was that Enda's party, especially in the Dáil, didn't really believe in him. Michael Noonan had left him out when he was leader. That helped Enda get himself elected almost as part of a backbench coup, but as soon as he was in, you could see them all thinking, 'What have we done?' There was Richard Bruton sitting beside him, who they could have had. He's very focused on the economy, finance and reform. He's obviously a strategic thinker and can give you a fair old tongue-lashing in the debates. I don't think Enda ever managed to lay a glove on me. He certainly never got a knockout punch.

Once the EU presidency was over on 30 June 2004, I set about trying to shake the party up, reconstructing the government and the National Executive. First I did an analysis of the recent election's numbers with the general secretary, Seán Dorgan, to see what they might mean for a general election. There would be a root-and-branch reform of the Fianna Fáil structures. We had around 55,000 members in 3,000 cumainn. That kind of local strength needed to be harnessed, including getting more people out canvassing throughout the year. We identified about ten constituencies that were going to be particularly vulnerable to new threats, including my own in Dublin Central. Sinn Féin had made good progress, with Mary Lou McDonald picking up an EU seat in Dublin. That was as clear a sign as we needed that the party would be under threat from Sinn Féin unless we changed tactics, emphasising that we were the real Republican party. I also wanted to get TDs and local workers to report back on what the voters had been saying on the doorstep.

The message I got from that was loud and clear. People felt that we had become too business-oriented. They were pleased that the country was doing so well, but there were other values that mattered too. Surely the point of a strong economy was that we could share things out a little more, helping the disadvantaged. Whether that was a right or wrong impression, it definitely seemed to be one that was strongly held. Clearly we needed to spend more time showing that we were helping the poor and the sick.

The way that events turned out, it looked as if I was happy to make one man the scapegoat for the government's popularity slump. Charlie McCreevy had always been a controversial figure. After the bad results in June, the usual suspects in the parliamentary party started gunning for him. When he left the government shortly afterwards to become Ireland's EU Commissioner, it looked as if he had jumped before he was pushed. Nothing could have been further from the truth. I had already known for a long time that Charlie was on his way to Brussels. The previous September, on his birthday as it happens, he had come to see me to discuss the vacancy at the commission that would be coming up the following year. He explained that he would be fifty-five, had been in Dáil since 1977 and had fought a few battles during that time. He had done seven years as Minister for Finance and implemented a reforming agenda. But he also had a young family and wanted to take account of that. 'Would you give me first refusal on the EU Commission?' he asked me outright. I told him that I would be sorry to lose him, but of course if he wanted the job, it was his. That was agreed between us. When I raised it subsequently with José Manuel Barroso, the president of the commission, he told me he anticipated Charlie getting an important economic portfolio. I passed this along and Charlie seemed excited about the prospect of going.

Then came a slight wobble in the middle of July. Charlie definitely felt some emotion about leaving the Dáil and his constituency. Then there was the thought of commuting to Brussels. But what really made him have second thoughts were those few individuals in the party saying it was time to get rid of him. Anyone who knows Charlie will tell you that he is a fighter who isn't afraid of anything. He had not left to join the PDs when there had been the chance and he had stayed in Fianna Fáil to defend his corner. He wasn't going to leave the government just because a few backbenchers didn't like him. Quite the opposite. He now began to think about staying just to show people that no-one pushed Charlie McCreevy around. I told Charlie that if he didn't want it, he didn't have to take it, although to be honest I never thought he was going to refuse. What I did tell him, though, was that he was going to have to make his mind up soon, because otherwise I would be offering it to Séamus Brennan. He asked to have the weekend to think about it and then phoned me to say that he would like to accept the nomination.

right. She would certainly be up to the job. The moment when I appointed her as Minister for Education was very emotional. Mary's husband, the barrister Eamon Leahy, had died suddenly the year before, aged just forty-six, so inevitably the real achievement of being appointed to cabinet was a bitter-sweet moment for her. Naturally there were a few tears as we talked about Eamon and how proud he would have been.

The press tried to create a row between Séamus Brennan and myself about where he was going. He was sorry to leave Transport, but I told him that Social Welfare had moved to the top of our political agenda and that I needed one of our biggest hitters in that department. A couple of weeks earlier, Fianna Fáil had been down to Inchydoney, Co. Cork, for a 'think-in' at which I had told the parliamentary party we needed to keep focused on issues of social justice and social inclusion. Father Healy from CORI spoke to us on strategies for addressing the growing poverty gap. It was one of the paradoxes of our open, competitive economy. Putting Séamus in at Social Welfare was a sign of how seriously I was taking that.

It bothered me a great deal that the government was presented as Thatcherite and uncaring. I wasn't going to apologise for the economic success that Ireland enjoyed under Fianna Fáil, but it was only one side of the equation. Since we had come to office in 1997, hundreds of thousands of additional people were at work in the country. We had brought forward some of the most progressive social measures anywhere in Europe. Child benefit had trebled, old-age pensions had increased by two-thirds and we had introduced the minimum wage. Record levels of funding had been pumped into education and the health service. Our inner cities were being transformed, with some of the poorest communities benefiting from a modern housing stock. These were real achievements making real differences in people's lives.

That was something we were never really given credit for. Sometimes I would look at people pontificating in the Dáil or writing in the papers who I knew for a fact didn't have the first idea of what poverty and deprivation really meant. I'm not saying that if you went to a private school and grew up surrounded by wealth that you can't know about these things – but it was obvious when you listened to a lot of these guys that they didn't have a clue. The truth is that I felt well qualified to understand what the issues were for the old, the unemployed, and those who were excluded, because I had been dealing with them all my political life in Dublin Central. Whatever the successes and failures of my time in politics, the one thing I've always done is try to help those in need.

I made a comment around this time that I was 'one of the few socialists left in Irish politics'. I might have meant it slightly tongue in cheek, because I certainly wouldn't be an ideological socialist. But it had a grain of truth. I was genuinely interested in helping the poor and making sure that we redistributed wealth to help the low-paid and disadvantaged. I pumped billions into the health service and social services. I worked with the unions on social partnership to deliver a better deal for workers. And I protected and improved the wonderful civic amenities that belong to all of us. I worked hard over the years, to take a local example, to invest in the Botanic Gardens, which were in poor repair and are now one of the glories of Dublin. The Farmleigh Estate was purchased by the state and is one of many houses we restored around the country that are used extensively by the public. Maybe it was naive, but since I was a child, I had always believed that when places like that were owned by the state, I owned them. These were the places that we shared together as a community. Perhaps it wasn't socialism exactly, but it was definitely a belief in society.

I had been influenced for many years by the work of a Harvard professor of public policy, Robert Putnam, and in particular his book *Bowling Alone*. The book's title drew on a statistic from the 1980s and 90s which showed that while the total number of bowlers in the US had increased by 10 per cent, league bowling had declined by 40 per cent. That was a neat way of showing that participation in community life seemed to be breaking down. Voter turnout, church attendance and union membership were all down. Fewer people bothered to attend community meetings. Membership in voluntary associations was declining. Over the previous twenty-five years, club meetings had declined by 58 per cent, the number of families eating together had dropped by 43 per cent and even having friends over had decreased by 35 per cent. These were depressing trends in social capital.

I wanted to avoid this happening in Irish civil society. Living in Drumcondra had given me a real appreciation of the importance of community life. In my first term, we had introduced a White Paper on community development to try and strengthen civil society, and in my second term I asked Mary Davis to head a Taskforce on Active Citizenship to encourage greater civic participation in Irish society. In 2007, it delivered an outstanding set of recommendations about how we can encourage people to remain active in sporting, cultural and voluntary organisations.

The whole question of society and values came to be more and more on my mind from this time onwards. I suppose early on in my tenure as Taoiseach, I was grappling so hard with doing the job itself, that it wasn't always easy to step back and see the bigger picture. As I went on, though, picking up little tricks along the way, the job became if not easier, then simpler to read. Experience has to count for something. That gave me time to think about some of the broader issues facing the country. One of those was religion. I had done my best to help Ireland become a more open, cosmopolitan society that respected the various traditions on the island and welcomed new ones. Around this period, particularly after we opened up our labour market to the EU accession countries on 1 May 2004, we were experiencing record levels of immigration. Approximately 70,000 people were coming into the country annually. I think we dealt with that well, making Ireland a good destination for anyone who wanted to start a new life. Many of those who came, particularly from Poland, were attracted to our Catholic and family values.

But the Church and the religious institutions had been going through a terrible time. Truly horrible things had been coming out about child abuse that turned many people against religion. The issue of child abuse in religious institutions in our society is a scandal of appalling proportions. The more I've learnt about these sickening activities, the greater my anger at those who perpetrated abuse and the greater my disappointment at those who allowed it to happen. The largest proportion of abuse occurred many decades ago, but for a number of reasons, the full extent of abuse in institutions has only become apparent in more recent years. One of the reasons for that was the failure of successive governments to face up to the extent to which the state was to blame for what happened. There was a reluctance to admit that as a state and as a society we failed many of the children of the nation by allowing them to be incarcerated in places where they were not cherished.

On 11 May 1999, I apologised to the victims of abuse. 'On behalf of the state and of all citizens of the state,' I said, 'the government wishes to make a sincere and long-overdue apology to the victims of childhood abuse for our collective failure to intervene, to detect their pain, to come to their rescue.' There were plenty of people telling me not to make that apology, that there were compelling reasons – financial and legal – why we should say nothing. But that did not hold water for me. I had listened to the sincerity and logic of people like Christine Buckley, who had campaigned on behalf of the victims, and I knew it was the right thing to do. It was one of the best decisions I made as Taoiseach. It was something I felt deeply about and I thank God I did it. There are many brave but vulnerable survivors of childhood abuse, whose young lives were shattered by terrible wrongs that were perpetrated upon them. The reality is that much of the abuse that occurred in the past was directed towards children who were pupils in residential institutions that were regulated and supervised by the state. An apology and a recognition of the wrong that was done to them in the state's care was the very least they deserved.

In the aftermath of the apology, it became clear that, if the words of the apology were going to mean anything, they would have to be followed up by actions. Those actions would have to be strong and meaningful, and performed on a scale that was big enough to make a difference for the survivors of abuse. At that time, we had just come to terms with the fact that awful abuse had happened in institutions, though we did not yet understand the terrible scale of what had happened. We established a Commission to Inquire into Child Abuse, which would later – after nine years of painstaking work – publish the full, terrible story.

There was also a clear need to compensate the victims of abuse for the suffering they had endured. Several hundred victims had started some legal claims in the first few years after the apology. The lawyers for all sides looked likely to make a handsome profit from that process because of the massive complexity of the legal issues. What was the division of liability between the congregations who inflicted the abuse and the state that failed to stop it? Would elderly victims have to wait years for court cases to come to hearing, and then have to face traumatic cross-examinations when they finally got their day in court? Could congregations – which are not like legal companies – even be made liable in law for the actions of their members? These and many other problems made it seem like the courts would not be a suitable place for victims to pursue justice.

For that reason, we decided to set up a compensation scheme for the victims of abuse. We wanted the scheme to be fair, easily accessible by victims and not be tied up in unnecessary legalities. I have heard that some victims later had issues with the Residential Institutions Redress Board, but it was designed to be as fair a place as it could possibly be for victims, and I believe that everyone who has worked there has done their best to make that design a reality.

Beside the question of whether there would be an out-of-court redress scheme was a separate issue. That was how much the religious orders should pay towards the scheme. That is a matter which has become very controversial in recent years, as the full, awful truth of institutional abuse has become clear. The view we took in the period between 2000 and 2002 was based on the information we had then, not the information we have now.

As I understood it then, the congregations took a confrontational negotiating position against the government side in those discussions. This was based on the fact that, if the congregations dealt with these cases through the courts, their liability would be limited because of all the legal complexities. The state had a high chance of being left with the bill, and many victims would be left with nothing. We were going to set up a redress scheme, but it was probably not going to be possible to force the congregations to contribute to that scheme. So the government side had to persuade the congregations to contribute, and to do that we had to offer them an indemnity in relation to the court cases from victims.

We were also conscious of the fact that we didn't want to bankrupt the religious orders who, though they had harboured many evil members over the decades, were doing some very good and important work. The congregations were still filling roles which the state would have to take on if they were bankrupted.

Michael Woods, when he was Minister for Education, had negotiated an agreement in good faith in those circumstances. The contribution towards the redress scheme which the congregations made was a large amount of money and seemed, at the time, to be a significant percentage of what our redress scheme was going to cost. That was based on the understanding we had of child abuse in 2002.

Looking back now, after the nine years of investigations by the Commission to Inquire into Child Abuse, we know that abuse was far more systematic and institutionalised than it appeared in 2002. The cost of compensating victims was also far higher. In the meantime, many of the orders have had enormous windfalls of cash by selling property during years when land was extremely valuable.

In light of those developments, the moral arguments recently made by Brian Cowen and others to the congregations are unanswerable. The congregations should revisit their contribution and make more of a financial commitment to right the wrongs that their members committed.

Over the years since we made the agreement, there have been all kinds of criticisms of it. It is easy to say with hindsight that we should have held out for a bigger contribution from the congregations, but there were no legal mechanisms to do that.

This issue was thrown back at me many times in the Dáil, especially by the Labour Party. Time and again, they tried to insinuate that we had done something wrong. Unfortunately, the truth is difficult to summarise in a three-minute reply during Leaders' Questions. The legal issues involved were enormously convoluted, though I got great assistance from Loughlin Deegan in the Attorney General's office, who helped communicate difficult legal concepts in language people could understand. My essential message was simple: this was an agreement reached in good faith to help clear away the legal blockages which might prevent victims of abuse from getting their fair redress.

There can be no doubt about the full horror of what went on in the Industrial Schools. The state and the religious institutions had failed many of the children of Ireland. It is inevitable under those circumstances that much of the good work and the contribution of so many religious across Ireland, and indeed the world, is now overlooked. But in truth we still owe thanks to many visionary priests, nuns and brothers across the country for facilitating our development as a people. They are the opposite of those who inflicted only cruelty and abuse in schools. They recognised the importance of an education for life. That did not mean education simply in the narrow sense of knowledge attained, but rather in terms of the values it instilled in us as members of a community. It was thanks to those men and women that many gifted children from less privileged backgrounds were able to realise their full potential in life. At a time when the expectations and opportunities for young women in Ireland were extraordinarily limited, religious sisters were the loudest champions of education for girls. The tremendously vibrant Gaelic Games of which we are so proud today would not have thrived were it not for the unpaid work of brothers and teachers, both lay and religious, in every parish across the country. Equally, it was impossible to quantify the debt we owed to successive generations of religious who nursed our sick and reached out to our poor.

Embracing those values did not mean turning back the clock, or sweeping the wrongs that happened in the Industrial Schools under the carpet. The truth was that for too many people, the 'good old days' were marred by destitution, powerlessness and despair. But it is worth recognising that the Church has been a force for good as well. Turning our back as a country on our living and vibrant religious faith would be a loss and a mistake. And now that we have a multitude of Churches, the dialogue between religions and the state must be conducted on a multi-faith basis. In July 2005 I announced, as part of an EU-wide process, the establishment of structures for formal dialogue between the government and the faiths operating within the state. 'Our country, our strengths and our weaknesses are all part of a long gestation of history, of culture and of religious belief,' I said when launching this initiative. 'We cannot understand who we are today, let alone where we hope to go tomorrow, if we do not first understand and listen with an open ear to the deepest influences within our national life.'

That ability to reflect on our history in an open and tolerant way was a central priority of my period as Taoiseach. From the outset in 1997, I had given particular support to the process of commemoration. This usually involved some kind of public ceremony as well as serious academic research to debate the important and often controversial issues surrounding the various anniversaries and historical landmarks. These would have been as varied as the seventy-fifth anniversary of the foundation of the Irish Free State in 1922, the bicentenary anniversaries of the 1798 Rebellion and the death of Robert Emmet, the reinterment of the remains of 'the forgotten ten', and recognition for the Irish regiments who fought in the First World War. The 32 counties of Ireland had been a divided society in so many different ways, but we had a shared past. If that history could be commemorated respectfully, I believed that would make an impact on our shared future.

There was one event in particular that I was always determined to revive. Looking back on my childhood, one of the great occasions in my life was the fiftieth anniversary of 1916. I only had to close my eyes to see the amazing pageant at Croke Park or to hear the guns as the army fired the salute from the roof of the GPO. Then the Troubles came, with the violence, the bombings and the killings. The Provos tried to claim they were the heirs of the Rising. The revisionists trashed the whole 1916 legacy. People got so uncomfortable with militarism that the annual military parade was scrapped. The Good Friday Agreement had changed this context. I was determined to take 1916 back from both the IRA and the revisionists for all the people of Ireland. That was why in October 2005, given great encouragement by Attorney General Rory Brady, I announced the reinstatement of the military parade, with the army marching past the GPO, and the establishment of a 1916 Centenary Committee to prepare for the hundredth anniversary in 2016. 'The Irish people need to reclaim the spirit of 1916,' I said, 'which is not the property of those who have abused and debased the title of Republicanism.'

This was not a popular move to begin with. Although the PDs were supportive, when I sounded out others, including Enda Kenny, there weren't many takers. That was a shame, I thought, because it ignored the fact that many of the important figures in his own party had fought in the Rising. By the time we got to the anniversary itself, I think most of them had changed their minds. There were huge crowds for the events, with 120,000 people out on the streets to mark the day. What made me especially happy was the number of young people who turned out, making a new connection with 1916. Obviously I had spent a bit of time worrying that it might not come off, wondering how the spectators, the army, the opposition would view the whole event. I had been going to commemorations for the Rising all my life, going to Arbour Hill and Glasnevin with my dad. It had hurt me when Sinn Féin hijacked these events, so I was anxious that the anniversary should be retrieved from all that. There would only be one army in our state and that was Óglaigh na hÉireann. This would be a commemoration by the state and the people for those who gave their lives for Irish freedom.

The march past was fantastic, but for me the most telling moment took place earlier in the day. There was a short ceremony held in the yard at Kilmainham Gaol where Pearse and his compatriots had been brought out and shot. That was such an eerie moment. The walls of the yard are so high, you could imagine how the shots must have sounded as they reverberated around. Inevitably my thoughts were with the fifteen men who were executed over nine days, but for a moment I found myself wondering about the emotions of the young soldiers who shot them. When the wounded Connolly was brought in on a stretcher, strapped to his chair and shot, it must have been an image that stayed with his executioners forever.

After the march past, I walked back to the Gresham Hotel, chatting to people along the way, to meet the relatives of the 1916 leaders. The highlight was talking to Father Joseph Mallin, the son of Michael Mallin, who had been just two years old when his father was executed. I had meet him previously in his Jesuit house in Hong Kong. Now, at ninety-two and the only surviving child of an executed leader, he was a bit embarrassed by all the fuss made of him. But he talked about his father and James Connolly, who was clearly such a hero to him. I spent hours there that afternoon talking to the relatives, being photographed and sharing stories. In a way, this was like the meeting of a great extended family. These were relatives of people

of this island, from all traditions, in the year of 1916. Everyone had their sides, but what mattered was that the sacrifice of all of those who died be acknowledged and commemorated in an appropriate and respectful manner. I saw that powerfully in 2006 when the famous words, 'At the going down of the sun and in the morning, we will remember them', were spoken at the restored memorial to the 131 men from Fermoy who died during the Great War. A huge crowd turned out in the rain. This was the heart of traditional Republican territory. Ned O'Keeffe, who had been closely involved in the project, was a TD from the Republican wing of the party. It was deeply moving to witness such a noble spirit of remembrance and commemoration.

Respect for our shared history was one of the ways that we were trying to build a shared future North and South. It was something that, probably to the surprise of both of us, Ian Paisley and I agreed about. It would turn out to be an important factor in implementing the Good Friday Agreement. In 2004, Tony Blair and I had been determined that we weren't just going to let matters 'drift on'. After a series of intensive meetings with the parties earlier in the year, talks resumed in the autumn at Leeds Castle in Kent. Paisley had been very ill in hospital. His son later admitted that his father had been 'at death's door'. That seemed to focus his mind a bit, because although he still wouldn't engage directly with Sinn Féin he was now saying publicly that we had 'never been closer' to doing a deal. Bizarrely, I think we might have made even more progress if Leeds Castle hadn't turfed us out because they were booked for a wedding!

When Paisley came to Dublin for a first official meeting at the end of September, that was an important moment. He wouldn't shake hands at this stage, which didn't bother me. More importantly, he was in great form, mingling with everyone and roaring with laughter. He was very businesslike and professional in the meetings, not doing too much grandstanding. Don't forget, this was the man who had been protesting outside Castle Buildings as negotiations for the Good Friday Agreement had been taking place. People are sometimes surprised that he's actually a very courteous man and he likes it when everyone's polite. He was pleased we showed him the respect due to the leader of the biggest party in the North. Slowly, slowly, it looked as if we might finally be getting him to agree.

I should have known better. When it came to the peace process, it paid never to get ahead of yourself. There was always something waiting to go wrong. From the end of November onwards, three things happened in quick succession that put us right back where we had started. First, Paisley made a speech to DUP supporters in Ballymena saying that 'the IRA needs to be humiliated. And they need to wear their sackcloth and ashes, not in a back room but openly.' There was an almighty row about that. When I met Tony in the margins of an EU summit in Brussels that December, I warned him that there wasn't even 'a glimmer' of that happening. Then a few days afterwards, on 20 December, a gang robbed the Northern Bank in Belfast of £26.5 million. 'This was a Provisional IRA job,' I said on *This Week*, after reading the intelligence report. 'This is a job that would have been known to the political leadership, that is my understanding.' I knew this would provoke a reaction, but it had to be said. I was happy to kick them all over the shop on that one, because I was furious. Nobody else was going to be able to conduct a raid like that and vanish with the money. Sinn Féin tried to take umbrage and tensions were high. They got worse on 30 January 2005 when Robert McCartney was stabbed to death and Brendan Devine was seriously injured outside Magennis's pub in Belfast. These attacks provoked revulsion in Ireland and around the world. When the day afterwards, Tony Blair and I said that the 'continuing paramilitary activity and criminal activity of the IRA' were the main obstacle to peace, we were just stating the obvious. Once again, we were nowhere.

I think everyone felt disgust about what had happened at Magennis's. The way it was covered up, the horrific offer by the IRA to shoot dead the perpetrators. Everywhere people were asking themselves, what is this horrendous place, has nothing changed? I met the McCartney family many times over the next while. They were very brave people. They had historically been Sinn Féin supporters, so for them to confront their own in the way they did caught the mood, especially in the United States. They met President Bush and Hillary Clinton, and their fight for justice had a big effect. And although I know they were angry that no-one was ever convicted for the murder, there was no doubt that their campaign had an impact on the IRA. A few weeks after the McCartneys' visit to the White House, Gerry Adams made a speech appealing to the IRA to make the 'truly historic decision [that] the struggle can now be taken forward by other means'. Soon afterwards the IRA ordered an end to the armed campaign and committed itself to completing the process of verifiably putting its arms beyond use. All Volunteers were ordered to help develop purely political and democratic programmes through exclusively peaceful means and specifically not to engage in any other activities whatsoever.

In the days leading up to this announcement, I had spent two long sessions with Gerry Adams at St Luke's. I noted how determined he was to make progress, and I admired that. He seemed to have made up his mind to get the job done. In the end it was a brave move by the IRA, because they were giving away the Republican movement's main card. I heard later that officials in the US State Department were impressed by Adams as well, noting how he had brought a terrorist organisation into the political process. There was no doubt the announcement was a historic development, one that we all hoped would herald a new era. That seemed to be confirmed in September, when the IICD reported that they had witnessed a fourth and 'very large' act of decommissioning, which they believed represented 'the totality of the IRA's arsenal'. It was a momentous day, I said, and one that showed 'the gun of the IRA is out of Irish politics'.

But Paisley was unconvinced. He criticised the lack of detail on the weapons decommissioned, calling it a 'cover-up', and accusing both governments of duplicity. I was astonished. When we met in November for the annual stocktaking on the peace process, I was amazed at how laid-back he was about moving the process forward. We had put ferocious pressure on the IRA to say the war was over and to dump their arms. They had now done that. If the DUP didn't respond, the process was over. For the first time I began to wonder if that was what Paisley had wanted all along. Had it all been a game? Was he just playing with us all? If the answer was yes, then we were in trouble. I really felt the time had come for the British to put pressure on Paisley in the way we had done with Adams and McGuinness. All through 2005, we had used the pressure that had built up on the IRA after the Northern Bank raid and the murder of Robert McCartney to try to force a comprehensive statement. I had put in a huge amount of time and effort on that. That had been a very tense time, but we had kept going. So I felt from the Irish side, in taking responsibility for getting the Republicans on board, that we had delivered. After all that work, it annoyed me to watch the Unionists sitting back in their chairs saying they wanted more. It was time for the British to get tough with them.

When Tony came to Farmleigh in January, I had to tell him that in fairly blunt terms. I said that we needed more pressure on the DUP. I also said that after almost eight years at this, we needed to get a deal within twelve months, or else scrap the Agreement and start again on something else. 'And with someone else,' Tony added, giving me the first sign that maybe he was thinking of packing it all in.

I think by this stage we both realised that, for better or worse, the peace process was now in its end game. By the time I met Tony again at Navan Fort in Armagh in April, we had agreed a way to try and force a result. The Assembly would be recalled on 15 May. If it failed to elect a First and Deputy First Minister within six weeks, we would allow a further twelve weeks after the summer recess to try to form an executive. If there was still no agreement by 24 November, there would be no elections and the MLAs would have their salaries stopped. When the Northern Ireland Assembly reconvened that May, Gerry Adams nominated Paisley and McGuinness as First and Deputy First Ministers. Paisley rejected the nomination. The clock was now ticking and everyone knew it. As Tony put it, 'This is the last chance for this generation to make this process work.'

When we all gathered at St Andrews in Scotland the following October, everyone knew the stakes. Naming a date wasn't just some cheap trick to apply pressure. We had been through years of slowly removing obstacles, dealing with the issues and squaring the parties. I felt very strongly that we had to put a timetable on the process or else it would just drift on forever. Tony had been sceptical to start with, but by now he was absolutely in agreement that it couldn't drag on any more. We had to get answers.

A few days beforehand, the Independent Monitoring Commission issued a report saying that the IRA had disbanded 'military' structures. That was good news, because it gave an impetus to the final intensive talks. These focused on the crucial issues of timing and sequencing, Sinn Féin's endorsement of policing, the devolution of policing and justice, and finalising changes to the institutions. Tony and I presented a draft agreement to the parties on the final morning, including a timeline starting from the nomination of First and Deputy First Ministers designate on 24 November leading to an election in early March and devolution restored on 26 March.

The atmosphere as always on these occasions was tough. It was lashing rain on the first day, which seemed a bad omen, although as the weather improved, so did the talks. Tony was in poor form, because the UK Chief of the Defence Staff had landed him in it with some loose talk about Iraq. My relationship with Gerry Adams around this time was frosty. In these particular sessions, he was more aggressive than usual and we had some rough encounters. Predictably, whenever it looked as if we were close to getting a deal, Adams would come back with more demands. It was frustrating, but years of negotiation had taught me the only way to deal with this was to keep cool and talk the issues through one by one.

Paisley on the other hand seemed happy enough. You could see there were real divisions within the DUP, but when I looked at him, I thought I could see a man who had decided to say 'yes'. For half a century, he had been saying 'no' to everything. Could he put that behind him and change? I was beginning to think he could. I had enjoyed a particularly warm discussion in a private meeting with him and his son, Ian Jnr. At the end of the last session, I gave Ian and his wife, Eileen, a gift to mark their golden wedding anniversary. It was a bowl carved from a walnut tree that had stood on the site of the Battle of the Boyne. I would like to say it was all my idea, but I think it came from Dermot Gallagher in Foreign Affairs. Tony thought it was a good idea as well, so good in fact that he even tried to borrow it. 'What did we get them?' he asked Jonathan Powell. 'A photograph album, Prime Minister,' Jonathan replied. 'Damn!' said Tony. 'Bertie, I wonder, should we give them the bowl from both of us?' It was a nice try.

Anyhow, the gift was a masterstroke. Paisley was genuinely moved. We had seen 'the first sign of a new light', he said in that incredible preacher's voice of his, 'and I hope that this light shines not just on those in this room but on our children and grandchildren'. It was an amazing moment. When Gerry Adams jumped up to lead the applause, looking about as emotional as he ever gets, Tony and I exchanged a look that said 'we might be in here'.

With the North, you never took anything for granted, not least, I couldn't help thinking on this occasion, because we concluded the St Andrews Agreement on Friday the 13th. But I left Scotland with some hope that we might be able to finish the process. That was good, because by this stage there was enough going on at home that I wasn't sure how much longer I would be Taoiseach.

In politics, the clock is always ticking.

15

HEADED FOR THE FUTURE

I had been here so many times before. TV interviews were my bread and butter. It was just part of the job and you got on with it. Sometimes they would go well, at other times it could be rough, but you accepted that. No one comes into politics expecting an easy ride. I've got no real friends who are journalists, because at the end of the day their job is to make yours hard. So you just have to go out there and defend what you believe in. This time it was Brian Dobson from the *Six-One News*. By and large he's one of the good guys. He gives you a fair interview and lets you get a word in edgeways without talking over the top of you all the time like some. It was ten minutes into the interview and I could feel myself starting to go. I was in St Luke's, which was home ground, but now as I talked about my personal life, perhaps being there meant it all came back too easily. That dark period in my life when this office really had been my home. No family, no house. Marriage broken. Seeing the kids once a week. Sleeping upstairs, taking my stuff round to the launderette. Living off a bad diet. As I started talking about the girls, putting money into an account to pay for their education, my voice started to break. You know that feeling, when you're about to lose it in public. That feels even worse on television. TV picks up every move you make. When the cameras are rolling, there's nowhere to hide. No discreet turning away or pretending to blow your nose. So I was just swallowing and swallowing, trying not to let it show. In the end I had to take one long, deep breath to steady myself, to say to myself, 'Get it together.' I could feel the colour draining out of my face. I bit my lip to sting myself back into action. That gave me a moment. I could see it in Dobson's face, him thinking I was going to break down. The minute I realised that, I got it back together. I wouldn't give anyone the satisfaction.

Events had started the week before with the *Irish Times*. On 21 September 2006, Colm Keena had written a story based on information before the Mahon Tribunal. It said that individuals had been contacted by the Tribunal concerning payments made to me in December 1993. And so began a period in my life and that of the country that would be dominated by the Mahon Tribunal and allegations against me. The soap opera that this became would not subside until after my resignation as Taoiseach in May 2008.

In fairness I thought I had already put all these false allegations behind me. On 10 July 2001, Judge John O'Hagan at the Dublin Circuit Court had said that ludicrous claims by Denis Starry O'Brien of a IR£50,000 bribe being given to me in 1989 on behalf of a Cork property developer, Owen O'Callaghan, were 'utterly, completely and absolutely false'. The judge found that I had been defamed by O'Brien and awarded me maximum damages for that defamation. To me, this judicial decision was a public vindication through the courts of my reputation and character. But it was not the end of a saga of untrue allegations being made against me. The allegation of the O'Callaghan bribe had also been made to the Mahon Tribunal, which I had helped set up in 1997 to investigate and report on corruption in the planning process. On this occasion the author of the allegation was a Luton-based property developer called Thomas Gilmartin. He alleged I received IR£50,000 in 1989 from O'Callaghan and a further bribe of IR£30,000 in 1992, although these dates were subsequently changed many times by Gilmartin in the course of his dealings with the Tribunal.

Through the evidence given in the court case, it was clear that a building society account book bearing O'Brien's name had been forged and an entry purporting to represent the proceeds for the purchase of a IR£50,000 draft was doctored. The account only ever held IR£500. Moreover, I was supposed to have received this IR£50,000 cheque on the day of the All-Ireland Final in 1989. This never happened. O'Brien alleged that it had been given to me in the car park of a hotel in Dublin, but it transpired that O'Brien was not even in Dublin that day for the match. A witness gave sworn evidence at the defamation case that he recalled meeting O'Brien in Cork that day and commenting on the fact of how surprised he was that O'Brien was not at the match in Dublin.

With the overwhelming evidence of my innocence, and the court adjudication on the bribe allegation, I expected that to be the end of the matter. Unfortunately I was wrong. The Mahon Tribunal decided to investigate the Gilmartin allegation against me that I was in receipt of a bribe from Owen O'Callaghan. The Tribunal was examining the affairs of O'Callaghan, in essence, because of a dispute between O'Callaghan and Gilmartin. I now became embroiled in that row.

The only allegation ever made against me that the Mahon Tribunal publicly investigated was the IR£80,000 bribe and it is untrue.

But not only did I find myself the subject of the allegation of a bribe from O'Callaghan. I was also the subject of a very sophisticated scam by unknown forces. This related to a document purporting to show that I had an offshore account with Deutsche Bank in Mauritius. Fortunately contact was made quickly with Deutsche Bank and they confirmed that the letter showing my ownership of the account – which had been sent to the Moriarty Tribunal – was a forgery and that I had no such account. It had a false signature. Separately, Gilmartin made wild and untrue allegations against me concerning bank accounts in the Dutch Antilles, the UK and Liechtenstein. He also alleged I had £15,000,000 in a bank account with Bank of Ireland, Jersey. He even accused me of blackmailing a TD in relation to rent boys. These allegations were baseless, untruthful and malicious. Nevertheless I was faced with a public inquiry.

Given that my personal finances became a matter of public comment I am glad to have the chance to explain myself again. It was common at this time for working people to cash their salary cheque or expenses cheque. That is what I did. Over the period from 1987 to 1994 or thereabouts, I did not operate a bank account. The reason for this was that I was splitting up with my wife Miriam, with whom I had joint accounts. My practice during this time was to cash the cheques I received. Out of the cash proceeds I paid maintenance and other expenses for the benefit of Miriam and the girls. I kept what was left in cash. There was nothing wrong about that. There was nothing illegal or unusual about cashing cheques and retaining cash.

One other aspect of the public proceedings of the Mahon Tribunal was that the cash lodgements to my accounts – investigated by them – all occurred within a period of about two years from the settlement of the matrimonial proceedings for me and Miriam. Throughout this period I did not live an expensive lifestyle. I was separated. I did not have my own home. I lived mostly with friends or at St Luke's. My whole life was politics.

With the conclusion in December 1993 of my matrimonial proceedings, I was in a position to formalise my financial affairs. Friends had organised contributions to help me with legal costs. With that money and the cash that I had saved, I opened a number of bank accounts. This, in many respects, is the origin of the problems that subsequently confronted me at the Mahon Tribunal. Cash has no earmark. Cash does not identify its source. Hence the investigation into the cash lodgements in my accounts by the Mahon Tribunal.

What is crystal clear from the public hearings of the Mahon Tribunal is that there is not a scintilla of evidence available to show that the monies lodged came, directly or indirectly, from Owen O'Callaghan. A trawl through O'Callaghan's financial records and dealings – which the Mahon Tribunal has engaged in for ten years – shows no contribution from him to me or for my benefit. That's because I never got any money from O'Callaghan. Notwithstanding this, the Tribunal decided to investigate, in public, the allegation that I received IR£80,000. In that regard, one of the most significant pieces of evidence that has been unearthed is that O'Callaghan did indeed make a contribution of IR£80,000, but it was to Fianna Fáil. It is fully receipted in the records of Fianna Fáil. It's a remarkable coincidence that Gilmartin would make an allegation that I received IR£80,000 from O'Callaghan, which is precisely the sum Owen O'Callaghan actually gave to Fianna Fáil.

I also had to go to court with the Mahon Tribunal. As part of its trawl through my lifestyle going back to the mid-1980s, the Tribunal sought access to my matrimonial file. I was, to put it at its mildest, surprised at this. In our legal system, matrimonial proceedings are held in private. The file is held by the courts and it is not accessible to the public. The only people who should have access to the file are those who are involved in the matrimonial dispute. The privacy of such proceedings is fundamental. But the Mahon Tribunal decided that they were entitled to the matrimonial file and I had to take them to court. Miriam also opposed access to the matrimonial proceedings being given to the Tribunal and she was separately represented in court. The president of the High Court, Mr Justice Finnegan, upheld the privacy of the matrimonial proceedings. I was shocked that I had to go to such lengths to vindicate the right to privacy of myself, Miriam and the girls. But even this was not the end of litigation. The Mahon Tribunal also challenged legal positions that I had taken.

It challenged the right to a constitutional privilege when speaking in the Dail, and asserted that there was no legal professional privilege applying to my dealings with my lawyers and expert witnesses, and denied me access to certain records in their possession. Again, I was successful in the case. It was heard by three judges in the High Court because it raised issues of legal importance. I had decided to go down this road again with reluctance. But I felt I had no choice. This was about upholding the constitutional legal principle that protects the right of TDs to speak freely in the Dáil without being cross-examined in the courts or tribunals on what they have said. And basic fairness dictated that I should be entitled to legal professional privilege and that I should be given Tribunal documents affecting my good name. I was glad to succeed in that litigation and to have vindicated a constitutional principle and my rights. I would have preferred not to take an action against the Mahon Tribunal. But that's the way it is – I did the right thing.

I made discovery of all of my records to the Mahon Tribunal from 1985. I was the subject of a lifestyle trawl. I gave thousands of documents, including invoices and receipts, even for the purchase of the carpets and curtains in my house. I would give evidence on oath for days and days. Throughout this whole period confidential information that I provided to the Tribunal was intermittently leaked, by persons still unknown, causing hurt to those closest to me.

As of now, I'm still waiting the report of the Mahon Tribunal that will deal with the allegation made against me. The only allegation was the alleged bribe of IR£80,000. And that is untrue. I did not receive any monies from Owen O'Callaghan. I did not receive a bribe. Gilmartin's allegations, like those of Denis Starry O'Brien, are false and untrue.

Inevitably, there would be a political cost in all this for me arising from the media's fascination with the Tribunal. Matters weren't helped by the departure of Mary Harney as leader of the PDs around the same time as the *Irish Times* story and my interview with Brian Dobson. It was sad to see her go. I had known Mary in her Fianna Fáil days, had liked her and was sorry when she left to found the

PDs. All told, I had worked well with her in government. We had enjoyed our fair share of barneys and she could be very tricky once she got into something. But by and large she had been steady throughout. I felt I could trust her. I suppose the fact that I liked her personally helped as well, because it always meant we were comfortable in each other's company. That definitely wasn't the case with her replacement as leader of the PDs, Michael McDowell. He was a different kind of a character, not just from Mary, but from most in Leinster House.

Michael never really seemed to have the thick skin needed for life on the front line of political life. He was highly strung, so you were never sure if he was going to lose his temper when somebody was riling him in the Dáil. There were times when having someone who gives it both barrels could be useful politically – Gerry Adams would discover that at the next election when McDowell made mincemeat of him in the debate between leaders of the smaller parties. Although his sharp tongue would sometimes get Michael into trouble, it could also be very effective. He had that ability to cut right to the heart of a matter. That had come in handy during the St Andrews talks, when he sat down and wrote out the timings for the sequence leading to devolution on the back of an envelope. That impressed the Brits, especially Jonathan Powell. But whereas Mary had been very steady, Michael was nervy whenever some issue or other came up in the press. I knew right from the outset that life was going to be more fraught now. So that was Michael: gutsy and jumpy, full of colour, lots of ideas, and never boring.

Whatever about agreeing a timetable for the North, that didn't mean there wouldn't be the usual jigs and reels along the way. The day of nominations, 24 November, began in confusion and almost ended in massacre. Paisley said that the circumstances were not right to nominate a First Minister. Adams then nominated McGuinness as Deputy First Minister. While all this was being debated in the chamber, Michael Stone, the Loyalist paramilitary, tried to storm the building. He was carrying explosives, a replica pistol and a load of knives. Thank

God security stopped him at the door and no one was seriously injured. But in a bizarre way the incident helped create solidarity between the sides. Afterwards, Paisley confirmed that he would accept the First Minister nomination if everyone delivered on St Andrews. That counted as progress. It was Tony Blair's job to keep applying pressure, to keep the DUP to the timetable. Mine was to keep Sinn Féin on board, although in fairness they didn't need much encouragement by this stage. At a special Ard Fheis in January 2007 they gave support for the PSNI and the criminal justice system and authorised Sinn Féin representatives to sit on the Policing Board and District Policing Partnerships. A few days later the Independent Monitoring Commission issued another report confirming the strategic shift of the IRA and the absence of activity. 'In all the areas that Sinn Féin said they would deliver on, they have,' I said. The responsibility to move the process forward now rested elsewhere.

On 30 January, I went to Downing Steet for talks with Tony. He was convinced that if we held elections on 7 March, the DUP would live up to their obligations and enter the power-sharing executive on the 26th of that month. I was sceptical. This would come in the lead-up to a general election in the South. 'You do realise, Tony, that if the entire thing collapses,' I told him, 'that's going to have an impact on me at home?' He understood that it was a massive risk. But at the end of the day he really believed after all his meetings that Paisley was ready. 'I'm not going to say "trust me", Bertie, but I think we have to take the chance.' In the end though, I did trust him. We had been through so much together. He had already announced that he would be leaving office by September at the latest, so this was really our final opportunity to achieve peace together. I had to put that before narrow party and political interest. This was a once-in-a-generation chance to bring peace to Ireland.

The Assembly elections on 7 March confirmed the position of the DUP and Sinn Féin as the largest parties. Sinn Féin were ready to go into government at the end of March. The British government put a generous financial package on the table for a new devolved Assembly. All eyes now turned to the DUP. I spoke to Tony on a regular basis, helping where I could and getting updates on his progress with Paisley. Some days he would be up – 'Paisley's moving into the First Minister's rooms.' Other days he would really be down – 'They want a two-month shadow executive.' I was furious when I heard that one. That was the point of the timetable – it was now or never. It helped that public opinion data showed popular support, including among DUP supporters, for a government by the deadline. When questioned, I kept repeating the same line over and over. Everywhere in the world people run for office to take responsibility for their own affairs. There had been revolutions for that same right. Why should the North be any different? These representatives had been elected and paid to run an administration for the people. It was time for them to get on discharging that duty.

In the end it all came down to one meeting that was out of my and Tony's control. The DUP executive met on Saturday 24 March. Whatever was said in that meeting, they formally agreed to open direct talks with Sinn Féin and agree a new date in May for the devolution of powers. Contact was made that same weekend. Tony had phoned me early on Saturday morning to say it looked like the DUP were proposing May instead of March. 'But,' said Tony, 'I think I can get Paisley to agree to a face-to-face meeting with Adams.' That would be a big deal. I told Tony that he should phone Adams himself and put it to him. 'Tell him that if he's all right with the delay, so am I.' Never mind about the executive, seeing those two men sitting side by side was worth a delay of six weeks all by itself. Not quite together as it turned out. There was a bit of a kerfuffle about the table for the meeting on 26 March, but someone had the bright idea of turning it on its diagonal to make a diamond shape. In the peace process it was always the small details that mattered.

The image of Paisley and Adams together went round the world. In the next few weeks, we would be falling over ourselves with 'historic' moments. It was an extraordinary time. On 4 April, Paisley came down to Farmleigh. That was another incredible day. His car came crunching up the gravel and before it had even stopped, he was out and hammering towards me. 'I have to shake hands with this man,' he boomed, 'and give you a firm grip!' We had heard that he might do this, but right until the last minute we didn't know if would or if he wouldn't. But no, there it was, the hand outstretched, a tight grip with a right auld thump on the back for good measure. We've come a long way, I thought to myself.

Our first meeting at the Irish Embassy in London in November 2004 had been OK, but it had been clear that Paisley was very suspicious of me. It had been a breakfast meeting and there had been a whole lot of fuss about making sure he got his boiled egg. Afterwards, he had said that had been because he thought we couldn't poison him with a boiled egg. 'You still drank the orange juice,' I joked with him, which made him roar with laughter. That had been an important meeting, not least because he impressed me by giving his own press conference standing under the Irish tricolour.

At Farmleigh in 2007, we had a very workmanlike meeting. All the substantive issues were discussed. There was no dodging questions or saying 'that's none of your business'. I think by now Paisley knew that although I differed with him on a lot of issues, I respected the way he spoke up for his community and his real Christian faith. Religion always played a big part in our discussions, which was surprising given that he had regularly denounced the Pope as the Antichrist. But I think he knew that I took my own faith seriously and he could respect that. We also shared a love of history and I know that he was deeply appreciative when I decided that the historic Boyne site should be purchased by the state and developed in a way that was fully sensitive to Unionism and Loyalism. So there was a trust between us and a real sense of shared commitment. For so long we had been outsiders who he had seen as unhelpful to him. Now he was talking about his family connections in the South. And to be fair, he was genuine.

We didn't get any reversals. He might have frustrated us at times and there had been real concerns along the way. But in the end, he had delivered, just as he had said he would.

The day when it all came together, 8 May 2007, was one of those moments that you come into politics to see. This really was history in the making. Thankfully there were no last-minute hitches. The world's press was out in force, as were many of the leading figures who had played a major role in getting us there. Dermot Ahern attended as Minister for Foreign Affairs. Also present was US Senator Ted Kennedy, whose death was sadly announced as this book went to press. Although John Major was unable to attend, Albert Reynolds was there representing the huge effort both men had put into the process. Father Alex Reid and the Rev. Harold Good, who had both done so much to persuade the paramilitary groups to renounce violence, also attended, as did the Attorney General, Rory Brady, who behind the scenes had been a key adviser to me.

There were many extraordinary aspects to that day, but perhaps the most amazing of all was the chemistry between Paisley and McGuinness – the First Minister and Deputy First Minister. There was the famous cup of tea beforehand, when somehow I ended up wedged next to Tony Blair and Peter Hain on the most uncomfortable sofa I had ever sat on. 'I suppose that's devolution,' Tony muttered. 'They get the comfy chairs.' Most of the time was spent with Paisley and McGuinness roaring with laughter, while we looked on like nervous parents at a wedding. I think the key to it was that from the beginning McGuinness had shown Paisley respect and spoke to him in a way that said 'we're for real'. Obviously Paisley had to get past McGuinness's background, but once he did, I think Paisley believed in him. All the way along he could see that McGuinness was supportive of the process, wasn't trying to pull a fast one or undermine him. It certainly wasn't that the two had decided they were on the same side. Far from it. But I think they both came to believe that the best way forward was to support each other, not do each other down, and air their disagreements on the basis of that respect. Paisley in particular seemed to set great store by the fact that McGuinness always showed great personal courtesy towards him. Watching them chuckling together may have been surreal, but it gave everyone faith that even with their differences the two men wanted to make the process work.

In my speech that day I quoted King George V when he had opened Stormont eighty-six years earlier: 'I appeal to all Irishmen to pause, to stretch out the hand of forbearance and conciliation, to forgive and forget and to join in making for the land which they love a new era of peace, contentment and goodwill.' The laughter between Paisley and McGuinness symbolised that. Each had stretched out the hand of conciliation and sounded the call for a new era of mutual respect and peace.

But they couldn't have done it on their own. Tony Blair's contribution to Ireland, North and South, had been immense. I don't think anyone really knows how much time he put into the peace process, and his complete dedication to it. In spite of all the different pressures on him, he never took his eye off the ball. He would always take the phone calls, sit through those long, long sessions as the various parties lectured him. Then there was the concentrated effort of conferences, such as those in Castle Buildings or St Andrews. He could just as easily have handed that all off to his ministers, especially when the Good Friday Agreement got bogged down for the umpteenth time. But no, he kept at it, bringing the full force of the prime minister's office to the process. So Tony was a true friend to Ireland. The peace process just would not have happened without him. I remember looking at him during the ceremony, while children sang, and he was in another world. I wondered then whether he was thinking, 'This will be my legacy.' I found out soon enough. Afterwards, I asked him what plans he had. He told me that in the next couple of days he would be announcing when he was standing down as prime minister. 'Make sure you watch the news!' he laughed. Sure enough, two days later he set out the timetable for his departure. It would mark the closing of a chapter, not just for Britain, but also for Ireland.

Before Tony left office, he paid me the highest compliment he could give an overseas leader by inviting me to address a joint session of the Houses of Parliament on 15 May. That was an extraordinary honour, and a first for a Taoiseach. It was a humbling experience to join the list of thirty-one world leaders who had spoken at Westminster since 1939, including Charles de Gaulle, Nelson Mandela, Mikhail Gorbachev and Bill Clinton. The speech was one to which I gave a great deal of thought. Once I had received input from the various departments, and made notes myself, I let Brian Murphy, my principal speech-writer, work on the final drafts. Gerry Howlin, my special adviser, and Martin Fraser, the key official on the North in the Department of the Taoiseach, were also heavily involved. Afterwards we had the world and its mother saying they had written it, but most of the work was done by those three individuals working with me.

While I was conscious of the honour of addressing the Houses of Parliament in Westminster, I also knew I had a job to do. The speech was an opportunity to bind up the wounds of the past, lock down the current peace process, and set the tone for British–Irish relations in the future. I was also keen that it should reflect the contribution that so many Irish politicians had made in Westminster. I wanted it framed with a real sense of history, because I felt that although I was speaking on behalf of my generation, I was also part of a line that included Daniel O'Connell and Charles Stewart Parnell. I might not have been an orator like 'the Liberator', but I was aware of the long and noble tradition of those who had furthered the cause of the Irish nation in that Parliament. This wasn't just me turning up for the day to give a speech. The Irish were already an important part of the fabric and history of Westminster. And after all, embracing our shared history in all its forms was how we had finally brought about peace. 'I call to mind,' I said towards the end of the speech, 'the words of another great Irishman, Edmund Burke, who served in this Parlia-

saying get out there, which seriously narked some of them. I think they thought I had done it on purpose. It was a lovely sunny morning to be out early, so I didn't make any apologies, but the reality was that the early hour was not chosen to inconvenience the press. As usual, it was more cock-up than conspiracy. We had wanted to go to the Áras the following Tuesday, giving an election date of 28 May. We had checked the President's schedule and knew she had an official visit overseas on the Wednesday. It was only on the Friday beforehand that we looked for an appointment and discovered that she was going a few days early in a private capacity. When the President is preparing her schedule, the government is notified of the destinations she intends visiting. But if she decides to take some downtime before the official visit, we don't need to know that. She's always contactable, but otherwise it's none of our business. Add in the necessary secrecy surrounding the date of an election and it's easy to see how the thing happened. There was no way that I was going to try to call an election while the President was out of the country, so that left us with no option but to get the reporters out of bed and call the election for 24 May. The press were even more annoyed when, as I came out from my meeting with President McAleese, I didn't stop for an interview. They had forgotten the convention, which I always observed during my eleven years as Taoiseach, that nobody should do an interview in the Áras except the President. So what with that and the early start, the media were on my back from the beginning. It was something I had to get used to in this election.

That made the campaign a tough experience for me. There's not much I enjoy more than canvassing, but this time that was hard enough to do. There is always a flurry of reporters at the start of a campaign, but then it usually eases off. Normally I would get about twenty journalists with me covering the campaign. A lot of them I already knew and the others I would get to know pretty quickly. They were there to follow the story and talk to me, but they didn't stop me meeting people. However, in this campaign there must have been three times that number. They would be pushing and shouting, which hassled the voters on the street who found themselves in the middle of the scrum. People were getting blocked off or having big sharp cameras thrust towards them. It wasn't nice for anyone.

After forty-eight hours of this, I started to get angry that I wasn't being let canvass properly. I tried jumping in the car and speeding off to a new, unannounced location, but of course the press pack found us soon enough. It just became impossible. Even when voters braved the mob to come and say hello, they could hardly get a word in before journalists would be shouting at me as I was walking along. I had never known such a hostile bunch in all my years of politics. I had seen enough tussles between canvassers outside polling stations during the 1970s and 80s, but this was something new from the media. I had expected, what with the Mahon Tribunal story, that they would give me a rough time, but this level of aggression really took me by surprise. Whether the British journalists who were covering the election brought that new element in I don't know, but definitely this time round it was almost impossible to canvass.

We were set on that collision course for the first ten days of the campaign. It seemed every question put to me was confrontational and it was all Tribunal, Tribunal, Tribunal. Even the odd question about something else was often aggressive. I've got no reason to be defensive about the media. For most of my career, I've been lucky enough to have had a reasonable press. In fairness, there were still commentators like Shane Ross in the *Sunday Independent* saying of me that 'he deserves credit for his management of the Irish economy', or others who were praising my efforts in the peace process. So I'm not tarring everyone with the same brush. But there was no doubt that, unlike 1997 for example, when the opposite was true, most of the media wanted me out by this stage. The reality is that after ten years they get bored of you. Give us a new story, they say. It had happened to Tony Blair in Britain. Now it was my turn. The Mahon Tribunal was the nearest stick to beat me with and they hit me with it hard.

A good example was someone many of us have a love–hate relationship with – the veteran commentator Vincent Browne. Like a lot of people I have a high opinion of Vincent, but not half as high as he has of himself. At the Fianna Fáil manifesto launch on 3 May Vincent was flying. He started with a question about the Tribunal – fair enough – but then came back with another question and then another and another. He wouldn't shut up. Someone told me afterwards I had put my head down, which I wasn't really aware of at the time. I was just thinking to myself, 'Jesus, keep your cool here.' No doubt that's what he was trying to do: provoke a reaction in me. He just wanted to keep coming back at me, not letting any other journalists get in with their questions. I had seen him do it many times before, getting himself worked up into a lather of self-righteous indignation. But immediately after the press conference, I did a one-on-one interview with him, which went fine. That's the way it is with Vincent and I admire him for that. He is honourable and at least you know where you are with him.

That was not true of everyone. The press were having a field day, because once again confidential information I had provided to the Mahon Tribunal had somehow found its way into the public domain. This happened around the time when the campaign began, and I believed then and now that the leaking of this material shortly before a general election was sinister. A senior media figure said that their news organisation had received the information in a perfectly bound copy. It seemed this could only have come via sources who had received circulated material from the tribunal. Obviously newspapers publish material like this when it comes their way, but the whole thing left a bad taste in the mouth.

The perception of dirty tricks in the media seemed to me to change the mood on the doorstep. I think people had seen pictures of reporters shouting in my face on the campaign. They were hearing leaks and innuendo. Voters had seemed positive when I had actually spoken to them and I kept hearing public fury about the media.

That was repeated to me over and over again on the campaign trail. The image of me with my head down really seemed to strike a chord with people. The consensus from canvassers all around the country was of voters saying, 'Who do these people in the media think they are?'

That public anger began to change the nature of the election. It certainly galvanised us as a party. Three of our biggest hitters – Brian Cowen, Dermot Ahern and Micheál Martin – went out and gave a brilliant, barnstorming press conference. That morning, before I met the three ministers in Treasury Buildings, I had given an interview to Sky News saying that I was going to make a comprehensive statement on the Mahon Tribunal, which I subsequently did. The ministers were then able to use that to great effect, hitting back at the opposition for talking out of the sides of their mouths. In the constituencies, we got reports that canvassers were volunteering for longer and longer hours. Other supporters were saying that they didn't do much in 2002, but they were going out this time. In that previous election, maybe we had eased off a bit. Not this time. The whole party went at it hell for leather. And every day, bit by bit, the election became less about me and more about the issues. As that happened, so the numbers from the media following me started to fall. And the reception on the doorstep was terrific, in many ways much more like 1997 than 2002. So although I still had to put up with a lot of agitation with the media on the campaign trail, I started to feel the tide was turning.

By the time we got to the traditional leaders' debate on TV, I was ready for a right battle. Enda, in my view, had been having it easy during the campaign, with almost all the focus on me. He had been running round the country with his 'Contract for a better Ireland', which was made up of ten specific commitments like free health insurance for children under sixteen and free GP care for children under five. It had irritated me during the campaign that, while I was getting flak, he wasn't probed to explain how he would deliver all this. As I was driving around the country, seeing these 'Contract' posters, I thought to myself, 'Right, let's see how you're going to do it.'

I actually did less rehearsal for this debate than for either of the previous two. I knew what I wanted to say. I knew that what he was promising did not stack up. In fact, it was all nonsense, something that became clear as the debate went on. Enda is an able politician, but he's not quick on his feet. He got more and more flustered as I tripped him up on the detail, with each answer more wooden than the last. The real killer, which he completely fluffed, was when I pointed out that no child born on the day of the debate would benefit from his plan for free GP visits for children aged under five. When I saw the look of panic in his eyes as he wrestled with that one, I knew at once that he had failed the 'Taoiseach-in-waiting' test.

I left the studio feeling brilliant and dropped into campaign HQ in Treasury Buildings. There was great euphoria among the campaign staff, who now believed the election had turned. However, it did cause me some amusement that the loudest praise came from a guy on my own team who hadn't seemed to have much faith in me earlier in the campaign. Afterwards, I headed away to Fagan's. One of the locals, a friend of mine who I know votes Labour, said to me, 'We took a straw poll in the pub and you've walked it.' Then he added, 'Mind you, there's a few guys on the TV saying it was a draw. Can't they get anything right?!' There were 1.4 million people watching that night and the tracking polls showed overwhelmingly that I had won the debate. The whole campaign had changed course.

Fianna Fáil had a couple of other good TV moments during the election. A party political broadcast featuring Tony Blair and Bill Clinton emphasised the role that I had played in the peace process. The fact that they were willing to jump into the middle of Irish politics showed how far they were prepared to go to help. I was grateful and humbled by that. Then on the Friday before the election, Eoghan Harris put in an unbelievable performance on the *Late, Late* by trouncing Eamon Dunphy. As the show was going out, my daughter

Cecelia phoned me to say, 'Are you watching this?' To be honest, there are times when you feel like saying, 'Look, I'm working hard and doing my best for the country,' but when someone stands up to say things about you in such an impassioned way, you say, 'Thank God!' So I was grateful to Eoghan, because there weren't many others in the media prepared to do it. Shutting Dunphy up was an achievement in itself.

By election day, I wasn't confident exactly as much as calm, because I knew that we had come right back into it. I had even managed not to take it as a bad omen that Chelsea had beaten Man United the weekend before in the FA Cup Final. I certainly couldn't imagine us losing, even though I knew the result would be tight. To be honest, I thought it would be closer than it turned out to be. As I cast my vote in the polling station on Church Avenue, I already knew that it would be the last time I would be doing so as Taoiseach. Win or lose this time round, I knew that come the next election I would have gone to the backbenches. I might not even be on the ballot standing as a TD next time. I had been a deputy for exactly thirty years. Whatever happened in the election, this day, 24 May 2007, was already a turning point in my life.

As the day went on, I started hearing more and more positive messages coming in from constituencies around the country. Everywhere people were saying they thought we were going to do it. In fact, as it turned out we probably failed to capitalise on the goodwill out there for the party. If the campaign had run another week, I think we could have got an overall majority. We had definitely gathered momentum after being on the back foot for the first half of the campaign. With a bit more luck and some better vote management and candidate selection in places like Dublin North Central, Dublin North East and Sligo/Leitrim, we might even have got that overall majority. There were places where people obviously wanted to give us the seat and we ended up throwing it away because of poor planning.

There was even fun and games in my own constituency. We had

considered only putting forward two candidates – Cyprian Brady and myself – to make sure we got the two seats. But Dermot Fitzpatrick, who was retiring as a TD for the area, wanted his daughter Mary to run to carry on the family name. That was fine, because I figured she would help sweep up votes at the Navan Road end of the constituency. But there was no doubt in my mind that Cyprian would win the seat. Our tactic was simple enough. I would get a good vote, the transfers would go back to Cyprian and we would both get elected. In the end that's exactly what happened. Why anyone was surprised or felt aggrieved about it I don't know. Cyprian had worked hard in the constituency for sixteen years, was a senator and was closely identified with me. It was obvious that my transfers would go to him. As for Mary, her day will come. She has since proved in the local elections that she has a bright political future.

On the day of the count, I did my usual thing of staying in bed for as long as I could. It's always a strange time, waiting for the people to come back with the verdict. There is not much you can do except sleep, watch an old match on the TV, eat some brown bread and Bovril. I was tired from the campaign, which had seen me out and about for around eighteen hours each day, so I didn't get out of bed until six. The girls phoned for a chat. Then I went for a quick walk round All Hallows for some fresh air. It seemed like the first time I had been out on my own for a lifetime. Around 7.20 I left the house with my security driver, John Byrne, to go to Mass in Gardiner Street Church. Then it was off to RTÉ.

When I arrived at Montrose the atmosphere was subdued. I don't know whether that was because they were all exhausted from the coverage, or if it was amazement and even disappointment with the result. Either way, the place wasn't exactly rocking. Saying hello to people as I went into the studio, I could see them looking at me thinking, 'How the hell did he do that?' Going into the campaign I expect most of them thought we would lose, and maybe they even wanted us to. I probably should have left it, but I did have a crack at the media during the interview. I felt that we hadn't had a fair shake during the campaign, except from the *Sunday Independent*. Being magnanimous in victory is one thing. But I knew a lot of this same crowd would be after me even more now that the result had left them with egg on their faces.

One interesting thing about the interview was that Mark Little looked genuinely upset by what I was saying. Anyone will tell you that Mark is one of the best and most honest journalists in Ireland, but his pained expression was nothing to do with what I was saying. What the viewers couldn't see was that the poor guy had his leg in plaster and was obviously in a lot of discomfort. I've been through it myself since, and it's awful, so I know how he felt. It did make a good image though: happy Fianna Fáil leader, sad media. The picture that spoke a thousand words.

Afterwards, I went to the Fianna Fáil campaign headquarters at Treasury Buildings to congratulate everybody and to thank them. The mood was one of great celebration. These people had really been through a lot during the campaign. Now they knew they were going to be on the winning side. In 2002 it had felt like business as usual. This time the atmosphere was more like scoring a goal (or two) during injury time to win the Champions League final. What a contrast to RTÉ.

I needed no reminding that this was an historic moment: I was the first Taoiseach since de Valera to win three general elections in a row. I was only sorry that my parents were not there to see it, because they had both worshipped Dev. Whatever about history and my place in it, this election also saw one political party consigned to the past. The election had worked out well enough for us, but our coalition partners, the Progressive Democrats, got absolutely blasted. As soon as the results came through, Michael McDowell resigned as leader and withdrew from political life. In some ways Michael had been difficult to work with, and maybe I had caused that too. But we had managed to stay together as Taoiseach and Tánaiste after Mary Harney resigned as leader of the PDs, and we had brought the government to a full term. Michael had also been an outstanding Attorney General and Justice Minister, so there was a lot to be positive about. I was sorry that the PDs were on their last legs. I asked Mary Harney to stay on in recognition of her abilities and the outstanding role she had played since 1997. I had been working in tandem with the PDs for much of the period since the summer of 1989. Together we had achieved a great deal in modernising Ireland. The PDs played a central role in that process and, in the challenges ahead, I believe we will miss them in political debate.

With the PDs down to two TDs, I had already been turning my thoughts to building a new coalition. The most exciting prospect was a coalition with the Greens, who I thought would bring new and interesting ideas. They were inexperienced, never having been in government before, but I knew John Gormley and respected him as a serious politician. He had been plugging his line before it was fashionable, which you always have to admire. Dan Boyle and Eamon Ryan seemed open to a coalition. But the leader of the Greens, Trevor Sargent, appeared more hostile to coalition with Fianna Fáil than the others. In the end, he tied himself into knots over that, resigning the leadership, refusing a seat in cabinet, but then joining the government as a junior minister. I'm sure there was a point of principle in there somewhere, although it was lost on me. In spite of this, Trevor played a major role in the negotiations to form a government.

The fact that we were ready to deal with the Greens was in many ways a tribute to Séamus Brennan. He had advised me over a year earlier that he thought highly of the Greens and believed they would make good coalition partners. We had agreed that he would try to nurture that relationship and talk about areas of their agenda that might overlap with ours. We had already been developing our environmental policy, giving over more discussion to green issues at the Youth Conference and the Ard Fheis.

Of course there were political calculations too. I knew that if we pulled the Greens away from Fine Gael and Labour, that would make it harder to put together a new rainbow coalition in the future. Sinn Féin were out on their own for the the time being, although I got a message through Sinn Féin that Fine Gael were making overtures to them. Going in with the Greens also left open the option of bringing Labour on board at some point down the line, which had always seemed a no-brainer to me. Unfortunately that was never going to happen under Pat Rabbitte, who to my regret was completely opposed to the idea. The key thing for me at this stage was to build a solid coalition. You always know there will be bumps along the way – although to be honest no one expected them to be so big – and you have to make sure that the buckles on the shoes are fastened down. Obviously it was a leap of faith going in with the Greens, because no one knew how they would perform in government. I could have done without their six votes in the Dáil, because I already had a majority with the independents and the two remaining PDs. But I wanted stability. This was an opportunity to put together a third coalition that was capable of running for another historic full term. I knew it would outlast me, and I wanted that to be the final piece of my legacy.

With a new partner in the Greens, I was also looking for continuity in my own party. I left most of the cabinet in place, with the main promotion going to Brian Lenihan at Justice. Mary Harney remained in cabinet and Brian Cowen became Tánaiste. He deserved that. He had really been out there battling in the election and had shown all the qualities you would want in a number two. Talking to the whips and people in the party, it seemed obvious that he was going to be the next leader. All through the seventies, eighties and early nineties, Fianna Fáil had been torn apart by heaves and divisions, with good men dying young from the stress of it all. Those were terrible times and as ever I was determined we would not return to them. One of my aims during this third term was to get a smooth transition to the next Taoiseach. I told the media that I would be withdrawing from political life when I was sixty years of age. Conveniently enough, I would not be sixty-one until after a potential five-year term in 2012. That meant I could retire from politics at the next general election if it went the full term. In my own mind, I was planning to leave as Taoiseach after the local elections in 2009. That would have given me time to achieve what I wanted. But it would also give the new Taoiseach a good run-in before the next election.

I got criticised even for saying that I would be going. I also got stick from some people when I said I thought Brian Cowen seemed the obvious successor. But I couldn't see how else to deal with the issue. Inevitably I was going to get the question over and over again. No one can go on forever. I could not flutter around the question for the next few years, and risk opening up divisions and fights in the party. It would have been chaos. I had been doing tallies all my life in Leinster House since I was a whip. I knew how to read the figures. Any number of candidates could have run against Brian and he would have wiped the floor with all of them. I also had no doubts that he was the person with the most experience and ability to do the job.

Not that Brian was in any particular rush for it. In fact, I think he was happy to know there would be a smooth transition. That would give him time to get his advisers together and map out his ideas. As it turned out, he had not been given the opportunity to do that when he came to take over a year earlier than we expected. That was exactly the situation I had wanted to avoid by coordinating a phased transition. I should have known that in politics you can prepare all you like, but events will always trip you up. Anyhow, when I said on RTÉ radio a few weeks after the election that I regarded Brian as an obvious successor, it seemed a straightforward enough comment to me. RTÉ didn't even bother to lead with it in their later reports, concentrating instead on what I had said about maybe bringing back Beverley Flynn as a junior minister. So it wasn't exactly headline news. One or two of the other potential candidates were disappointed, although in fairness the only one with any right to be annoyed was Dermot Ahern, because he alone could have mustered a decent vote. Dermot is a great friend of mine and I felt bad for him. There's no doubt he would make an outstanding leader, but Brian was ahead of him. Micheál Martin didn't have the numbers either. I thought Mary Hanafin's day would come, but not this time round. The die was cast.

Part of the reason I wanted to settle things down early was because there were still issues I wanted to deal with before I went. For most of my tenure as Taoiseach I had been caught up on the North sometimes forty hours a week. Now the Assembly was up and running, I had so much time on my hands that I might have eased off and enjoyed my last couple of years. But there was plenty of work to be done. Obviously with the Greens on board, the government's environmental agenda was sharper, with exciting new developments coming on track, especially in completing our public transport programme, which I had coordinated all the way since 1999, when I set up and chaired the infrastructural cabinet subcommittee. The other issue that I really wanted to give time to was health, which despite billions in extra funding over the previous ten years was still not at the high standard I thought our country deserved. There were several issues that I wanted to push forward, working with Mary Harney, including a range of health developments to deliver on the commitments we had made in the 'Towards 2016' partnership agreement. These included further provision for cancer care and 'fair deal' legislation that would provide upfront state funding of nursing-home care, with costs only recouped from the estate of a resident after death.

The disarray in the opposition during this period was there for everyone to see. They had put their ideas for change to the people and got knocked back. Pat Rabbitte resigned as leader of the Labour Party over the summer. There were murmurings in Fine Gael that Richard Bruton would make a better leader than Enda Kenny. When the Dáil came back in September, both parties took the only option left open to them: play the man and not the ball. That meant personal attacks on me. Those would continue until the day I resigned in 2008. The opposition could not beat me fair and square in a general election, so it was time to play dirty instead. On 26 September, Fine Gael put down a motion of no confidence in me as Taoiseach, and in January they came back with another one. Both were defeated, but I was disappointed that they were trying to use my personal situation for political gain. I suppose I should not have been surprised. I certainly had not come to expect consistency from the opposition. One day they wanted to leave my affairs to the Tribunal, the next they wanted to pre-empt its work. They condemned me because I had only partial recollection of events in my life almost two decades previously, and yet here was a party that had conveniently destroyed its own financial records. Its members preached integrity in public office, but that was a standard they didn't match themselves. They were spinning to the newspapers, and then saying, 'Who, me?' when challenged on it. To me it seemed that, for Fine Gael, integrity had become a tactic not a principle.

In September 2007, I was finally given my chance to appear before the Mahon Tribunal. 'All I can do is recount the circumstances to the best of my knowledge,' I said in my opening statement. The line of questioning that followed from Des O'Neill, counsel for the Tribunal, I thought was just out of order. Questions about which friends stayed loyal to me or to Miriam when we separated had got nothing to do with planning in Dublin. Neither had questions about me forming a second relationship and who had access to the bedroom in St Luke's. To my mind that just seemed prurient.

This was only the start of it. I went back to the Tribunal again in December, and in February. Then they hauled in every one of my friends all the way up to Easter. There was endless material to be dealt with each week by correspondence. And that was just the formal side of it. Every day was like a media circus. Press conferences were all about the Tribunal. Every politics programme was about the Tribunal. Questions to ministers were about the Tribunal. Slowly it was dawning on me that it was never going to end. No matter what good we were doing – or even if we were getting things wrong – no one was interested. We might have been heading into the credit crunch, but that was not the story leading the news. Tribunal issues had completely hijacked the political agenda. That really started to frustrate me. Apart from anything else it raised serious questions about the nature of the Tribunal itself. More than ten years they had been at it, without a final judgement. When I set it up in 1997, it was intended to last no longer than six months. In 2004, its terms and conditions were amended to give a specific end date of 2007. Yet here we were, still waiting. The Tribunal was established to address matters of 'urgent' public concern. But as Gerry Hickey used to point out, there had been two world wars fought in a shorter space of time.

The turning point for me came when my former secretary, Gráinne Carruth, was called back into the witness box, where she broke down. All they had to do was write to her and ask her to clarify her earlier evidence. They threatened her with jail. And she cried on the stand. It was real lowlife stuff, picking on an ordinary mother of three who by bad luck had found herself right in the middle of a massive story and dealing with issues from fourteen years earlier relating to a job she had long left.

That convinced me. For some time I had been growing more and more concerned that the work of government was being overshadowed. But it was now clear that the incessant publicity about the Tribunal was going to continue unabated. There and then I thought: 'It's not worth it.'

It had always been my intention to review my position as Taoiseach in the aftermath of the local and European elections in 2009. I now decided to bring forward that date. I was not going to let issues relating to myself go on dominating political life. As it happened this was the Easter weekend, so everybody was away from Leinster House. I thought I might ring a few people, but nobody was around. I tried calling Mary Hanafin, but her phone was off. Then I started talking to my family and my own guys. I had a chat with Tony Kett, who had just been diagonosed with cancer. I spoke to Mandy Johnston, Brian Murphy and Cyprian Brady. I talked to the girls and my two brothers and two sisters. I spoke to my cousin, Kieran O'Driscoll, whose advice I have always valued. The view from the family was that they didn't know why I put up with all the rubbish thrown at me anyway. Nobody was saying pack it in exactly, but I think they felt that since Christmas it had gone too far. It seemed endless. The media were hassling me every day. There was the strain of the constant demands from the Tribunal itself. It was too much.

Cecelia and Georgina were both upset about the treatment I was getting. It must have been hard for them to watch this every day. No one wants to see their family going through the mangle. Some of the gang in Drumcondra wanted me to fight on, because they didn't want the pack to bring me down. But I knew this was about more than just me. The credit crunch was already under way, and we were trying to grapple with that. Too much government business was getting caught up in the controversy surrounding the Tribunal. I started looking at the events coming up in the diary. I had been invited to speak to a Joint Session of the United States Congress in April, which would make me one of just a handful of people to have spoken both on Capitol Hill and at Westminster. There was the scheduled opening of the Boyne site with Ian Paisley. If there was a bright side to what was about to happen, it was that I could finish on a positive note.

On the evening of Good Friday, I had a number of private conversations with my closest supporters and some of them came round to my house off Griffith Avenue to kick the issue around over a few beers. Chris Wall and Tony Kett. Paddy Reilly, Liam Cooper, Paddy Brazil, Joe Burke, Danny O'Connor and Noel Mohan. If anyone formed my circle of closest friends, it was these people, who had been with me through thick and thin over a long political career. Most of them thought by this stage that the aggravation over the Tribunal would be endless. When I went to bed that night, I still hadn't decided.

But by the time I woke up the next morning I had my mind made up. I was going to resign as Taoiseach. I informed Tony and Chris, and then hinted as much on the phone to the girls. Over the next few days I spoke to Miriam and to Celia Larkin. I also told Cyprian Brady. Once I had made the decision, I just felt all the tension leave me. In my head, the clock was already counting down. I watched the highlights of Man United thrashing Liverpool. I went racing at Fairyhouse. I had a few pints in Fagan's. I could feel my old self returning. For better or worse, my time as Taoiseach was coming to an end.

I wanted to announce my decision when the Dáil returned on Wednesday 2 April. That gave me eleven days to plan my exit. It also meant I had to play for time. Brian Cowen had been away on official business combined with a few days holiday and only got back the Wednesday after Easter. He came over to my house the following day to discuss Finance matters. His uncle had died recently and he was obviously upset about that, because they had been close. At the end of our discussion, I took him through what had happened while he had been away. I told him I would be assessing things over the weekend and that I would give him a call on Sunday. Knowing that he was about to attend his uncle's funeral, I did not tell him I intended stepping down. It didn't seem the right time. Brian said a few fellas had been ringing him moaning about the situation, but he didn't seem overly bothered about it.

There's been a lot of speculation since then about whether Brian Cowen tried to push me out during this meeting. If Brian had wanted me to go, he definitely didn't say it to my face, and that's how he would have done it. Brian in my experience is not one to be talking about you out of the side of his mouth. He was absolutely supportive throughout, and was never anything less than loyal. In fairness, I think it was clear that he was going to end up Taoiseach, so he had no need to force my hand. In fact, I felt that he was keen for me to stay a bit longer. He was still preparing at this stage and I think he would have preferred it if I had stayed on.

A number of the parliamentary party were at the funeral of Brian's uncle later that day and, as he had promised to do, Brian gave me a quick buzz afterwards, reporting back that there was some concern but no real problem. Again he didn't seemed bothered. That was the only conversation we had until I phoned him at the weekend. Dermot Ahern called around this time as well and I had a good chat with him. He was up for a fight and said I couldn't let the media circus drive me out. I appreciated his support, but warned him that I was going to have to reflect on the situation. Looking back, I should have said that I would phone him on Sunday as well, because if he did want a crack at the leadership, he would have needed time to prepare himself. That was probably unfair to someone who was loyal to me to the end.

Dermot is made of stern stuff. Others were more wobbly. Brian Lenihan was edgy. Mary Coughlan was definitely not on board. That disappointed me, because these were people I had brought on and promoted through the ranks.

All week I had kept my peace, knowing that I was going to make an announcement on the day the Dáil returned after the Easter recess. That weekend, I started telling more people. I spoke to Mandy Johnston about how we would inform the media. On Sunday morning I asked Charlie McCreevy to come into me at St Luke's. Charlie and I didn't agree about everything, but there was nobody in politics I was closer to. We had a good chat and he reassured me that I had made the correct decision. 'You're here eleven years, Bertie,' he said. 'What more can you do?'

In the afternoon I phoned Brian Cowen at home in Offaly and told him that I was going to resign. I asked him not to say it to anyone and invited him to come to St Luke's the following Tuesday to talk about the practicalities. He seemed shocked and said some kind words.

Then I met the girls for Sunday dinner at the Grand Hotel in Malahide. They more or less knew what was coming, but I confirmed my decision to them. They were emotional but relieved. They both thought I was doing the right thing.

Starting that Sunday, I began working on my resignation statement with Brian Murphy. I had a draft already sketched out, because I had been jotting down ideas throughout the week and reflecting on what I wanted to say. As we sat there writing together just as we always did on an important speech, it didn't feel like any kind of a big deal. This was just another week at the office. On the Tuesday, I spoke to the former Attorney General, Rory Brady, whose common-sense approach to politics I had always admired. I also had a word with some of the guys who had been close to me for years. Around mid-afternoon, Brian Cowen came to St Luke's. Our meeting was all very calm and businesslike. That night I had a few jars in Fagan's with friends and watched Man United beat Roma in the Champions League. I went to bed happy as Larry and fell into a deep sleep straight away.

The next morning was just like any other. I was up just before 6 a.m., went into St Luke's to catch up on a few bits of paperwork and to look over my statement again with Brian Murphy. I could see Sandra, my secretary, was upset, but she did her best to be her usual cheerful self, fussing round me with cups of tea and plates of toast. I spent time with Mandy Johnston going over the exact sequencing of events. There was to be a meeting of Fianna Fáil cabinet members at 9 a.m. before a meeting of the full cabinet at 10.30 a.m. I arranged with Mandy that as soon as I walked through the door to begin the first meeting, she would ask the government press secretary, Eoghan Ó Neachtain, to call a press conference in one hour. Amazingly, not a word of what was to come had leaked out and there was nothing in the papers.

As I left St Luke's, I was surprised at how relaxed I felt. Heading through the traffic into Government Buildings, I had a chat with Brian and John, my driver, about the match. Looking at everyone heading into work, I knew that no one had any idea what was coming. I was pretty confident about what was going to make the news that day. As I watched people hurrying about their business, thinking their own thoughts about work, friends and family, I wondered how they would react to my going. No doubt some would be pleased to see the back of me and others might be sorry to see me go. In the modern 24/7 news world, having a Taoiseach around more than ten years is a long time. Eventually the country needs a change and that is the beauty of democratic politics. It would be left to history to say how I had done. But as I watched those faces, young and old, men and women, kids off to school, I knew in myself that I had worked hard and done my best.

We drove through the gates of Government Buildings, and pulled up under the archway. A private lift took me straight into my own office. For most of the staff it was business as usual, so I got the familiar smiles and 'Good morning, Taoiseach'. I had left it until quite close to the meeting to avoid too much chat, so almost immediately I was heading through the outer office, turning left into the corridor where Gerry Hickey had his office and then right into the usual hubbub of the long corridor that I had walked hundreds of times to get to the Dáil. This time though I stopped halfway along and entered the Sycamore Room. It was here almost eleven years earlier that I had welcomed my first cabinet as we gathered to go into the Dáil. That scene had been repeated after the election victories in 2002 and 2007. There had been a fair few dramatic moments in this room over the years. Today I was about to add to them.

Inside, I started the meeting of Fianna Fáil ministers on time and went through business in the normal way. The previous day the Chief Whip, Tom Kitt, had announced the legislative programme for the new Dáil session, with seventeen bills scheduled for publication. About forty minutes into the meeting, I started to notice people getting restless. Colleagues were sneaking looks at their mobile phones under the table, looking really puzzled. I just ignored it and carried on with the business. Eventually it was Mary Hanafin who spoke up. 'Taoiseach, is everything all right?' That was when I told them. I had no long statement prepared. There was no speech. I just said, 'I've made my decision. That's it, I'm going on 6 May. I'm giving a press conference at ten o'clock.' It was now a quarter to.

There was stunned silence in the room. Everyone looked totally shocked, with the exception of Mary Coughlan I noticed. I guess Brian had told her. A lot of colleagues looked genuinely affected by the moment. Mary Hanafin welled up. Noel Dempsey also looked shaken. Brian Cowen, even though this meant his day had come, was very emotional. He said a few words: 'Obviously this is a hard decision for you, Taoiseach, but we all respect it. There will be another day for tributes, but I want to thank you for your service to the country. And if you are going out to do a press conference, I want to stand beside you and I'm sure all my colleagues will want to as well.' I appreciated that.

I left the room quickly, because I wanted to inform Mary Harney and John Gormley before word got out. They were waiting in my office as arranged. Like the others, they had been getting texts saying there was a press conference and so they wanted to know what was going on. When I told them, they were both very gracious. Mary was upset and gave me a hug. We had been through a lot together. 'It's the right thing to do for yourself,' she said. John was also very sincere and thanked me for the way in which we had worked together in the coalition. Each of them said they wanted to join the other ministers at the press conference. That was a nice touch, I thought, and I was glad of it. Both of them had been good partners in government. I also sent word for Conor Lenihan to be invited to join the cabinet ministers at the press conference, because he had batted so hard for me in the media.

As the whole cabinet headed down the steps to the front entrance of Government Buildings for the press conference, I felt ready in myself for what I was about to do. I had been privileged to serve as the leader of Fianna Fáil since 1994 and as Taoiseach from 1997. I was the second-longest-serving leader and Taoiseach after Dev. Now my time was up. 'Here we are then,' I said to Dermot Ahern as I was going down the last step. I put my speech on the lectern and took a deep breath. Then I ploughed in, announcing my intention to submit my resignation to President McAleese on 6 May 2008.

'Today I want to say that I am humbled to have been entrusted for over a decade with the great responsibility of leading our nation,' I said. 'The Irish people are innately decent and I have been privileged to serve them.' I hoped that I had served Ireland well. On taking office in 1997, I had promised that the priority I would put above all others would be to work for peace on this island. 'I kept my word and I have given my all to that cause,' I noted. But it was the right time to go. 'The constant barrage of commentary on Tribunal-related matters has and I believe will continue to dominate the political agenda at an important point for our country,' I explained. 'The vital interests of Ireland' demanded our full attention without 'being constantly deflected by the minutiae of my life, my lifestyle and my finances'.

When the statement was over, I turned and headed back up the stairs. 'Cabinet in ten minutes,' I called out to my colleagues behind me.

That night I went out to Georgina's house. She and Nicky were supposed to have gone on holiday, but they had changed their flights to be around for me. Cecelia came over as well. The four of us sat round chatting about all sorts that had nothing to do with politics. It was great. The girls were in brilliant form, laughing and joking. There was some football on in the background. I had a beer. Later, I headed back to Drumcondra and got a bit of air and a walk. Then I went down to the Goose pub in Marino for a quiet drink with a few close friends, including Paddy and Camilla Reilly. I started getting calls saying that people were gathering in Beaumont House and would I go down. People wanted to show their support. I thought I would drop in, and by the time I arrived there was a huge crowd spilling out onto the street. That was an extraordinary night. I didn't get home until the early hours. There was no dwelling on anything as I climbed into bed. It had been a hell of a day. Five minutes later, I was asleep.

The next few weeks, my last as Taoiseach, seemed to pass in a blur. I went out to UCD the day after my statement to address a conference to mark the tenth anniversary of the Good Friday Agreement. I got a standing ovation, which I hadn't expected, and it made me realise there were going to be these moments along the way that would catch me out. There was a great reception from the crowd at a Dubs match at Parnell Park, and another at a Westlife concert at Croke Park, which I went to with Georgina and the twins. But for the most part it was business as usual. I worked every hour of every day. I kept on top of the briefs. I think some of the officials were a bit shocked that I was still interested, but I was determined not to slack off. On my final day the girls and their fellas, Nicky and David, came into the Department of the Taoiseach for a last visit. My grandkids, Jay and Rocco, came as well and they were crawling around under my desk, making everyone laugh. I finished my remaining paperwork when they left. My last letter as Taoiseach was on the Stardust Inquiry and I was glad that my final signature came on a issue that meant so much to me.

By the time I had completed those five weeks I had put in so many long shifts I was exhausted. There were some standout moments, two of which turned out to be highlights of my time as Taoiseach. On 30 April I became the sixth Irish leader to address the US Houses of Congress. I also became only the fifth international leader to have addressed both Congress and the Houses of Parliament in Westminster, joining Charles de Gaulle, François Mitterrand, Haile Selassie and Nelson Mandela. The day began dramatically when I was woken by the Secret Service at 4 a.m. to be told the hotel was on fire. I could smell the smoke and this was no false alarm. A generator on the roof had caught light. When I eventually returned to the room, I was too awake to go back to bed. In a way it probably helped keep me calm. What was an address on Capitol Hill after being hustled out of a smoke-filled building in the early hours? The previous year I had really felt the 'hand of history' in being the first Taoiseach to speak at Westminster. This time I felt a strong bond with a former Taoiseach, John Bruton, who had delivered an excellent speech to Congress in 1996. He was there for my speech in his role as EU Ambassador and could hardly have been more gracious, including by offering glowing praise to the press. 'What's life like in the former Taoiseachs' club?' I asked him afterwards.

There were some tough words that needed to be said in my speech about the status of the undocumented Irish who were living in the US. I wanted to tie that in with the role our country had played in their history. After all, I reminded Congress, 'The Irish helped to build America.' There were thanks too for America's role in the peace process. They had played their part in getting us to the situation where I could make a statement that some thought never could or would be made. 'After so many decades of conflict,' I said, 'I am so proud, Madam Speaker, to be the first Irish leader to inform the United States Congress: Ireland is at peace.'

Afterwards at the reception, Paul Kiely, a friend since the early 1970s, slipped in beside me. 'We've come a long way, Bertie, haven't we?'

By the time Tuesday 6 May arrived, it seemed just five minutes ago that I had been standing on the steps inside Government Buildings announcing my intention to resign. I had purposely coincided my last full day in office with the official opening of the Battle of the Boyne site with the First Minister, Ian Paisley. Who would have believed eleven years earlier that my time as Taoiseach would end in an embrace with 'Dr No' on the site of the most famous battle in Irish history? It turned out to be a great day. The sun was scorching. Paisley was in great humour. Both he and his wife, Eileen, were very gracious in their speeches, talking about our shared patriotism, 'a love of this island we jointly hold together'. Ian presented me with a beautiful eighteenth-century King James Bible. The project itself was a good example of why it's worth sticking with an idea even when it gets criticised. It had originally been the brainchild of David Andrews and Dermot Gallagher. We were attacked for it at the time, but here we were now, standing beside members of the Orange Order, and everyone showing respect for shared traditions. The picture of the day came when those Orangemen asked me to pose with them for an informal photograph. It was just another in a long line of small but symbolic moments in this extraordinary process.

That seemed the perfect way to go out. One way or another I had given so much of my endeavours to the North. Now as Green and Orange came together on the grassy banks of the Boyne on this beautiful day, it seemed the right way to go. Afterwards, I travelled back to Dublin. There were handshakes, photos and farewells at Government Buildings. I had been served with such loyalty, dedication and commitment. Our public servants sometimes come in for stick, but anyone who has worked as closely with them over the years as I have knows we have a civil service to be proud of. For most of my time as Taoiseach, I had worked with one of the very best: Dermot McCarthy, the secretary general of the department and the government. A lot of the officials who came out on my last day had worked with me for eleven years. Some of them, like Mick Sludds, had even been with me at Labour and Finance. A few were crying, which was amazing for usually calm civil servants. Then it was off to the Áras for a meeting with the President. She was very kind, thanking me for my contribution to the life of our state. She brought her family in with her, which was a thoughtful gesture, and that gave me the chance to thank them too for their support. The moment of resigning was almost an afterthought. To be honest, it didn't even feel real. Afterwards, I returned to St Luke's, with Brian Murphy, Olive Melvin and Gerry Hickey all crammed into the back of the one car that had replaced the Taoiseach's two.

There was still one last duty to perform the next morning before my resignation was formally announced. I had been going to the 1916 Commemoration at Arbour Hill all my life. What better way to finish than in my own constituency honouring the Republican dead who had set our independence in train.

EPILOGUE

As I was sitting in the sunshine on the bench in All Hallows, nobody fully appreciated the extent of the storm clouds that were gathering over Ireland and the world.

I have often been asked if I resigned because I foresaw the downturn in the economy and got out while the going was good. This could not be further from the truth. Anyone who knows me understands that I relish a challenge and I have to admit I would willingly have got my teeth into the big issues the country currently faces.

When I resigned, I did so because the ongoing obsession with issues surrounding the Mahon Tribunal was distracting from the work of government. I believed then and I still believe now that my decision was in the best interests of the Irish people.

On 6 May 2008, the day I returned my seal of office to President McAleese, nobody was talking about the worst global recession since the Wall Street Crash. Although the credit crunch was causing alarm, nobody had predicted that the international financial system would implode. The prevailing criticism from the opposition about my government was that over our tenure in office we did not spend enough.

History has to be analysed by looking at events in their own context. The policies I pursued as Taoiseach should be seen in the perspective of a time when an average growth rate of 4.5 per cent was projected for the period 2007–12 and when nobody envisaged an international recession on the scale we are currently experiencing. Those who are rewriting our recent economic history, labelling my governments profligate, would do well to check back over the Dáil record from the last decade. I could write another entire book on all the times when the opposition asked me to increase expenditure and I refused to countenance it.

I like to think that throughout my time as a politician I have always taken full responsibility for the decisions I have made. I am proud of what I have done in over thirty years in politics and in the service of my country, particularly during my time as Taoiseach, Minister for Finance and Minister for Labour. I didn't get everything right. But I am adamant that any fair study of the facts can only show that the vast majority of the policies I implemented brought immense and continuing benefit to the people of this country.

Rather than recite a ream of statistics, I want to refer to one achievement that means as much to me as anything from all my years in government. My parents, like so many others, raised their family at a time when Ireland was one of the poorest states in Western Europe. That's why it is a great source of pride to me that Ireland during my period as Taoiseach finally caught up with and then surpassed average EU living standards. Despite the severe downturn, all of the indications are that this convergence of our living standards will be retained if we continue to follow the right budgetary policies and do not repeat the mistakes of the 1980s, when large budget deficits were not tackled decisively.

It is a sizeable national achievement to have raised our living standards from a historically low base of two-thirds of the EU average to a point where, even now, Ireland can maintain its status as one of the best-placed countries in the EU. Given this fact alone, I find it hard to accept the assertion that we somehow blew the boom. I certainly won't apologise for an unprecedented period of economic advancement in our country's history. Not only did that achieve record economic growth and raise average Irish living standards across the board, but it drove social progress. This rising tide was essential in lifting hundreds of thousands of our people out of poverty, to reversing forced emigration, to significantly increasing pensions, child benefits, disability and carer allowances, to modernising schools, health facilities, roads and communications infrastructure around our country, and in creating well-paid jobs for our young people at home.

These are not just words. They represent real change in the lives of our people. We put huge amounts of money into regenerating traditional areas of poverty such as Ballymun, Fatima Mansions in Rialto, and parts of Limerick, Cork, Waterford and other cities. We put money into the islands, improving the electricity supply and the sewage system, and building new piers. Throughout the country people now drive on better roads. We travel on better trains. Our schools and hospitals have more staff working in better buildings. Our leisure time is spent using vastly improved amenities, from the redeveloped stadium at Croke Park to the Wexford Opera House, and the vast network of sporting and cultural facilities throughout the country that encourage greater local participation. All the time, we worked to improve the quality of life for ordinary people and to provide services that many had never seen before. It was an unprecedented time for us as a nation.

I've never claimed to have done all this on my own. The main credit lies with the hard work and ingenuity of the Irish people. But taking the right policy approach and making smart strategic decisions were also instrumental. Politics does matter. Ireland benefited from the upsurge in the world economy by choice not chance. Those who say we squandered the boom forget that in my time as Taoiseach we actually recorded budget surpluses in ten of our eleven budgets.

We balanced sustained increases in spending with the need to reduce our national debt. As a result, Ireland paid over a billion euros less every year in interest payments. For generations, our national debt had been an unsustainable millstone around the neck of taxpayers. It was a barrier to national progress as huge sums of revenue had to service interest payments. In 1997, the year I became Taoiseach, 20 per cent of all taxes raised in the state were used to service the national debt. In 2007, my last full year as Taoiseach, that figure stood as low as 4.3 per cent. Had we not taken the far-sighted decision to cut significantly our national debt when times were good, millions and millions more euros today, tomorrow and every other single day through this recession would have to be diverted away from vital public services to fund massive interest payments. Prudently we continued to pay into the National Pension Fund so that when the downturn came we had €20 billion saved to help us through these harder times. We also retained one of the lowest government debt ratios in the EU.

There is no credibility in suggesting that an open economy like ours could withstand a global recession and the collapse of the global investment banking system. This is a worldwide recession affecting America, Japan, Britain, China and most of the developed economies in the world. The Irish are not the only ones experiencing tough times.

In 2007, the International Monetary Fund (IMF) maintained that Ireland's economic growth would be strong over the medium term. The IMF directors said our economic performance was robust and was supported by 'sound economic policies'. When I left office a year later, the IMF and other international organisations such as the OECD, along with national ones such as the ESRI, were all predicting growth in the Irish economy in the region of 3 per cent for 2009. In June 2009, little more than a year on from my resignation, they were predicting a contraction of between 8 and 10 per cent. That illustrates how unprecedented and unforeseen this global crisis has been and how quickly it took root.

It is true that we had some warnings about over-reliance on property, but it is important to be clear about the record. In October 2004, the IMF alluded to a possible overheating in the housing market even though, subsequently, they themselves and other economic commentators implied there was no bubble. In the Budget two months later, Brian Cowen, as Minister for Finance, announced a review of tax incentive schemes. In the next Budget, we announced a termination date for all existing property-related tax incentive schemes with the exception of private hospitals, registered nursing homes and childcare facilities. Our stamp duty was already the largest transaction tax on property in the EU. Despite a concerted campaign by some to get rid of that tax, or to reduce it too substantially, I refused to go down this route. If I had listened to these calls, this would have added fuel to the housing market and we would be experiencing greater difficulties than we are now.

We were able gradually to remove incentives from the property market, but membership of the euro meant we were unable to raise interest rates. According to the IMF report in the summer of 2009, the housing boom was caused mainly by cheap credit due to low interest rates, along with rising incomes and a strong demand for housing. There is no doubt that this created a structural weakness in the economy and the international downturn has ensured this has changed from a soft landing into a very hard one.

Today we are faced with a severe economic challenge. But in so many ways we are better placed to tackle it than we were in the late 1970s and early 1980s when I was young man starting out in public life. We confront today's world of fiscal uncertainty from a position of strength relative to where we were just a generation ago. We have over a million more people in employment and years of record investment in individuals and training mean that we also have the most talented and educated workforce in the history of the state. This gives us some insulation from the ravages of the global recession. And it gives us confidence that we have the scope to accelerate rapidly again when the global economic storms are over.

I make these points not to breed complacency about the scale of today's challenges or to downplay the real suffering that many are enduring. We are in a battle for our economic and social stability, but we should never forget that we have been here before and overcome longer odds. The enormity of the struggle we faced in the 1980s – whether in terms of national debt, inflation, unemployment, hopelessness or emigration – were on a massive scale. But we got through that and Ireland prospered.

We need to remember that in getting out of the hole this country was in during the 1980s, and in enjoying in recent times the best and most prosperous decade in the history of independent Ireland, that we didn't get there by chance or divine right. We did it by tackling problems proactively, in a creative way, and by building consensus. This period shows the value of a disciplined and patient approach to problem-solving. Perhaps most importantly, it highlights the value of social dialogue.

I know given the scale of the downturn we are experiencing that some people now question all this. But to me social partnership is an essential component of modern Republicanism. Partnership has its origins in people from all sectors pulling together for the good of the country. We would be crazy to go back to the bad old days of industrial chaos, social disorder and mass strikes. This would not benefit our national productivity or our people. It would certainly do nothing to restore our prosperity. That's the challenge that now confronts us.

People say I was lucky to be Taoiseach during the boom times, but in many ways I made my own luck. And the same is true for this proud nation. We make our own luck. We are going through a bad patch, but if we buckle down and hold our nerve, I know we will see better days.

It's still an odd feeling for me that I will not be at the sharp end of that process. I have been involved on the front line of Irish political life ever since I was appointed Assistant Whip in January 1980. Now from the backbenches I give the government my full support, but I find it prudent to say very little. The last thing my successor needs is a former Taoiseach making regular speeches for the media to pore over, looking for any points of difference where in fact there are none.

I am happy to help Brian Cowen in any way he sees fit, but that will be done in private and with no expectation that he should follow my advice. I have had my go at the helm. Now it's the turn of the next generation.

That has meant a personal as well as a political readjustment for me. Right up to and including my final day in office, I was working hard on behalf of the country. For all of my time as Taoiseach, I was giving long hours every week to the North. Opening my diary almost at random, I can see in one month nineteen meetings scheduled on that issue alone, with one of those being an all-day summit. Then there was the ordinary business of government to conduct, with meetings to chair and speeches to give. There were frequent visits to different parts of the country and regular overseas trips.

Just to take the year 2000 as an example, I was in the United States three times for visits to the White House, the UN Millennium summit and another UN meeting on Aids. There were EU summits in Lisbon and Nice. I visited Australia, East Timor, South Africa, Egypt, Poland and Norway. There were trips to the Balkans to discuss issues of conflict resolution. And that was just an average year, unlike the period of really extensive travel that I undertook in association with Ireland's presidency of the EU. On top of these duties as Taoiseach, there were others on behalf of the party, which involved getting around the constituencies. Take all this together and I think I would have dropped if there had been time to think about it.

To go suddenly from a regimented diary where you're always looking to make space to one where you start out with a blank page definitely requires a gear shift. The brain knows that you've moved on, but somehow the old reflexes are still in place. For decades I had been waking up before six every morning. It took me a while to realise that the world wasn't going to worry if I had an extra hour in bed. The best aspect of a more relaxed lifestyle is getting Sundays back. I used to work seven days a week and Sunday was the only day when I begrudged my time. I knew it was the difference between me being on top of my game and not, so I would do the work, fitting it in around whatever suited the girls. But I never liked putting in those extra hours. Now on a point of principle I make sure that nothing gets written into the diary for Sundays. At last, I'm allowed my day of rest. The grandkids and the garden are seeing the benefit of that too

There's been a great deal of speculation in the media about what my next job might be, but to be honest they've been thinking about it more than I have. To begin with, there wasn't very much I could do, because I fell and broke my leg in October 2008, which left me immobile for months. Initially that was a frustrating time, because I had extensive plans in the United States. But something good came out of it, for me at least, because I started reflecting on the course of my life and began the process of writing this book. Whether I would have been able to sit still for long enough to write it otherwise I don't know, but it was a challenging and satisfying experience to try and put my own life into some kind of perspective.

What opportunities may arise for me in the future is anyone's guess. I decided against the Tony Blair route of withdrawing immediately from the domestic political scene after resigning as head of the government. I will serve out my term as a TD. If the government goes the full term, as I hope it will, then I expect not to run again. I always said I would retire from active politics at sixty. In the meantime, I am enjoying my role as a TD for Dublin Central. This is where I started out and I would have achieved nothing without the people of the constituency.

Whatever the future may hold for me, I feel proud of the achievements I have to my name. I came into politics as a member of Fianna Fáil, the Republican party, and I hope I served it well. I became a whip when the party was going through a difficult and traumatic period. There was a series of heaves. The party was divided. There was even physical intimidation. In the end a group of members who felt so strongly that they couldn't accept the democratic will of the majority in the parliamentary party split to form the Progressive Democrats. Later there was another heave backed by Albert Reynolds, and after that the bad blood surrounding the downfall of Reynolds himself. All in all, it was not a happy time. My period as leader was different. From the moment I became leader, I said there would be no room for factions in Fianna Fáil. I hope I brought a new sense of unity and comradeship to the party. Together we rebuilt the organisation and won three successive general elections. And because we had stability within the party, we were able to build coalitions with others that stayed the course for two full terms of government and have the potential to complete a third.

Reflecting on my broader legacy, I hope I served the image of Ireland abroad. I became a well-known figure in the EU, at the United Nations, and in political circles in Britain and America. Whenever Ireland had the opportunity to play a leading role on the world stage, such as during our EU presidency, I feel that I did not let anyone down.

Perhaps the most significant contribution I made is in the peace process. This is the single most important issue of my political lifetime. I gave it more energy, thought and commitment than any other issue. If anything defines my legacy, I believe it is this. By negotiating and implementing the Good Friday Agreement, I, along with others, helped bring an end to an era of death and destruction in the North. For all my adult years, Ireland was seen throughout the world for the violence of the Troubles. Now it has become a model for peaceful conflict resolution. Even today I still find that the peace process is constantly referred to at my meetings of the World Economic Forum's Global Agenda Council on Negotiation and Conflict Resolution. Success in the peace process does not mean that all the issues surrounding the North have been solved. But we have a settlement in place that has been accepted by both communities. The nightmare of killing, murder, torture and people living in fear has ended. Some of the bitterness remains, and from time to time it has raised its head sporadically through violence and disturbance. But there is still a strong belief on the island North and South that the words I spoke in Congress shortly before leaving office can endure: 'Ireland is at peace.' That is why since my resignation I have put many hours into helping the peace-building charity, Co-operation Ireland. The political settlement is in place in the North. The next phase is to tackle sectarianism and social exclusion. Peace must be built upon and protected.

Even as I think about the achievements of my time as Taoiseach, I am aware that a theme runs through them that illustrates how my personality has shown itself through my political actions. I think I'm able to deal with people who have totally opposing views, get them to work together and to move forward. Sometimes the individuals involved can be very difficult. The kind of circles I have moved in are not always short of big egos and even bigger mouths. But whether it is in the North, the South, or abroad, I have often managed to find a way to move individuals from a position of complete hostility to one where they are doing and saying things that many thought impossible.

That does not come without considerable effort. It requires patience and forbearance. Sometimes that meant taking a whole lot of abuse before getting down to business. At times I found that rough. But because I always remembered the bigger picture, I was prepared to put up with harsh words. At times my critics said that meant I was indecisive. But I like to think I achieved more than most who took a 'bull in a china shop' approach to politics. In my experience of decision-making, people will negotiate as long as you let them have their say. I was always prepared to give someone a tactical win if it meant they bought into the overall strategy. It's results that matter, not column inches.

In the end, the strategic aims that I have always worked towards are based on the same Republican values that informed my father's generation and those who came before him going right back to Wolfe Tone. For each of us the challenge has been to live up to the spirit of those Republican ideals of liberty, equality and fraternity. The language might seem old-fashioned, but the meaning behind those words is as important today as ever. It is about tolerance and respect for the individual. It is about social solidarity and building a better and fairer society for all. That's why I always tried to carry people with me during a transformative period for our country rather than ramming change down their throats. We are a small island on the periphery of Europe and a transatlantic bridge between two vast continents. We have not been given great national resources. Our best resource is our people. And they are sovereign.

Each successive generation adapts Republicanism for its own times. The values remain constant. But society is dynamic, and as the times change, so must we. I understood this from an early age. I saw it in my father. And I recognised it in my political heroes. These were men of principle who adapted to their times. Eamon de Valera was a commandant of the Easter Rising and the leader of the Anti-Treaty side in the civil war, but he was the same man who led Fianna Fáil into government and committed himself to constitutional Republicanism. Seán Lemass carried the stretcher of James Connolly during the Rising and saw action against the British military forces, but as Taoiseach half a century later he extended the hand of friendship to Unionists in the North. Lemass was also the protectionist who became an advocate of free trade and membership of the European Economic Community. He saw no contradiction between his boyhood self of 1916 and the Taoiseach of the 1960s. Those Republican values in which he and Dev, like my father, believed so passionately and for which they risked their lives, remained intact. But the circumstances had changed. And they adapted with them.

Change has always been the thread running through our tradition. From the Proclamation in 1916, to the Constitution of 1937, to the ratification of the Treaty of Rome in 1972, to the Good Friday Agreement of 1998 – the living generations have time and again renewed their hope in the future of Republicanism.

This has always been underpinned by the vibrancy and deep roots of our local communities. One of the strengths of Ireland through the ages has been that communities have been strong and people look out for each other. That is something I have always valued in my own life. Since childhood, I have been part of a community in Drumcondra where people are embraced, where they are not unknown to each other or living in a vacuum. That's society as I understand it and it is a vital part of our Republican tradition. This can show itself in simple ways, whether through the teams we play for or the churches we attend. It shows itself in the welcome we give to those who come to this island from overseas to make new lives for themselves in our localities. These are the ties that bind. They create friendships and relationships. Connections are made. And that's where the life of the nation is cherished. For me, a good community makes a good society and a good society makes a good country.

That has to start somewhere and in my experience it all begins locally. Growing up in Church Avenue, I lived beside Protestants and Catholics, young families and pensioners – but we all felt a bond of friendship and neighbourliness that ran deep. That was why people came out onto the street to welcome me home in 1977 when I was first elected. It was a shared moment for us all. Home was not just 25 Church Avenue. It was the wider family of my own community. We shared our successes and our misfortunes. And in between we gave each other the time of day and enjoyed together the experience of our daily lives. We may not have had much money, but we had a social capital that was beyond price.

It is the strength of our communities that will sustain Ireland into the future. The single-mindedness of those previous generations who imagined another Ireland into being in the decades after famine and emigration should inspire us. When Pádraig Pearse stood at the GPO he understood that the fate of every republic is defined by its citizens. We need to use the current moment in our history to renew our sense of citizenship. We should all claim a greater sense of ownership in the life of the country. We must all seek a greater knowledge and understanding of the values and rights that citizenship brings for us all. We are not simply individuals living in our own private worlds. Together we are joined in a common project: Ireland.

For my part, I am proud to have served the Irish people and content that I did my best on behalf of my generation. And I hear the words of Pearse: 'We have kept faith with the past, and handed on a tradition to the future.'

INDEX